City Images and Urban Regeneration

The European City in Transition

Edited by Frank Eckardt
and Dieter Hassenpflug

Band 3

PETER LANG
Frankfurt am Main · Berlin · Bern · Bruxelles · New York · Oxford · Wien

Frank Eckardt/Peter Kreisl (eds.)

City Images and Urban Regeneration

PETER LANG
Europäischer Verlag der Wissenschaften

Bibliographic Information published by Die Deutsche Bibliothek
Die Deutsche Bibliothek lists this publication in the Deutsche Nationalbibliografie; detailed bibliographic data is available in the internet at <http://dnb.ddb.de>.

This book has been realized
by the generous support of the
Forschungs- und Entwicklungsgesellschaft Hessen GmbH
(FEH).

ISSN 1619-375X
ISBN 3-631-50701-1
US-ISBN 0-8204-6415-5

www.peterlang.de

The European Cities in Transition Series

Cities are a mirror of society and a motor of change. Especially the challenges produced by the growing interconnection of people and places find their spatial organisation in the world's metropolis. Globalization shapes new forms of economy, culture and social life and it comes all together in the historically grown European city. The increasing of mobility and communication brings forward the key questions of urban life again: How can the heritage of a European city been transmitted to a city in times of profound changes? What does it mean for political, cultural, social and architectural decision makers to act in an urban setting transformed by major societal trends?

The "European Cities in Transition Series" aims at publishing answers from all disciplines that are dedicated to find theoretical and practical solutions for the European City under the circumstances of the globalization and the unification of Europe. Edited by Dieter Hassenpflug and Frank Eckardt who both work at the Bauhaus-Universität Weimar, the tradition of the first Bauhaus is remembered: The Bauhaus architects like Mies van der Rohe and Walter Gropius have been searching for adequate solutions for the city of modernity. Today, this spirit has to be brought in, again. The post-national age requires new approaches for understanding the European city. Bringing together the findings of research of scientists, city planers and architectures, the series will focus on different aspects of the current transition of urban life.

First volume: Consumption and the Post-Industrial City
Second volume: Urbanism and Globalization
Third volume: City Images and Urban Regeneration

Forthcoming:

The City and the Region
Paths of Urban Transformation

Contributors

Rob Atkinson is a Professor and an Urban Research Director in the Cities Research Centre, Faculty of the Built Environment, University of the West of England, Bristol. His research interests are primarily concerned with cross-national work on urban regeneration, community participation in urban regeneration partnerships, urban social exclusion and European urban policy. He has presented papers and published widely on these issues throughout Europe.
Contact: rob.atkinson@archit.uni-weimar.de

Lars Bölling is working as an architect and urban planner at the Bauhaus-Universität Weimar, where he is responsible both for design classes and for research projects in the field of urban planning. After his studies inDarmstadt, Mainz and Vienna in architecture and social science he practised as an architect for several offices. For two years now he is part of theresearch-project "In the Centre of the Edge" financed by theDaimler-Benz-Foundation. The transdisciplinary international project is aimingat strategies for the improvement of the periphery. Contact: lars.boelling@archit.uni-weimar.de

Lars-Erik Borgegård was professor in social and economic geography at the Institute for Housing and Urban Research, Uppsala University. He had a special interest in migration and segregation and was coordinator of the ENHR working group on migration, residential mobility and housing policy, areas on which he had published extensively over the years.

Antonella Bruzzese is an architect and urban planner. She has worked as urban planner in Milano, Genova and Trieste with Stefano Boeri, after her studies in architecture at the Faculty of Architecture in Genova (1995) and urban planning at the Politecnico of Milano where she finished her PhD (2002) with a research about the construction of the "image of the city" in urban renovation processes. Since 1993 she is part of *gruppo A12*, a team of architects involved in describing and experimenting through different tools (architecture and urban projects but also art installations and exhibitions) the condition of contemporary city. Contact: antobrz@tin.it

Frank Eckardt is working as an urban sociologist at the European Urban Studies programme of the Bauhaus-Universität Weimar, where he is the local organizer of the European Cities in Transition Conference Series. He has finished his PhD at the University of Kassel in political science. Besides contributing articles to several journals, he has recently published a book on "Rotterdam. Konturen einer globalisierten Stadt" (2001). Contact: Frank.Eckardt@archit.uni-weimar.de

Leonel Fadigas (1947), landscape architect (1971) and agronomy engineer (1978) at the Lisbon Technical University. PhD in Urban Planning (1995). Professor at the Faculty of Architecture / Lisbon Technical University where he teaches urban planning and urban regeneration and is the director of the master course in urban and environmental regeneration. Contact: fadigas@fa.utl.pt

Philippe Fayeton received both diplomas for architecture (dplg, 1969) and urbanism (diuup, 1969) in Paris, worked till 1999 as an architect and town-planner, and as professor assistant (1993 – 1998) at the Ecole d'architecture de Languedoc-Roussillon. 1998 he began studying semiology and received (2001) his Dr. SC.I.C. in Lyon university for his doctorate thesis : "Ecrire dans la ville, prolégomènes à une pédagogie de l'architecture urbaine". He is author of several contributing aticles and recently published a book on « Les rythmes de la ville » (2000).
Contact: phf_archi@yahoo.com

Dieter Hassenpflug is Professor for Sociology and Social History of the City at the Bauhaus-Universität Weimar. He studied ecomomics, sociology and philosophy at the Free University Berlin and Kassel University. He was a lecturer at the Technical University of Berlin, the Berlin College of Economics, Kassel University and at the J. W. Goethe-University, Frankfurt. He was curator of the EXPO 2000 projects in Saxony-Anhalt 1995 – 2000 and is Spiritus Rector of the postgraduate European Urban Studies at the Bauhaus-Universität Weimar and director of the EuroConferences Series "The European City in Transition" at Weimar 2001 – 2003.
Contact: hassenpf@archit.uni-weimar.de

Jörg Knieling, Prof. Dr.-Ing., professor for urban planning and regional development at the Technical University Hamburg-Harburg. He holds an engineering degree in urban and regional planning and an M.A. in political sciences and sociology. Current research topics are theory and modernisation of spatial planning, regional and metropolitan governance, and regional knowledge management. He is member of the German Academy of Spatial Research and Regional Planning, and partner in the private consultancy KoRiS, Hanover, for communicative urban and regional development. Contact: joerg.knieling@t-online.de

Peter Kreisl is Director of the land-use planning division of the Planungsverband Ballungsraum Frankfurt/Rhein-Main. He has worked as consultant in the fields of urban renewal, community economic development and urban land development before.
Contact: Peter.Kreisl@pvfrm.de

Mikołaj Madurowicz is a post-graduate student, MA in Human Geography at the University of Warsaw, Poland, in the Department of Geography and Regional Studies. He is currently completing a PhD thesis on the city inhabitants' perception of city space and its identity. He has recently published a book on "Sacred Sphere within the City Space of Warsaw" (2002). Contact: mm@uw.edu.pl.

Julia Müller is an architect and has completed the post graduate program "European Urban Studies" at the Bauhaus University Weimar. For the master thesis she did a visual study on gentrification, analysing its influence on the city space in Prenzlauer Berg, Berlin. Currently she is joining an international documentation on spatial development in Shanghai, Peking, Paris and Berlin. Contact: juliam74@gmx.de

Thomas Niedomysl is a Ph.D. student in Human Geography at the department for Economic and Social Geography and at the Institute for Housing and Urban Research, Uppsala University. He is currently working with his thesis on inter-regional migration and place attractiveness in Sweden. Contact: thomas.niedomysl@ibf.uu.se

Ivonne de Notaris is an architect and a PhD student in Public Policies and Territorial Planning at IUAV – Istituto Universitario di Architettura di Venezia. In 2001-02 she took part in a research promoted and guided by the Italian Ministry for Public Works on the evaluation of the efficacy of the Urban Programme within which she studied the case of Salerno. She is currently completing her thesis on 'Istituzioni e sviluppo locale' ('Institutions and local development') in a local government of Southern Italy. Contact: i.denotaris@tin.it

Marek Pieniążek is a post-graduate student, MA in Socio-Economic Geography at the University of Warsaw, Poland, in the Department of Geography and Regional Studies. One of his latest publication is a book on "Spatial Development Conceptions and their Realisations in Ciechanów 1918-1998". He is preparing a PhD thesis on the changes of former voivodship capital cities in województwo mazowieckie.
Contact: mapi@uw.edu.pl

Elisa Pozzoli is a planner and a PhD student in Public Policies and Territorial Planning at IUAV – Istituto Universitario di Architettura di Venezia. She is a lecturer at the Politecnico di Milano. She took part in several research activities in Milan and in Venice and she is author of some articles. She is part of the organising group of the European Young Researchers Network on EU Spatial Policies. She is currently completing her PhD thesis on 'local development in rural areas, social capital and identity', for which she did periods of in-field study in Ireland. Contact: elisapozzoli@tin.it

Achim Prossek works as a Research Assistant at the Faculty of Spatial Planning at the University Dortmund. From 2001 to 2004 he was a Research Assistant at the Department of Geography at the University Duisburg-Essen. He held a scholarship by the Initiativkreis-Ruhrgebiet-programme "Structural Change in the Ruhr. An International Comparison" in 1998/99, doing research on the image and marketing of Glasgow. His doctoral thesis is about images, constructions and representations of the Ruhr Area.
Contact: achim.prossek@uni-dortmund.de

Angelika Psenner is university assistant at the Institute of history and theory of architecture and historic building survey, at the Technical University Vienna. Technical doctor's degree in urbanism and sociology at the Technical University, Vienna. Postgraduate diploma in sociology at the Institute for Advanced Studies, Vienna. Her publications include: Sozialwissenschaftliche Studiengesellschaft (ed.) SWS Rundschau 1 (2002) "*'Also unten ist's schön und oben ist's Bibione' (Visuelles) Wahrnehmen...*" and IWI Kulturverein zur Förderung der Interdisziplinarität (ed.) dérive nr.7 (2002) "*Stadt–Raum–Wahrnehmung*. Areas of interest: urbanism, space-perception, architectural theory, transdiscipline communication and research.
Contact: angelika.psenner@utanet.at

Brigitte Schwab is actually completing her PhD in political science at the University of Lausanne, where she is a teaching assistant in Swiss politics. She worked as a researcher at the Swiss Federal Institut of Technology and is actually guest resarcher at the Deutsches Institut für Urbanistik, Berlin, Germany. Contact:: Brigitte.Schwab@etu.unil.ch

Contents

City Images and Urban Regeneration *(Introduction)*

Frank Eckardt/Peter Kreisl

The term "regeneration" suggests that urban planning is able to achieve a state of affairs that (it/the city) once had. In a broader sense, it generally applies to the concept of generation in a way that means that the sole objective of urban planning is to let something happen, something which is qualified as a process of generation. As it is difficult to trace the connection between a particular intention that is followed in urban regeneration policies in certain cities and a general understanding of what the term "generation" could mean, it might be worthwhile to engage in a broader discussion about the patterns and different approaches followed by urban regeneration and how these approaches attempt to achieve results. Either one could bring the debate into a position where either the restoration of a lost past is more accented (the "re" in generation), or the emphasis could lie in initiating new projects and plans. In the first case, it seems easy to understand where urban politics and urban planning is heading for, although everyday practice in urban conservation is more difficult to apprehend than in an antagonistic dualism between a past and a future orientation of urban planning. It is, moreover, questionable whether or not it is future oriented to restore past building areas and zones of cultural heritage.

Beyond this often very polemic debate in urban policies, the essential request for a guiding principle in urban planning becomes obvious. Where do we go and which principle leads there? Referring to a more German understanding of urban planning, the principles of planning are an expression of a broader cultural approach to urban life. In this way, planning principles are embedded in an "image" of how life in cities should look. The editors of this book have conducted some of the actual debates regarding the issue of "guiding images" for urban planning. Most of the studies represented here are the result of an international workshop at the Bauhaus-University Weimar, October 2002. On this occasion, the European Urban Research Association and the Forschungs- und Entwicklungsgesellschaft Hessen GmbH (FEH) joined the University in Weimar to discuss different approaches in order to examine the issue of "city images" and "urban regeneration". In this way, the three organizers wanted to reflect upon extant and experimental concepts as to how we could see the relationship with our perception of urban life, society and development to the planning processes. Therefore, the volume now presented integrates contributions deriving from both points of departure: namely the reflection on urban regeneration processes and the visual perception of urbanity. In addressing both approaches to urban development, the editors invite readers to allow themselves to get a little bit off the beaten track of their quotidian ways of discussing urban life. It might, for example, be challenging and even confusing to start the reconsideration of the future of urban planning by looking at the city from a more theoretical point of view, as it is clearly a stimulus to find one's way through the jungle of existing planning practices, when one has a certain idea of how urban policies should look. Nevertheless, the interference between both sides of the debate is hopefully of use especially in a situation where urban planning has reached its limits in many cities. It is the overall objective to stimulate controversial insights, so as to avoid the premature conclusion of an open debate regarding the future of urban planning, which might be frightened away as a consequence of fiscal crises of the cities and other powerful concerns.

With this book, the editors want to take up the long debate on "guiding images" in urban planning and present some new approaches to them. First of all, the debate is placed foremost on a European level of experience with examples from Sweden, Italy, Poland, Portugal, Switzerland, Austria and France, among others. Secondly, the contributions are written by authors with backgrounds in a variety of disciplines, most of whom are not engaged in urban planning research as such. Thusly, a scientific stance is taken, which posits that urban planning cannot be exclusively a field for specialists. On the contrary, the necessary dialogue between economists, sociologists, artists, historians, architects, political scientists and planners is essential for developing an understanding about the ways in which principles, images, concepts, fantasies, politics and planning theories lie at the heart of urban development. We feel that we are only just beginning to enable the transdisciplinary debate of urban research on the future of urban planning, although we are well aware of the long history of modern planning for the city.

The emphasis on these two points has neither led us to repeat nor discuss in length what other important considerations within the field of urban planning have already achieved. It goes without saying that we benefit from the results of the debates in all the disciplines. Instead, this volume is meant to add, at least to a certain extent, the level of transdisciplinarity and Europeanization to the outstanding research of others. We do not consider others' works to have neglected what we focus on, but it the specific focus that is probably not addressed in the sense as this book aims.

Particularly within the German context, many publications from the last forty years have more or less discussed the role of "guiding images" for urban development and planning. For describing the role of images for orienting planning processes, the German language offers the term "Leitbilder" which might be impossible to translate in the full sense of the word. As it is a key word in many outstanding publications on recent urban development and as it has become a tool for urban policies, it seems to be unavoidable to give the international reader a short explanation of the word's connotation. With "Leitbilder" we can describe a certain set of assumptions of future development that allows a flowing understanding of necessary tasks and a common perspective of the challenges ahead. The term expresses a kind of vision in a more focussed way. "Leitbilder" are therefore advantageous in comparison to loose ideas and utopias on urbanity. It might be argued against them that they are politically (or at least socially) constructed planning philosophies with a certain focus on suppressing other views.

The re-emergence of "Leitbilder" has often been traced to broader changes in society such as the ecological crisis, political transformation, economic restructuring, new space-time-dimensions, social change, cultural development and the crisis of local administration (Becker/Jessen/Sander 1997, 11-13). In general, "Leitbilder" are seen to motivate the actors of urban planning to concretize the objectives of a common vision on urban development, to broaden the platform of engaged citizens and political actors, to create transparency, and to allow the control of urban planning (Schnell/Walser 1995). There is a considerable amount of literature on how these "Leitbilder" should be formulated and integrated so that they are really meaningful for the processes of urban planning (Eckardt/Kerkhoff 2000): To only mention a few often cited aspects, one must take into consideration that the complexity of the objectives is in accordance with the abilities of the planning instruments. This leads to a focus on certain problems and avoids being overloaded with wishful but non-realistic orders (Maurer 1995).

With the German "Leitbild", it seems to be expressional that strategic development of the city is necessarily more than just a marketing product sold to the outside world to attract tourists and investors. It is, however, worth debating in which way both elements of urban politics can be combined and used for mutual benefit. To identify a corporate image of the city can trap one into a too literal translation from the sphere of enterprises onto something as complex as a city. On the other hand, it has often been argued that the definition of common goals for a city should be longer lasting than the next round of local elections. Here, the openness to learning from experiences with the economy has been widely achieved in many communities and cities. It remains unclear why there is so little attention given to the extension of marketing processes for the internal world of the city (Schückhaus 1997).

Although the term "Leitbild" appears to be attractive as it is apparently a means of communication in urban planning which brings the heavenly wishes for a "good city" down to the earth of realist pragmatism, the history of the "Leitbild" shows in which way these processes construct our planning approaches and pre-select perspectives, options and solutions for problems in urban life. It would take a longer effort than this introduction should allow, but it is certainly worth a debate as to whether some of these "Leitbilder" have only created problems that have not been recognized as such before. It is certain, however, that some of the general assumptions of the "Leitbilder" have delivered restrictions on our view on urban life which are problematic in their turn. As a result of these processes of communicative practice in urban planning via "Leitbilder", remaining scepticism about the adequacy of the selected view on the city should be advocated. As some of the contributions in the volume demonstrate, urban life is wider, broader, more colourful, complex and even paradoxical than can be captured by one single image, regardless of how sophisticatedly it was taken (Naegler 2003, 255-257). If these reservations are necessary to prevent strong believers from creating self-fulfilling prophecies, why should we stick to producing and following these guiding ideas, principles and images? If they are meant to organize a framework of orientation, then it becomes crucial to identify the political field of the construction of these principles and to compare the different images possible with those selected.
To underscore our basic endeavour, we would like to draw the reader's attention to a few of the common "Leitbilder" from post-war urban planning history. All of which are presumably still influencing our perception and regulation of urban planning, and in this sense worth a debate about their selective mechanism. While one would assume that it would make sense just to turn to the most recent "Leitbild" and to promote ourselves as real followers of fashion, in planning reality we are confronted with the heritage of a long durée (drawn-out succession) of many "Leitbilder" simply not melting into the air because of others that follow. So, if we want to point out what still is the most powerful guiding image in urban planning, politics, and research, the discussion comes to the idea of the compact and dense city. "Society by Density" was the slogan of the German Urban Planning Conference in 1963 and the new edition of the then "new initiatives for a new Leitbild for urban planning" in 1995 argued for the need to "revitalize the self-consciousness of urban planning against unlimited neo-liberalism" (Boeddinghaus 1995). In that debate, many aspects of urban planning were addressed and some of them sound like today's commentary. If we want to summarize the basic idea and simultaneously point at the problematic connotation of it, the following quotation might be helpful: "We should be aware that

that density, which we long so much for, can only be achieved with more control and discipline", stated the Professor for Landscape Architecture, Erich Kühn (Boeddinghaus, 27). To live together in diversity and on a limited scope of place is a basic concept of urban life still dominating our perception of what a city looks like. At the same time, the massive limitations of individual life are obviously a consequence of this urban life. And urban planners, who are children of this "Leitbild" spreading throughout in society, do not consider the necessity of addressing the unbinding of density and social control. Instead, they plead for emphasis on both the support for individualisation and community building. Is that a realistic perspective on urban life? The following massive suburbanization processes at the end of the sixties might be considered as an answer to a "Leitbild" that had to carry out the "mission impossible". Urban planning became critical because of its inability to foresee urban sprawl and, more important, to understand its dynamic. As it was guided by the concept that the compact city can achieve the integration of individual and communitarian lifestyles within the same bit of town, urban planning answered in an aggressive tone for a long period regarding the visible restructuring of urban settlements. In the following years, suburbanization and urban sprawl have been seen as something wrong and negative which had to be fought against.

The concept of the complex city created the problem of urban sprawl and contributed to it within the realisation of its own "Leitbild". A side effect was the "car-friendliness" of urban planning, which enabled easy commuting to and within the city and to sustain the compact ensembles of the inner city. In the next round of formulating "Leitbilder", this particular problem was addressed, whereas the basic assumptions regarding life in a compact city was not touched. In the seventies, the concept of participatory and scientifically evaluated urban planning was developed to readjust urban planning for the sake of the urban inhabitants. To take the stake of those concerned about and affected by urban planning seriously became a major political vision that found its expression in party programmes and planning law (Müller/Niemann 1971). But, once again, the conceptualization of a "Leitbild" was bound to a vision of urban life that had been grounded in a single experience – the resistance against certain types of urban planning projects while allowing others through. In other words, while it has certainly adequately reacted to the overarching and dominant features of urban planning and its neglect of elements of direct democracy, the focus on this special part of urban life could not deliver a realistic new guiding principle. It was already then clear, that "pluralist processes can hardly be integrated into the requirements of integrative planning and will be, in particular, not stopped by alternative planning proposals. Instead, single projects will be changed in bargaining situations as fitting to the interests of the strongest lobby." (Scharpf 1973, 185). It is obvious, that the limitations of participatory planning are not considered part of the "Leitbild" of the seventies. To mention only a few unaddressed obstacles, this "guiding picture image" has not foreseen the non-area based problems urban inhabitants are struggling with. Unemployment, borderless ecological threats, and urban development on a larger scale are transcending the mechanisms of regulation, participation and discourse between the urban planning authorities and the neighbourhoods, the direct objects of planning.

In the eighties, the mechanism on how to react to a failing "Leitbild" can be observed as still powerful and decisive. Reflecting major developments in society, principles of urban planning have added aspects of ecological and technical concern. A perfect example of this is the "General Tracts of a Theory of Leitbilder for Urban Design", published in 1988 by Bernd Streich. In a first attempt, this publication aims at understanding societal circumstances of the "Leitbild" development and ends up with a scientifically designed listing of "indicators" for "Leitbilder". In this way, the author reflects the modernist belief of solving the problem in a cliché-like manner of scientific pragmatism. In his concluding outlook for new "Leitbilder", the author focuses on three issues: shrinking cities, implementation of new technologies and ecological concerns are to have been combined in order to take advantage of the new situation (Strech 1988).

During the course of the eighties, predominantly ecological aspects shaped subsequent Leitbild-debates. Different concepts have been discussed to "concretize" these, particularly focussing on urban life. Most famous and with broad international attention (for many: Haughton/Hunter 1994) were images like the "car free city" or the "city with short distances" (Brunsing/Frehn 1999). In an even more powerful and integrative way, the concept of "sustainability" has shaped a whole new body of literature and "Leitbilder". This is not only true with regard to the issue itself, which might be considered as predominantly ecological and integrative with regard to the social and economic sphere of urban life, but it has also brought other voices in. The so called "Local Agenda 21" and other related social groups have been actively advocating for new guiding principles in urban planning and urban politics. As a result of these redirections, a highly sophisticated description of new fields for urban planning and sets of indicators have been proposed. The initiative of incorporating ecological issues into the guiding principles of urban planning has, in its turn, reassured the necessity and the legitimacy of "Leitbilder" as such, and even of urban planning as an instrument of urban policies. In this way they have contributed to the reestablishment

of both after a decade of a critical public attitude towards them (Schäfers/Köhler 1989, 111).
To a certain extent, the sustainability discourses shift urban planning in a paradigmatic way. Nevertheless, it speaks very much to the imagination while keeping to the old idea of a compact city (Wolf 1996, 96). In practice, the application of ecological perspectives on urban planning is based on a "narrowed perspective on ecology using a deformed concept"(Betker 1992, 199). As it might sound like another round of desperation regarding the fact that reality is not what the principles have asked it to be, the reaction to the failure of this second basic concept of the complex city, the "Leitbild" becomes enlarged and remains uncorrected. One might feel sympathy with the fact that sustainability has become an extended concept expressing the awareness for the social circumstances of urban life. Meanwhile, the question appears to be justified: how can the concept of sustainability be formulated in such an imprecise way (Dangschat 2001)? The concept of sustainability with its amalgamation of "empowerment strategies" aims at a new quality of urban participatory politics (Evans/Rydin 1997) and we could therefore consider this new "Leitbild" as cumulative of all that existed before. This means that it not only reintegrates all desirable aspects of planning, but expresses the uselessness of these wishes at the same time, thereby heavily questioning urban planning based on "Leitbilder": "Unfashionable (and, in many quarters, unthinkable) concepts such as intervention, collective action, socialism, communitarian values, the public interest and social equality will have to revivified if we are to secure survival in the long run. All this may sound hopelessly unrealistic at the present (...) it is a task that planners, above all, must be capable of fulfilling." (Blowers 1997, 168).
The recent development of "Leitbilder" under the paradigm of sustainability is therefore a very ambivalent political process. On the one hand, it has shaped a new faith in and encouragement for engaging the citizens and the administration for an all-including vision. The exclusionary processes often visible in everyday urban planning have become reflected with regard to its effects on future options to plan and political room to manoeuvre. The process of the debates about the sustainable city itself has already had positive effects on the sustaining of planning processes, although many actors of planning authorities have, at least in the beginning, seen these new and external actors as simply disturbing. Taking social networks and their effects into account, it often becomes very likely that planning as such and urban politics have gained credibility and support for specific projects and planning strategies when they have gone through the test of their sustainability. On the other hand, it seems that the Leitbild-process has come to a

critical point that is comparable to the late sixties where the concept of the "compact city" had not reflected on its "side-effects". This is even truer as the sustainability discourse is based on and repeats a different perspective of the old idea of the city of density.

It is, at present, hard to say which aspect of these highly sophisticated guiding philosophies does not fit with the urban reality of the 21st century. Clearly, this conceptual failure will harm the encouragement of many citizens to engage their urban environment, as soon as it becomes apparent that they remain paper tigers. Reduced to the limited scope of this introduction, only one, presumably important aspect can be considered here. It has been argued above that our basic understanding of urban life is based on the contradictory assumption of urban life combining individual freedom and communitarian solidarity within a spatially limited area. This image of the city has not been corrected in all fields of urban life, especially those regarding urban planning. Forty years after the Gelsenkirchen conference, we are confronted by a process that has led to a high fragmentation of urban settlement, a regionalisation of cities, a high level of interference between different levels of social, economic and cultural life. Many of these aspects are caused by an accelerated speed of exchange and a global flow of goods, services, people, and images (Eckardt/Hassenpflug 2004). It has been shown that the development of larger urban structures, the so-called "In-between-cities" (Sieverts), are not as influenced by the inhabitants preference for the suburban life and a disgust for the cities, as by the medial discourse on lifestyles that shapes other expectations towards the urban infrastructure (Eckardt 2003). Still, many authors are hoping that fragmentation and urban chaos will not be the last word and that "even in the 21st century, Paris will be the urban capital of the world" (Marquart 1999, 79). As this point of view does not offer any perspective for urban planning, practice in the times of post-modern planning can be seen as a kind of abolition of "Leitbilder" and a self-limitation to the aesthetics of single buildings and projects. City planning seems to follow an unformulated "Leitbild" where city design is the solution for the urban development complex (Jencks 1978). A sensible debate on architecture, however, seems to repeat the history of the Leitbild-development where dialogue, sustainability and identity politics have occurred to be major aspects, too (Ungers 1983). But this perspective is also one which is and can only be realised in a limited way and is reluctant to address major problems of contemporary urban societies. The post-modern approach, a "Leitbild" without "Leitbild", has not lost its influence and is convenient for those who do not want to put the heavy load of any kind of transparent and consensual objective on urban planning. The critical reflection, however, looks at it as another type of the "myth of guiding principles" (Müller-Raemisch 1990, 139-169). One other point of departure is leading to the developing of guiding principles that do address the metropolitan landscape in recognition of their pure existence. While landscape planning still seeks to purify the "periphery" from being absorbed and wasted (see f.e. DRL 1997, 21), other authors are pleading for a "qualification" of the broader urban realm (Bölling 2003) or are discussing a "decentralist concentration" (Aring 1997). "Leitbilder" are, in this attempt, placed on a larger scale and are seen as an instrument for regional management. Does that help to solve the principal problem that guiding principles are seemingly expressing an expectation that exceeds the existing capacities of urban planning? In a preliminary conclusion, Jörg Knieling stated that regional "Leitbilder" are enlarging the dimensions of expected activities of the planning bodies, as well (Knieling 2000, 230).

We might have a more realistic version of a vision for urban planning when we consider the inclusion of the periphery and the regional as crucial aspects of recent urban life. But is then the quality of a "Leitbild" proven to capture dynamics or urban images? Far from being conclusive on this point, the following contributions address in different ways the balance of urban images and urban planning, "Leitbild" and urban regeneration. Some focus more directly on the topic of this book, whereas others take the long road to give us some clues for practical uses. In practice, we will have to find a way to reflect upon the different images and their applicability for processes of urban regeneration. In this way, this volume seeks to stimulate the necessary debate about urban images in planning procedures without delivering a vast definition of what a Leitbild – neither a simple tool, nor a theoretical construct – may be.

References:

Aring, J. (1997): Die dezentrale Konzentration – ein tragfähiges regionales Leitbild gegen die Auflösung der Stadt in der Region? In: Bose, M. (ed) Die unaufhaltsame Auflösung der Stadt in der Region? Dortmund: Dortmunder Vertrieb für Bau- und Planungsliteratur, S. 101-118.

Becker, H./Jesse, J./Sander, R. (1997): Auf der Suche nach Orientierung – das Wiederaufleben der Leitbildfrage im Städtebau. In: Becker, H./Jessen, J./Sander, R. (ed.): Ohne Leitbild? – Städtebau in Deutschland und Europa. Stuttgart/Zürich: Karl Krämer, S. 10-17).

Betker, F. (1992): Ökologische Stadterneuerung: ein neues Leitbild der Stadtentwicklung? Aachen: Alano.

Blowers, A. (1997): Society and Sustainability. The context of change for planning. In: A. Blowers/B. Evans (eds) Town Planning into the 21st Century. London/New York: Routledge, 153-168.

Boeddinghaus, G. (ed.) (1995): Kritische Initiativen zu einem neuen Leitbild für Planung und Städtebau 1963/1964. Braunschweig/Wiesbaden: Vieweg.

Bölling, L. (2003): Gestaltung der Zwischenstadt. In: polis. Zeitschrift für Stadt und Baukultur. Nr.3 , S. 24-27
Brunsing, J./Frehn, M. (1999): Stadt der kurzen Wege. Zukunftsfähiges Leitbild oder planerische Utopie? Dortmund: IRPUD.
Dangschat, J. (2001): wie nachhaltig ist die Nachhaltigkeitsdebatte? In: Alisch, M.(ed.) Sozial - Gesund - Nachhaltig. Opladen: Leske+Budrich, 71-94.
Deutscher Rat für Landespflege/DRL (1997): Leitbilder für Landschaften in "peripheren Räumen". Meckenheim: DRL.
Eckardt, F./ Kerkhoff, M. (2000) Von der Verwaltungsmodernisierung zum kommunalen Leitbild. Eine praxisorientierte Darstellung von Leitbildern in der öffentlichen Verwaltung, im Rahmen von Stadtmarketing-Konzepten und der Lokalen Agenda 21. Universität Kassel.
Eckardt, F. (2003) Eine periphere Gesellschaft. Regionalentwicklung zwischen Weimar und Erfurt. Marburg: Tectum.
Eckardt, F./Hassenpflug (eds) (2004) Urbanism and Globalization. Frankfurt: Peter Lang.
Evans, B./Rydin, Y. (1997) Planning, Professionalism and Sustainability. In: A. Blowers/B.Evans (eds) Town Planning into the 21st Century. London/New York: Routledge, 55-70.
Haugthon, G./Hunter, C. (1994): Sustainable Cities. London: Regional Studies Association.
Jencks, C. (1978): Die Sprache der postmodernen Architektur. Stuttgart.
Schnell, K.-D./Walser, M. (1995): Räumliche Leitbilder – Hilfestellung zu Kommunikationund Kooperation. In. RaumPlannung, 70, 262-272.
Knieling, J. (2000): Leitbildprozesse und Regionalmanagement. Frankfurt: Peter Lang.
Marquard, C. (1999) Stadt-Konzepte. Planungstheorien zwischen Utopie und Sachzwang.Stuttgart: dva.
Maurer, J. (1997) Strategische und organisatorische Anforderungen zur Konkretisierung und Umsetzung von Leitbildern. In: H. Becker/J. Jessen/R. Sander (ed.), Ohne Leitbild? – Städtebau in Deutschland und Europa. Stuttgart/Zürich: Karl Krämer, S. 72-80.
Müller, C.W./Niemann, P. (1971) Stadtplanung und Gemeinwesenarbeit. München.
Müller-Raemisch, H.-R, (1990): Leitbilder und Mythen in der Stadtplanung 1945-1985. Frankfurt: Kramer.
Naegler, D. (2003): Planung als soziale Konstruktion. Leitbilder als Steuerungsmedium in Stadtplanungsprozessen. Berlin: sigma.
Schückhaus, U. (1997) Kooperative Leitbildentwicklung im Rahmen des Stadtmarketings. In: Becker/Jessen/Sander (ed.): 143-150.
Scharpf, F. (1973): Planung als politischer Prozeß. In. Schäfers, B. (ed.) Gesellschaftliche Planung. Materialien zur Planungsdiskussion in der BRD. Stuttgart:, 169-201.
Schäfer, B./Köhler, G. (1989): Leitbilder der Stadtentwicklung. Pfaffenweiler: Centaurus.
Streich, B. (1998) Grundzüge einer städtebaulichen Leitbildtheorie. Bonn: Institut für Städtebau, Bodenordnung und Kulturtechnik der Universität Bonn.
Ungers, O.M. (1983) Die Thematisierung der Architektur. Stuttgart.
Wolf, J. (1996): Nachhaltige Raumentwicklung. Ein Beitrag zu einem neuen Leitbild der Raumordnung. Berlin: Verlag für Wissenschaft und Forschung.

Some Remarks on Urban Signs and Symbols in History

Dieter Hassenpflug

The title of this workshop "City Images and Urban Regeneration" is resulting from discussions at another EURA-Meeting in October 2001 in Prague. All participants were still severely affected by the terrorist raids against US facilities on September, 11th. With a shock the incredible attack demonstrates to the public all over the world that not only two big and tall buildings, filled with thousands of people from all over the world providing a huge number of different services and functions collapsed, but also a very important symbol of the leading economical role of the United States of America. Evidently the terrorists knew about the enormous symbolic meaning and power of this monument and the

Figure 1

media value of their operation. They could rely on the fact that people take the Twin Towers as iconic codes sending out messages that extend the functions of the two buildings. The ensemble could be interpreted as a sign of the greatness, significance and strength of a globally acting Atlantic super power. In this respect they could trust on the fact that a successful attack against these buildings will be taken as a humiliating

blow against the predominance and strength of this power. Those who set fire to this symbol and, may be unexpectedly, make it collapse could at least for a historical moment nurture false certainties about own greatness and glory. Expressed in terms of semiotics the Twin Towers did not only denote specifically economic and public functions. In addition they connoted far extending meanings like power, greatness, superiority, transparency, self-consciousness and openness to the future.
Yet the Twin Towers were not placed anywhere. They were embedded in the meaningful context of the socio-spatial and cultural body of the city of New York. Being a significant and imposing statement of the skyline they did not only refer to the global acting business machine called New York, but also to an archetype of the modern western big city and, as demonstrated by the presence of the UN-Headquarters, to the secret capital of the emerging global society. Condensing the symbolic landscape of New York to a single architectural sign, the Twin Towers put the city into terms. So the attack reasonably appears and even worked as a stroke against the self-assessment and self-awareness of the city in a whole. In this respect the action of striking the buildings out of the New York skyline is comparable with erasing a keyword from a written sentence. The murderous action definitely aims at changing the semantic of the urban text of New York. Thus all the efforts to give the place at Ground Zero a new meaning and destination can be interpreted as means to give a text that has become partly incomprehensible a new meaning and understanding.

Figure 2

Cities are texts. They are written in an urban code. This code is multi-dimensional, it encloses social, functional and aesthetical aspects. (Hassenpflug 2003) As this code is of iconic provenience, it produces a pictorial context. Anyway, the usage of this iconic code by architects, urban designers, planners and sociologists do not necessarily produce good urban results. As to the mastering of this code (the usage of urban iconology) I'm very doubtful. The first reason is: It is not considered enough that all disciplines being engaged in urban development and construction are inevitably communicative, i.e. context oriented. They cannot prevent from being engaged in producing at the same time social, functional and aesthetical spatial contexts because its impossible to separate one dimension from the others. The second reason is: It is necessary to distinguish two kinds of iconic messages: a *denotative* and a *connotative* one. Denotative messages refer to direct functions (usage of a building, its services etc.), while connotative messages refer to the wider range of social and cultural meanings (very popular: architecture of power, of equality, of transparency connoting democracy etc). (Eco 1972, 301ff)

Figure 3

In his Introduction into semiotics, titled "Function and Sign" Umberto Eco dedicates a whole chapter to the semiotics of architecture. It ends with a definition of the professional identity of the urban designer: He has to accept variable and open socio-spatial functions in his blueprints. Eco discusses this definition taking the example of the Brasilian capital Brasilia, designed by Lucio Costa and Oscar Niemeyer. He summarizes his semiotic analysis as follows: *"Summing up we may say that the intended socialist city has turned into a manifestation of social difference. Primary functions has changed into secondary functions and the latter have changed their signifier (the idea of equality): The ideology of community which should emerge from the urban net and the appearance of buildings made way for other interpretations of social life. This happened although the architect (Niemeyer) has made no mistake according to his first model of Brasilia. While real change affected the circumstances of interpreting the architectonic signs and by this the total signifie of the city as a sign of communication, the first blueprint was based on the idea of an invariable system of social relations."* (Eco 1972, 355)

With all due respect to the broadly conceptualised cultural semiotics of Eco he is wrong when saying the architect has made no mistake in a semiotic sense. Although the blueprint of Costa transcends the functionalist urban design of modernity by using symbolic and narrative elements, he failed in defining the term 'city' properly. The socialist idea of equality (Eco calls it 'ideology of community') is no genuine urban idea. In contrary, it is 'difference' or 'inequality' that (in terms of semantics) obviously refers to the idea of urban life. So the term (the signifie) 'equality' was already *un*usable for defining functional urban destinations before it was changed by reality.

Figure 4

Both, Costa (Niemeyer) and Eco, fail in explaining what a city really denotes functionally and connotes symbolically.
The equation of 'function' and 'meaning' is one of the big faults of modern urbanism. Qualifying urban designers and urban managers for mastering significant urban forms and structures - and by this make them ready to serve for changing ways of urban reception an urban life - needs more than functional competence: it also needs an idea of what a city is in a social and aesthetical sense. This competence reclaims knowledge about what the urban text has to denote **and** to connote.

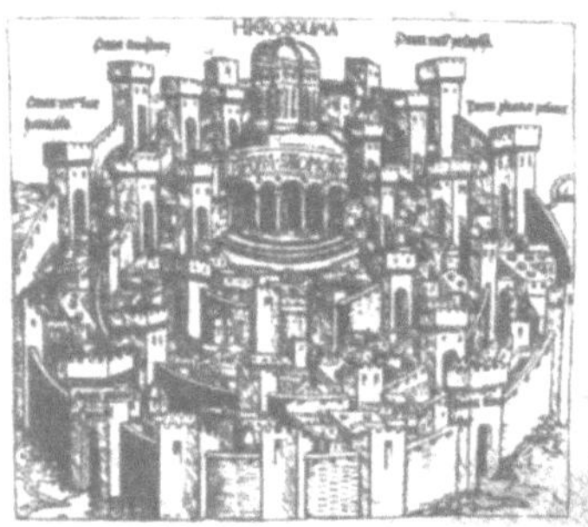

Figure 5

Lets go back to the interrelations between urban images and urban renewal and let's start with a brief look back at history. Urban history informs us about the fundamental, direct and very old interrelation of urban renewal and urban images. Let's take the period of medieval

urban renewal from the 11th to the 13th century. At that time about 80% of the still existing European cities were founded in an exceptional cooperation of feudal elites and early bourgeoisie (mainly interregional operating traders). The leading model which grounded this urban resurrection was the vision of the Holy Jerusalem, the city of God. This, by the way, explains the outstanding role of church construction in medieval cities. First of all the cities were taken as sacral spaces, although their foundation primarily aims at a profane goal: it aims at creating the best conditions for an expanding market economy. This dualism of sacral and profane space produces e.g. the bipolarity of church and city hall or of church yard and market place which still shapes the images of our European city centres. (Hassenpflug 2000, 24ff)
According to the differentiation of faith and knowledge (of Platonic realism und bourgeois nominalism) the visions of Holy Jerusalem were substituted during the epoch of Renaissance by those of the rationally derived city, the so called 'ideal city'. Later the proto-bourgeois absolutism took up the intellectual material of Renaissance urbanism to mould the shape of the new residential and capital cities from it. At least the huge stock of courtly images got a decisive influence on the urban productions of the early industrial society. (Elias 1978, Vol. II) You can easily find this interrelation in the way of the Parisian renewal by Baron Haussmann. (Benevolo 1984, 835ff)

Figure 6

During the period of early capitalistic restructuring of the market economy and the connected emergence of big city development images and visions lost control over urban development. The old iconic urban codes grew pale. The more the social and spatial conditions grew unbearable in the exploding industrial cities, the louder the cry for another urban renewal could be heard. Again images have to play the role to give strategic orientation to the social, functional and aesthetical urban process of restructuring. Ebenezer Howard for example blended traditional images of the Arcadian and Bucolic landscape with the rational radial-concentric urban visions of early modern times into a garden-city model which combines the advantages of rural life (light, air and sun) with the advantages of urban life (labour, industrial performance and mobility). By this he created the most lasting, image mediated reformulation of the modern city.

Those who think that the heroes of classic modernism, Le Corbusier, Gropius, Hilbersheimer, Neutra, van der Rohe etc., being influenced by Protestantism and Cartesian traditions, had rejected the influence of images forever, are wrong. The modern vision of the machine city, condensed in the Charta of Athens to a manifesto, only pretends to be a result of another 20th century-iconoclasm and so to do without images and ornaments for the sake of pure functional aesthetisation. Yet, in reality the aseptic spatial appearance of the industrial laboratory and fabrication hall serves for a new type of a non-pictorial world of images. When urban design follows functions only, the result is not the absence of images but a built, i.e. a 'frozen-to-sign-misunderstanding' of the real functional dimensions of the urban body.

Most mistakes of modern urban design and modern space production in the whole are grounded in this misunderstanding of the interrelations between spatial function and spatial image. The art of urban design, planning and construction has always been, not only closely but also fatefully, related to imaging (Disney called it "imagineering"). The city is not only made of functions. It is also a significant iconic and pictorial representation of peoples idea about "good life".

In these days the call for renewal strategies for our cities is to be heard almost frequently and most emphatic. The reason for this has to be seen in the advanced transformation of the labour-intensive industrial society into the capital-intensive consumer and service society. More and more the "fordistic" shaped spaces of the old industrial society get into conflict with the spatial demands of the new leisure society. This conflict results from two problems:

1. The one-dimensional fordistic fixation on functional efficiency, acceleration and specialisation runs more and more contra-productive. What once has been a hard spatial advantage turned into a disadvantage. Unstable frequencies being the result of mono-structuring turn urban spaces into insecure and dangerous spaces. (Jacobs 1963) Spatial specialization turns the urban realm into numerous spatial islands which instead of supporting mobility and identity promote long distances and fail in supporting identity constructions. The modern vision of the urban machine and the city as high performance space has definitely exhausted its possibilities.

2. The complementary visions of the Garden City, the Broad Acre City, the Green City and all the other city/country-concepts have also had their days. In the end they supported space devouring suburbanisation, peripherisation and urban sprawl. By this the urban and rural landscapes are turned into a pulp of settlements getting more and more entropic. (Fishman 1996/97) Facing ongoing low birth rates (below 2.1) the suburban migration supported by government with grants, subsidies, tax-reductions etc. rises the pressure on the shrinking cities.

Figure 7

Against this background the incredible success of the leisure and media industry in commercialising urban fakes and images is not astonishing at all. The people living in the suburban housing deserts are longing for places, for spaces which contribute to meeting und communication and provide a multiplicity of mixed functions in a mesocosmic, comprehensible physical space. Urban places are also spaces that

Figure 8

quote pictures and set them free, that tell stories and while doing this, activate our memory and imagination. It has to be accepted that the leisure and media industry - Disney ahead - was the first to notice this missing of such communicative, multi-functional and narrative spaces and to realize the demand coming out of it and even to take the logical step. The leisure industry did not only react on but also produced a huge world wide market for urban fakes. Today we can admire the offers in Disney's theme parks, in different kinds of entertainment parks, suburban malls, urban entertainment centres, in Las Vegas (the world capital of urban fakes) and last but not least in the form of a growing urban tourism offering old European urban shapes for consumption purposes.

Figure 9

Today the production, consumption and commercialising of theatrical, staged urban fakes is a boosting branch of industry, initiated by the absence of narrative, meaningful and picturesque places caused by "fordistic" space production. (Hassenpflug 2003)

In the meantime we are right in the middle of a change of the urban paradigm. The most important characteristic of this transformation is the rehabilitation of distinctive urban images and forms and, related to this, the restitution of a distinctive dualism of urban and rural space. Dedifferentiation and reintegration of functions, designing and staging of public spaces and encouragement of urban centrality by turning the centrifugal to a centripetal urban development, all these measures of the new urbanism are naturally linked with spatial narratives and images which give them a focus.

Mainly in the United States, having no feudal and courtly urban traditions, the faking of old European urban images became a forerunner of a new public discourse about urban renewal called New Urbanism. The roots of this debate and its already numerous practical consequences go back to the City-Beautiful-Movement. (Hall 1988)

Figure 10

Meanwhile the debate has led to a fundamental critique of suburbanisation and all the supporting ideologies like Wrights "Broad-Acre-City" or the different kinds of neighbourhood-ideologies (communitarism etc.). At the beginning of the 21st century we notice that the idea of the city is not only related to functions but is also very closely interwoven with the figurative dimension of urban space. Its image and pictorial equipment is an indispensable part of its cultural capital.

Figures:

Fig. 1: Azure Communications, Inc. Professional Web Design since 1996 Albuquerque, New Mexico http://www.azurecom.com/wtc/

Fig. 2: http://www.greatbuildings.com/buildings/World_Trade_Center_Images.html

Fig. 3: Lucio Costa, Blueprint of Brasilia showing a bird or airplane

Fig. 4: Hartmann Schedels Weltchronik (1493), in: Kruft, H. W., Städte in Utopia, München 1989, S. 48

Fig. 5: Ludwig Hilbersheimer, Studie 1924, The Art Institute of Chicago, Schenkung George E. Danforth 1983, 992

Fig.6: Le Corbusier, La ville contemporaine, Lichtenberger, Elisabeth, Die Stadt, Darmstadt 2002 (Wissenschaftliche Buchgesellschaft)

Fig. 7: Fake Urban Space in a Mall in East London, South Africa, advertising leaflet

Fig. 8: European Signs and Symbols in Chinese Theme Park "Window to the World", Shenzhen

Fig. 9: Mainstreet Disneyworld, Tokyo

Fig. 10: Fake Urban Space in a Theme Park in Shenzhen, China

References

Benevolo, L. (1984) Die Geschichte der Stadt, Frankfurt/M., New York

Eco, U. (1972) Einführung in die Semiotik. München

Elias, N. (1978) Über den Prozess der Zivilisation - Soziogenetische und psychogenetische Untersuchungen, 2 Bde., Frankfurt/.M.: Suhrkamp

Fishman, R. (1996/97) Bourgeois Utopias: Visions of Suburbia, in: Fainstein, Susan S., Campbell Scott (eds) Readings in Urban Theory, Malden (USA), Oxford (UK): Blackwell Publishers

Hall, P. (1988) Cities of Tomorrow - An Intellectual History of Urban Planning and Design in the Twenties Century, Oxford, Cambridge: Blackwell

Hassenpflug, D. (2000) Die europäische Stadt als Erinnerung, Leitbild und Fiktion, in: Hassenpflug, D. (ed.) Die Europäische Stadt - Mythos und Wirklichkeit Münster: LIT-Verlag

-, (2003) City and Consumption, in: Hassenpflug, D., Eckhardt Frank (eds) Consumption and the Post-Industrial City.Frankfurt/M.: Peter Lang-Verlag

Jacobs, J. (1963) Tod und Leben großer amerikanischer Städte, Berlin/Frankfurt/M.: Ullstein

Marling, Karal A. (1997) Designing Disneys Theme Parks - The Architecture of Reassurance, Paris-New York: Flammarion

Urban Policies in Europe: the Development of a New Conventional Wisdom?

Rob Atkinson and Frank Eckardt

Introduction

In this chapter we provide an overview of the `urban policies' developed to address urban problems in a number of different European countries. We do not attempt to cover all European countries, merely to examine a range of countries that illustrate the different, although sometimes broadly similar, approaches each country has developed. First of all we provide an overview of the European context, outlining the general problems affecting urban areas in Europe and identifying the response of the EU, principally through the actions and activities of the European Commission.

The European Context

This section will briefly outline the forces currently affecting `Urban Europe' and those likely to influence it in the immediate future as well as identifying the key policy responses at EU level.

There is a general recognition that urban areas/regions do not exist in isolation from wider forces originating in the national, European and global spheres. Indeed it has increasingly been argued that the process of globalisation has rendered the nation state redundant and that the `national economic space' no longer exists as an independent unit. The implications of such a position are that there is little national governments can do to control their own economies or counter the forces creating urban decline. Interestingly one of the related arguments frequently developed is that, whilst national governments are largely impotent, cities (and city regions) can act to attract inward investment to improve their position through the development of new forms of social and cultural capital, efficient infrastructure systems, etc. This involves cities engaging in forms of competition with one another through place marketing or boosterism to convey their potential advantages to investors, what Harvey (1989; see also Paddison, 1993) terms `urban entrepreneurialism'. Clearly there is an `urban hierarchy' within Europe and cities do compete with one another to improve their position in this hierarchy by attempting to attract investment, prestigious events and important political institutions (see Lever, 1993; Meijer, 1993; Wegener, 1995).

Whilst there is undoubtedly considerable truth in these arguments it does appear that the extent of globalisation and its effects are sometimes oversimplified and overstated (see Hirst and Thompson, 1996). The processes of deindustrialisation and economic restructuring have produced major changes in the economic structure of Europe (e.g. from manufacturing to services; growth of ITC) and in its corresponding spatial structure (see Lever and Bailly (eds), 1996), yet many of these developments pre-date the current wave of globalisation. While recognising that in order to understand what is happening to our cities we need to be aware of the `global context' in which they operate (see Dicken and Öberg, 1996), we also need to recognise that these forces will have a differential impact upon cities depending upon national policies and their position in the European urban hierarchy (see Hall, 1995).

Hall (1993, p883) has identified the following factors that affect Europe's urban hierarchy:

1. Globalisation and the formation of continental trading blocs.
2. The transformation of Eastern Europe.
3. The shift to the informational economy.
4. The impact of transport technology.
5. The impact of informational technology.
6. The new role of urban promotion and boosterism.
7. The impact of demographic and social change.

Clearly many of these factors operate on a global scale, although even these are likely to be mediated by national, regional and local factors. But others may equally operate on a purely European scale, for instance the integration of Eastern European countries into the EU combined with the move of the German government to Berlin could shift the centre of gravity within the EU eastward with corresponding implications for Europe's urban hierarchy (see Lichtenberger, 1995). Another example is the development of trans-European high-speed transport networks that have important implications for cities and are strongly influenced by both national and EU policy (see Wegener, 1995). The point is that distinctly European and national developments can have important spatial impacts and implications (both positive and negative) for cities and city regions. Thus it seems premature to write off the implications of national policies for urban change and development, particularly when one recognises the different national political, social and policy traditions that continue to exist with member states.

In response to the developments outlined above the 1990s witnessed a growing interest in Europe over how to address these issues at both EU-wide and national levels. Within the EU this has led to a range of initiatives attempting to both facilitate the adaptation of cities to these changes and to ameliorate the resulting problems (e.g. social exclusion, social segregation, industrial decline, and unemployment). While these problems are not unique to cities it is widely acknowledged that they are often most sharply expressed in urban areas. This process culminated in the publication of two Urban Communications by the Commission - Towards an Urban Agenda in the European Union (Commission of the European Communities, 1997) and Sustainable Urban Development in the European Union: A Framework for Action (Commission of the European Communities, 1998) - and post-1998 the holding of EU `Urban Forums' by successive Presidencies. Thus the EU has recognised that there is a specific `urban dimension' within the EU that needs to be addressed in a coherent manner at European, national, regional and local levels (see Atkinson, 2001 and 2002).

Simultaneously it has been recognised that the processes transforming Europe, and the policies developed to facilitate adaptation and attenuate the most severe by-products of change, require the adoption of an explicitly spatial view of Europe in order to fully understand the effects of these ongoing changes and to help develop appropriate responses at all levels of governance. Since the late 1980s there have been informal meetings of the ministers from Member States responsible for spatial planning (Committee on Spatial Development or CSD), along with others from the Commission, sub-national government and the research community, attempting to develop a coherent spatial perspective for the EU. Thus we have seen the development of the European Spatial Development Perspective (ESDP) that has gradually taken on a more coherent structure starting with the publication of the first Official Draft in June 1997 (ESDP, 1997), the Complete Draft in June 1998 (ESDP, 1998) and most recently the `definitive' ESDP (ESDP, 1999) in 1999. A meeting, in Tampere in October 1999, of the CSD formally adopted the `definitive' version. As one might expect of any spatial perspective the `urban dimension' figures prominently in the ESDP's analysis and its proposals for future activities by the EU.

Central to these developments has been the Commission's emphasis on the importance of building partnerships to carry forward urban regeneration. Thus the Commission argues that it is "...becoming more important to engage the participation of local participants to ensure their

needs are addressed in implementing legislation or programmes." (Commission of the European Communities, 1997, pp7-8).
It is therefore vital to:

> "...build partnerships through which residents and key local actors can influence the future of their communities, at the same time counteracting the trend towards low levels of participation and increased alienation from the political process." (Commission of the European Communities, 1998, Annex, p7).

In particular the Commission has strongly emphasised the role of Area-Based Initiatives (ABIs), albeit as part of an integrated and holistic strategy, in tackling these problems.

Despite this apparent consensus on the means to achieve the aim of urban regeneration we do need to take care when comparing policies in different countries. It is notoriously difficult to make meaningful comparisons between similar policy areas in different nations (see Heidenheimer et al, 1990), but urban policy presents particular problems given its often ill-defined nature and peripheral relationship to mainstream welfare and economic policies. What this should caution against is attempts to make any simplistic attempts at `policy transfer' between countries. It may well be possible, as the Commission hopes, to identify examples of best practice in particular policy areas, but to transplant these examples from one country to another is fraught with danger given the, still significant, political, institutional, economic, social and cultural differences between nations.

Urban Policy in the UK
From the late 1960s concern was growing about the situation in parts of British cities, although the problems were largely thought to have their origins in the `problem areas' themselves and were addressed through small-scale ad hoc ABIs. However, in 1976 the then Labour government instituted a major review of urban initiatives, the outcome of which was the 1977 White Paper - Policy for the Inner Cities (see Atkinson & Moon 1994a, chs 4, for more detail). It identified four key problems:

1. Economic Decline;
2. Racial Discrimination;
3. Environmental decline.
4. Social decline - high concentrations of poverty

A central government department, the Department of Environment, was responsible for coordinating this new Urban Policy in order to ensure that a unified approach, rather than a fragmented one, was developed. It was hoped that other central government departments would give their policies an urban dimension. In essence it was intended to form partnerships with sub-national bodies operating at local level and develop a coherent strategy bringing together local government and local representatives of central government departments (e.g. the Health Service, the police) and voluntary bodies (for more detail see Atkinson and Moon, 1994, chs.4). Before these partnerships could be fully developed in 1979 the Labour Government was replaced by a Conservative Government headed by Margaret Thatcher.

During the 1980s British urban policy was dominated by an approach which prioritorised the role of market forces in urban regeneration, in particular the approach know as property-led regeneration was dominant (see Turok, 1992; Imrie and Thomas, 1993; Atkinson and Moon, 1994, chs.7). This approach emphasised the economic and physical renewal of run-down urban areas and relied on the `trickle-down effect' to bring the benefits of regeneration to the poor and socially excluded. Urban Development Corporations were perhaps the best example of this approach (Imrie and Thomas, eds, 1999). They essentially represented a partnership between the public and private sectors, in which the public sector attempted to create the conditions that would encourage the private sector to invest in run-down urban areas that the market would otherwise by-pass. In essence the public sector was underwriting the private sector. Other problems included a multitude of urban initiatives, often located in different government departments, the lack of policy coherence and organisational coordination and the marginalisation of local government and local communities (see Atkinson and Moon, 1994, Chs.5-7).

Urban policy in the 1990s attempted to address many of these issues. In particular City Challenge and its successor the Single Regeneration Budget (SRB) sought to allocate local government and deprived communities central roles in the regeneration process. The key notion was that of multi-sectoral partnership; partnership between the public, private, voluntary and community sectors. The underlying rationale was that by creating multi-sectoral partnerships new innovative methods of tackling urban problems would be developed. Thus the notion of `social learning', whereby the different partners learn from one another and adjust their thinking and operating procedures accordingly, was an essential element in the process. It was also hoped that each partner will bring additional resources to the partnership. The inclusion of the community sector reflects the belief that deprived communities `know the problems of their areas' and therefore can help ensure that activities are better targeted. Resources would thus used more efficiently and effectively and new innovative methods of tackling problems developed. When taken together it is hoped these developments will create synergy. Sustainability is also a central element and partnerships are encouraged to think about `exit strategies' to sustain activities once government funding has ceased (for more detail see Atkinson 1999a and 2003).

Another characteristic of SRB was the attempt to strive for greater policy and organisational coherence by bringing together all the key urban initiatives under a single department and budget heading. Simultaneously at central level a Cabinet sub-committee was created as part of an attempt to develop a more strategic approach while at the regional level Government Offices of the Regions (GoRs) were set up. In the late 1990s Regional Development Agencies (RDAs) were created with a remit to address economic issues, including regeneration. It was hoped that GoRs and RDAs would work together to create a more strategic approach at the regional level. On coming to power in 1997 the new Labour Government emphasised the need for SRB to compliment its wider initiatives on welfare, social exclusion, crime, drugs, etc.

The other major urban policy development since New Labour's election was the New Deal for Communities which was developed as part of the strategy entailed in the Social Exclusion Unit's report Bringing Britain together: a national strategy for neighbourhood renewal (Social Exclusion Unit, 1998). In many ways this document contains a remarkably frank acknowledgement of urban policy's past failures, arguing that these include:

> "...the absence of effective national policies to deal with the structural causes of decline; a tendency to parachute solutions in from outside, rather than engaging local communities; and too much emphasis on physical renewal instead of better opportunities for local people. Above all, a joined up problem has never been addressed in a joined up way. Problems have fallen through the cracks between Whitehall departments, or between central and local government. And at the neighbourhood level, there has been no one in charge of pulling together all the things that need to go right at the same time. "(Social Exclusion Unit, 1998, p9).

In November 2000 an Urban White Paper was published – *Our towns and cities: the future. Delivering an urban renaissance* (DETR, 2000). Essentially the White Paper contained very little which was new. In the foreword to Urban White Paper the Deputy Prime Minister, John Prescott, stated:

> "Our guiding principle is that people must come first. Our policies, programmes and structures of governance are based on engaging local people in partnerships for change with strong local leadership." (DETR, 2000, p5)

The White Paper attempts to do two things: 1) to create a *vision* of urban living; 2) to create a *framework* in which all of the various initiatives and themes previously announced can be brought together and operate in a holistic and coherent manner. The *vision* `...is of towns, cities and suburbs which offer a high quality of life and opportunity for all, not just the few.' (DETR, 2000, p7). The *framework* is one that aims to facilitate co-ordination, collaboration and partnership; these are the means by which effective policies and programmes will be delivered and resources directed at problems. Thus joined-up strategies and joined-up working are the keywords of the White Paper. To this end government at national, regional and local levels are exhorted to work together.

Significantly for urban policy a report by the Treasury -*Government Interventions in Deprived Areas* (HM Treasury, 2000) - has argued that the primary responsibility for tackling (urban) deprivation should lie with main programmes and that this requires a refocusing of those programmes. The report argues:

> "Targeted initiatives, including holistic regeneration programmes, have a role to play. But they should be part of a clear framework for tackling deprivation, rather than the main tool for doing so." (HM Treasury, 2000, p2)

Urban Policies in Germany

It is essential to recognise that two important aspects of the German constitution play a key role in structuring urban policies in Germany First of all the constitution contains few explicitly formulated principles that guarantee the autonomy of communities particularly with regard to urban planning. Secondly, urban policies are strongly constrained by the position of cities in a Federal system in which the "Länder" (regions), as intermediate policy bodies, play a major role. As a result there is a limit to the degree to which it is possible to identify German urban policies in general as the autonomy of cities and the federal system play an important role in creating and sustaining diversity.

However, within the established pattern of interactions between national, regional and urban actors there are features that can be identified as characterising the German situation. First of all, there is a limited ability for national governments to directly intervene in urban developments. Moreover it is almost impossible to implement a single top-down strategy on urban policies in general. This can be seen as an opportunity to adjust general policies to local situations and to prevent national politicians from having a major input on urban questions. However, the development of the European Union has influenced the situation of German communities and will, as a more explicit European urban policy is developed, have a major impact in the future. Despite this it remains difficult to predict exactly how this situation will develop. What could emerge is a situation that is increasingly characterised by an ambivalent relationship between the different governmental levels. On the one hand the principle of subsidiarity, which is deeply embedded in the German system, will continue to support the self-regulation of urban affairs by cities. On the other hand cities are likely to be increasingly influenced by the norms and principles agreed at the European level (Eckardt, 2003b).

A second factor structuring German urban policies is the influence of national policies concerning issues that are not, at first sight, urban policies but impact on the development of cities in crucial ways. This is especially true with regard to tax policies. The political and organisational weakness of cities in the constitutional framework prevents them from objecting to national legislation that disadvantages the urban level. Whereas the Länder have a second chamber of parliament ("Bundesrat"), where a restricted number of legislative procedures can be debated and blocked, cities have to negotiate their share of the tax income at the level of the Länder. Nevertheless, national government has to consider the equal distribution of revenues at all three levels. In fact the policies of the last twenty years have shifted the tax burden from the national to the local level while simultaneously reducing the ability of local authorities to raise local income taxes. For instance since the 1980s high unemployment has been a continual problem in Germany but the number of people ineligible for the nationally provided support facilities has been constantly growing. These people are dependent on the Minimum Care system ("Sozialhilfe") that is financed by local authorities. At the same time national reforms of the tax systems have led to a shrinking contribution by the wealthy and big companies. As a consequence all German cities are bankrupt or overburdened with financial consolidation policies leading to the curtailment of "extra" services for citizens and the termination or reduction of their financial contribution to public libraries, swimming pools or special social projects. Contrary to previous practice privatisation of core communal institutions and established social provisions has been argued for in the context of this `fiscal crisis' and such strategies have been implemented, albeit reluctantly, by left wing mayors.

A third specific feature is the negative side of urban autonomy, which is most clearly illustrated by intensified inter-communal competition. In this difficult financial situation cities are seeking a solution by attempting to attract large-scale investment by companies with special incentives. Scarce fiscal resources are thus used to offer special deals to companies if they invest. This leads to a situation which neighbouring cities attempt to outbid one another other with firms often investing in the outskirts of bigger cities. This is especially true in the larger metropolitan areas such as Frankfurt Rhine-Main where the city remains a special place for limited use and "edge cities" are attracting investment through their low tax rates.

While this situation has, to a certain extent, been counterbalanced in West Germany, it occurred in a more extreme fashion in East German cities after reunification in 1990. Without attempting to fully describe the special situation of the former GDR-cities these issues are even more intense and extreme in Eastern cities. Within the complex situation of the political transformation of the institutions, policies, practices and political culture there continues to be major social and economic problems in eastern cities. Since the late 1990s the gap between East and West Germany has increased rather than decreased as many had assumed would happen. With the exception of Weimar all East German cities witnessed dramatic declines in their populations, losing up to one third of their 1989 population, with those leaving being the best educated and most socially active sections of the urban population. Moreover, increasing levels of social segregation in cities and the abandonment of high-rise estates ("Platte") is creating new challenges for city planning and urban politics (Eckardt, 2002).

As a consequence of the specific situation of German cities in the national political framework the development of urban regeneration politics have been strongly influenced by local political, social and economic factors. If local developments are not congruent with the power relations established at the level of the Länder and the national government, all policies that require negotiation can be blocked by the conflictual overlapping of the different interest expressed in the three fields of power relations. This is made more problematic because the German political system has traditionally been structured by a dichotomy between conservative and social-democratic spheres of influence and political organisation. Although this still largely remains the case, since the 1980s the links between social actors and political representation has weakened. This has enabled new political coalitions to emerge that have undermined formerly stable local arrangements. Most prominently, the stronghold of the Social Democrats in the cities of the Ruhr, Hamburg and Northern Hessia have switched to Christian-Democratic mayors. Elsewhere new political alliances have developed in cities such as Cologne where the Green Party and conservatives formed an alliance to end social-democratic mismanagement, or in a medium-sized city such Konstanz where a Green Major was elected. These developments are producing complex effects, creating new opportunities for policies unrelated to party preferences. These unexpected new alliances are bring into question existing urban politics creating a situation that threatens to undermine the political support of local politicians. Thus urban regeneration policies face a number of uncertainties in the political arena.

The situation facing German cities is made even more complex by the fact that social policies have been designed to disregard territorial and local situations. The major objective of the German welfare state, laid down in the constitutional framework, is to ensure equal living conditions in all parts of the country. At national level policies such as "Sozialhilfe" are developed, but implementation is left to local authorities who have limited discretion to decide the volume and forms of delivery. This situation means that at local level there are incentives to social movements to articulate their interests and make them an issue in local elections. The creation of the Green Party focussed attention on urban change and its impact on neighbourhoods, such as in the west of Frankfurt and in areas of Berlin.

Another important implication of the German political system is the insertion of many social issues related to the national government into the framework of city building programmes. The main weakness of this arrangement is that all regeneration programmes are based on negotiated contracts with the Länder and communities. As the willingness and ability of communities to support urban regeneration programmes from their own resources has been dramatically reduced, national programmes have only been accepted as long as they provide additional funds. These programmes have been most easily accepted if they restrict themselves to infrastructure related forms of urban regeneration. Starting with the Urban Development Act at the beginning of the 1970s, urban regeneration policies were linked to the Ministry for Infrastructure ("Bau"). Debates drew attention to the need for a more `socially sensitive' form of modernisation, especially of old "Jugendstil" areas in the inner city. Physical regeneration has increasingly been focussed on reconstruction rather than demolition and those managing the schemes were told to permit citizen participation. With the institutionalisation of the act as a part of the new Building Act Legislation mechanisms were developed and formalised laying the foundations for future urban regeneration.

Although this process was only concluded in the mid-1980s the need to renew the policies was soon recognised. It had already become obvious that the impacts outlined above would find their spatial expression in the resurgence of depressed neighbourhoods. The Kohl government created circumstances whereby the construction of new social housing declined while the demand for such housing increased. While welfare state reforms increasingly reduced support for those most affected by the societal changes created by de-industrialisation, cities have been experiencing the most extreme impacts of these developments.

A few social democratic controlled Länder began developing urban regeneration programmes for urban areas with special needs. After the victory of the Red-Green coalition the newly established national government wanted to demonstrate its social sensibility and hurriedly introduced a new programme - "The Social City". This programme has been implemented in almost 160 cities and has a budget of 750 million Euros over a three-year period, although the programme cannot compete with the major resources available through the "normal" urban regeneration policy of the affiliated ministry. In contrast to its financial resources, the objectives of the "Social City" are ambitious, aiming at the improvement of run-down housing areas and contributing to meeting the social needs of families and young people while also seeking to develop local employment strategies. The programme focuses on the neighbourhood level and follows an empowerment approach. Resources are provided to autonomous projects, but they have to co-finance the projects. However, as many social organisations are already dependant on local funding sources to carry out their day-to-day activities only a few projects can apply for the "Social City" money without the backing of the political elite of a city. In effect the programme is mostly administered by urban authorities and integrated into existing urban management or private offices run the projects. The legitimisation of the "Social City" programme is achieved through the establishment of a formal system of co-operation with steering groups that include different social groups and operate as participative organisations which locally produces very varied outcomes.

The situation described above significantly reduces the impact of social issues and community involvement at neighbourhood level, arguably limiting the possibilities for the development of new and innovative ways of addressing the problems of these areas. Evaluation studies show that the mixture of top-down and bottom-up networks envisaged by the programme has not occurred and this represents a major obstacle to the development of a genuine neighbourhood based strategy. Basically the programmes are `successful' when managed by urban elites; this reflects the political situation in which the neighbourhood approach is embedded. As a result such an approach is largely used as a form of legitimation when applying for funds, but it also brings into question the approach as a whole and raises the question: "is it enough to address the neighbourhood's social needs though a programme that is merely intended to improve the physical environment?".

In practice one third of the programme is directed to the "Jugendstil" areas and another third is dedicated to renewal of high-rise building areas. The scope of the "neighbourhood" can range from 500 to 40,000 inhabitants. The evaluation of the 214 projects that have competed for "Social City" funding has shown that few projects propose developing links between infrastructure investments and social initiatives (Eckardt, 2003a). In those instances where the link between uses of places and neighbourhood interests have been discussed physical intervention was mainly limited to symbolic activities. While this can have a positive effect on neighbourhood life the scope of activity is so restricted that many consider these outcomes could have achieved using existing building codes.

The new building policies of the Red-Green national government have attempted to support social developments in cities with the help of an infrastructure oriented urban regeneration policy, but this is organised by utilising a project-oriented policy. The "Social City" has been accompanied by the "Urban Regeneration East" programme, the most generously supported programme for urban regeneration in German history. To ameliorate critics in West German cities a pilot phase called "Urban Regeneration West" has also been initiated. The latter is only meant to produce some studies and so far has had no implications for further policy development. But the "East" programme might provide indications for the future development of the "project approach". As this project clearly shows the problems of the housing market have provided the necessary impetus to introduce the whole programme. While the intention of creating a more vibrant city has been placed on the agenda the design of the programme and its underlying rationale may contradict this. The crisis of the property market in cities with shrinking populations and the oversupply of accommodation has been the real reason for this "demolition project". Using national resources "Platte" buildings will be demolished, the number of dwellings on the market will be reduced and rents will increase. This will have differential impacts on the urban actors in Eastern German cities. Housing investment firms and those remaining better-off households will be given incentives for further investment while those urban dwellers depending on low rents will find affordable housing more difficult to obtain.

In particular the "Urban Regeneration Project" reduces the social dimensions of urban regeneration to insignificant proportions and supports the approach of city planners which views the improvement of the physical environment as automatically a positive contribution to the social coherence of a city or neighbourhood. Most significantly there is a lack of any concept of participation by urban inhabitants. Instead, there is a competition for the most youth oriented projects through which only marginal additional funding is provided. The East German regeneration programme foresees a dual application structure that clearly splits up into a Part A and Part B system. Part A provides an overall plan for the form of urban development a city wants to achieve, here there is a degree of planning consultation via the internet, though this is largely rhetorical and has little impact on the outcome. In Part B the community applying presents concrete plans for a chosen neighbourhood. The coherence of both parts is not required.

In sum, German urban policies are in a critical phase of development, the most obviously failing is the lack of any link between urban policies and the need for cities to adapt to the new challenges posed by post-industrial society. There is no urban agenda in Germany and the good intentions expressed in the programmes of the Red-Green government may lead to a backlash against urban policies.

Urban Policies in Hungary

The Hungarian case should not be taken as a typical example of the situation facing cities in the former socialist countries, but it does indicate some of the difficulties they face during the transition to a market oriented society. Foremost among these was the question of land ownership and the transfer of state properties into private hands. Also there was a need to change the normative framework on how to organise the spatial order of cities and their relationship to the countryside. This logic has been expressed especially with regard to social housing where the state regulated private initiatives to build one's own home. The degree to which different forms of building activities were permitted varied between the different socialist states, but has been assumed to be the greatest in Hungary. Nevertheless the state did seek to streamline private housing plans through a system of huge state subsidies. Beyond the high rise buildings so closely associated with social housing in the socialist countries private interests found a space in which to exist when the economical crisis deepened in the 1970s.

However, from a general perspective city development was the result of socialist planning and in particular the notion that industries had to be concentrated in urban centres. In a way this was an anti-centre policy that sacrificed the existing urban heritage by settling worker households in the periphery and under-investing in urban infrastructure. The deterioration of the old inner-city stock of Budapest only became a concern for architects in the 1980s. Financial restrictions hindered city council attempts to renovate areas that were threatened by decay. The most urgently needed regeneration and renovation projects are still in the urban fringe and remain unfinished. Although privatisation of the stock has been completed very quickly, the rescue of the heritage of the turn-of-the-century houses has not been completed to date. This is not primarily due to a lack of awareness on the part of the urban planners and politicians but more the result of limited financial and legal resources.

The transition of Hungarian cities to a market economy has lead to a situation that can be compared to that experienced by many West-European areas during the processes of de-industrialisation in the 1970s and 1980s, but in Hungary the whole process took place more rapidly and under uncertain political circumstances. Urban life has been strongly influenced by the simultaneous appearance of joblessness, declining social benefits and the depopulation of urban areas. Increased social mobility has found spatial expression in previously unknown forms. For instance the number of inhabitants able to build their own homes has increase while at the same time the number of urban dwellers searching for affordable housing has increased. The later resulted in homelessness, a phenomena that had not been experienced by post-war Hungarian society. Free choice of location has speeded up the suburbanisation processes and the emptying of the prefabricated tower blocks resulting in an increasing loss of city inhabitants.

The new politics ensuing from the move away from the socialist system have undergone different phases of transition producing a variety of attitudes towards urban planning. Initially the shift of powers from a centralised to a more decentralised form of urban government was the primary objective in reshaping local policies. In a very early stage of political transition the requirement to address urban issues on a local level was acknowledged. Within this newly formed political structure of autonomously organised local authorities the success of this political re-direction was generally accepted (Bennett, 1998, p38). The principal achievement was the reduction of the influence of national politics on urban affairs and the creation of a general legitimacy for urban planning procedures. This was not achieved without conflicts with forces at the state level. Budapest has been in favour of this situation, compared to other Hungarian cities, because, to a certain extent, the capital city has been strong enough to play the role of a counterweight where urban affairs have interacted with national politics. In the course of this conflict the national government accepted that housing policies needed to be better organised at local level.

Similar debates regarding the government's responsibility towards aspects of spatial politics have occurred over the last decade, however there is no formal urban policy as such. Instead urban policies have emerged out of the difficult reorganisation of the political landscape in general and the outcomes of this process for urban aspects of economic and social life. Hungary's first right-wing government supported the autonomy of small local authorities and enabled them to apply for state funding for rebuilding public buildings and physical infrastructure. As a result little attention was given to larger urban areas. The next, left wing government, continued the political efforts to improve local government structures by introducing meso-level institutions. With the 19 county governments the priorities of urban policies differed little from the smallest to the largest communities (Temesi, 2000). Nevertheless, the urban agenda has still not recognised the importance of paying special attention to the large cities, especially Budapest. By continuing a policy that aims to create equal conditions in all parts of the country urban issues in the capital are ignored. This was even more so after the return of right-wing parties to national power in 1998 as Budapest was governed by opposition parties. Nevertheless the government announced programmes in 2001 that recognised the need for certain urban subsidies, in particular to support the rehabilitation of inner-city blocks and large housing estates.

The greatest impact of these developments has been on the housing market. Decentralisation, privatisation, and the restitution problems have changed the living conditions of millions of Hungarians. Although this process has proceeded step by step the accompanying social policies have been rather vague and have been not been in force in all cities. Since 1998 the subsidy system has favoured families. This also indicates a particular perception of what the social needs of cities are, although whether it addresses them in an adequate manner is open to question. In sum, private initiatives have been supported by state funding while the remaining state-owned rented flats are left for the cities to maintain. And as urban councils are short of funds a dual housing policy outcome emerged; those not able to leave the tower blocks are the losers in the new housing market (Tosics, 2001).

For the less favoured social groups the urban transition to a market logic has been painful in a double sense. Firstly, they are not able to participate in the upward movement of those who can afford better housing conditions and they suffered from the apparent dis-investment policies that resulted from the new political situation. Secondly, existing social facilities and support systems have been eroded by the cuts in local resources. As the state no longer sees it as its overall objective to ensure the equal living standards of all citizens there are now other priorities on the national agenda competing with social equality issues. State led social security systems had to be redefined and new legislative frameworks for childcare; retarded people, family provisions and others have been developed in recent years. As these systems are under the control of central government local authorities are only obliged to provide professional services. Continued national support for these activities is in doubt and this has led to uncertainty for local planning. As a consequence there is an ongoing selection process in which those social groups able to pay for any social support are given preference. In this way, better-off inhabitants are attracted to use the inner city for their daily living and lower strata-families have to compete with them in gaining access to urban services.

After the implementation of the 1990 Law on Local Government, Budapest's political responsibilities were reorganised by creating a district level of local government. Over the following years communications, or their lack, between the city and the districts created new challenges for decision-making. The failure to define each level's responsibilities and a general lack of resources means Budapest's urgent need to halt urban decline has not been addressed. The political weakness of the city has been physically visible in the massive decline of housing estates on the edge and the inner parts of the city. This was exacerbated by the failure of newly established departments to support one another. It was not until 1996 that a communicative structure was established between the most important actors in the relevant departments. With the Urban Development Program Budapest Council took up the rehabilitation plans drawn up in 1985. Within a period of a decade 125 buildings have been "gentrified" and others demolished to save the physical quality of the 9th district. The rehabilitation program was successful in integrating different actors, in particular private investors and the non-profit organisation SEM IX. In sum, the project has been realised by a combination of activities following the rules of the market supported by local government. This experience created trust on both sides of the public-private partnership and more private investment in the physical stock of Budapest followed. Budapest has therefore achieved a position as one of the preferred locations for foreign investment in the cities of formerly socialist states.

Urban Policies in the Netherlands

Writing about the political situation of the Netherlands after the events of the year 2002 is a risky enterprise. Traditionally the Dutch political system has been regarded as one of the most sophisticated and stable in Europe, but the sudden emergence and subsequent murder of Pim Fortuyn has indicated that populist forces can be influential even in the emblematic polder society of the Netherlands. It was of symbolic significance that as one of their first governmental acts the coalition between the Fortuyn successors and the conservative-liberal parties cancelled the 5th Law on Regional Planning (vijfde nota). Seen as part of the "old politics" the comprehensive planning policy of the previous social-liberal government was abolished with little debate. After the elections of January 2003 political discourse will have to address the situation in the urban areas of the big cities once again. It is probable that the likely coalition of Christian and Social Democrats will continue policies that have embodied promising perspectives for urban renewal. Nonetheless, policies associated with the "Big Cities" programme remain in question as they are closely connected with the issue of integration of ethnic minorities. The later field of politics has been a key issue in the political upheavals in recent elections and public debates (Eckardt, 2003c).

With a legacy of urban and regional planning that is one of the foremost in Europe, Dutch urban policies have been well aware of the complex challenges that faced cities since the 1970s. A wide range of factors has been taken into account during the formulation of urban policies. The Netherlands has undergone significant changes in its economic structure with the process of de-industrialisation has particularly affecting urban agglomerations. Accompanied by major trends in society, the big cities have experienced a complex set of problems. The four big cities have lost significant numbers of their populations, mainly as a result of suburbanisation. The densely populated western part of the country has a highly integrated spatial structure that has led to the provinces of South and North Holland being viewed as part of a single undifferentiated region, the so-called Randstad. Although urban policies have never treated it as such (Cortie, Dijst and Ostendorf, 1992) As the Randstad idea has only limited significance in the everyday life of many inhabitants of urban conglomerations regional planning has had to include those smaller communities unwilling to be absorbed into a single metropolitan body. Moreover, organisational reforms intended to weaken the position of Amsterdam and Rotterdam have been rejected by a referendum. As a result obstacles remain to the development of a more integrated approach to the problems arising from the high-density of building and population in both the big cities and the suburban or peripheral settlements. The "vijfde nota" wanted the provinces outside the Randstad to share part of the burden of addressing these issues.

Suburbanisation and the movement out of the city have to be discussed in the context of the individualisation and upgrading of households during the economic boom of the last decade (although it slowed down in 2002). While the upward movement of large parts of Dutch society lasted for a considerable time the problems facing inner-city area in the four big cities have persisted. Most notably in the former working class housing areas close to the centre that have been the focus of urban regeneration programmes in the past. Under the urban renewal policies of 1970-1985 the physical quality of the social housing stock in pre-war housing areas was the main target of urban policy. The demolition of derelict houses and the replacement of the former inhabitants of these neighbourhoods were the main aims of these regeneration strategies, leaving social issues largely untouched. After criticism of this physical renewal strategy the 1980s witnessed a shift of urban renewal policies, projects focussed more on renovation and rehabilitation of the existing stock. In the late 1980s social issues came to the fore. Since then the improvement of living conditions has been the focus of the so-called "social renewal" policies. With this ambitious programme job opportunities, educational facilities and other social infrastructure improvements was recognised as crucial for the further development of the neighbourhood as was the active participation of affected communities. This policy shift was the result of an increased tension in the old inner-city neighbourhoods which were vacated by those who could afford to live in the suburbs and which then became the entry point for foreign immigration (Eckardt 2001, 43-70).

Concerns over this issue formed the background against which the latest urban restructuring programme started in 1997. It sought to address the significant residential concentrations of low-income groups and ethnic minorities in particular areas, although anti-segregation policies were part of earlier urban policies. In the government paper "Housing in the 1990's", the Ministry of Housing developed another attitude toward housing policies. Up to then the social housing system in the Netherlands could be seen as one of the most extensive in Europe containing a high percentage of socially supported households. Rent controls, individual housing allowances and the provision of social housing by state owned agencies made the housing sector a major pillar of the post-war welfare state. Even today the number of available low rent-flats is unequalled throughout Europe. Widespread social housing not only supported the less favoured but has also made a substantial contribution to the shaping of a Dutch middle class that remained in the social housing sector even after taking part in general economic upgrading (Dieleman, 1992).

With the above mentioned White Paper housing policies moved towards greater deregulation of the housing market, less state subsidy and the intention to prevent the development of a situation in social housing in the inner cities that was restricted to the lowest income groups. To discourage the exit of the middle class to other areas the so-called VINEX policies were implemented. High quality housing was provided in neighbourhoods with a high percentage of lower income groups so that movement would be easier and restricted to the surrounding areas. As a consequence the social mix of the neighbourhood would also be maintained.

The effects of this anti-segregation policy can be viewed from contradictory perspectives (Musterd and Ostendorf, 1998). Those in favour of the restructuring policies have pointed to the influx of better-off households into formerly homogenous poor areas. Critics have argued that it inevitably decreased the housing opportunities available to low income groups. Furthermore, the underlying logic of preventing segregation by restructuring the housing market has been questioned. The debate on segregation has highlighted a complex process with ambivalent effects that can only be fully understood by taking into account other factors that influence urban opportunities as well as housing. Housing policies have thus been the object of new legislative initiatives and broader political debates. The flexibalisation of the housing market in 2000 introduced fiscal incentives that favoured home owners and house builders.

At the same time the “Big Cities” policies were being formulated. This programme carries forward the aims of “social renewal” and seeks to improve the social and economic quality of urban life. In scope and design the Big Cities Policies surpass their predecessors. Special attention is paid to those urban areas that have been identified as the location of cumulative social problems. This area-based policy represents as aspect of the "Big Cities" programme designed to bring about an improvement in an area's living conditions through integrated activities directed at improving the physical environment, social infrastructure and local economy.

To ensure cohesion between urban restructuring and the "Big Cities" programme all available resources are combined together into a single fund and allocated in such a way as to support the achievement of social and economic objectives. More than thirty cities have signed a contract to co-operate with the Ministry of Big Cities Policies and thereby promised to exercise their discretionary powers so as to ensure the successful implementation of the projects. At present it is not possible to draw any substantive conclusions on the outcomes of this integrated and area-based approach.

In some urban areas the "Big Cities" policies can be seen as a continuation of urban regeneration policies since the 1970s. This is especially true with regard to those areas where physical renovation was started earlier, in inner-city neighbourhoods such as the “Indische Buurt” in Amsterdam. Here, the objectives of the broader agenda for urban renewal have been realised in a defensive way by focusing on public safety, improvements for business activity and youth care (Ostendorf, 2002).

The integration of an economic dimension into the Big Cities Policies can be seen as progressive compared to older approaches that ignored this aspect of urban life. The same can be said about the attention paid to safety and other “weak” aspects of urban policies not easy to target.

As part of the innovations developed by this integrated approach it is possible to support local initiatives for improving shopping facilities, refurbishing squares in the neighbourhood, intensive training courses for deviant youngsters or child care for the Moroccan minority.

A weak aspect of the programme is illustrated when considering that next to the socially weak neighbourhood of the "Indische Buurt" a residential area for white and better-off households has been constructed. There may be an integrated approach evolving from the partnership between the district council, the city management and the ministry, but this does not appear to have impacted overall urban development in general terms. Although it is much to early to analyse the contribution of the Big Cities Policies to improving the opportunities of the selected areas, the need to integrate with social and economic renewal process beyond the territory included in the projects is clear

Urban policies in Sweden

Considered within the context of Western Europe as has a whole Sweden has been `late' in developing b urban policy to address the challenges facing its urban areas. It was not until 1995 that government planning recognised the need to support certain urban neighbourhoods. The political recognition of specific urban needs was signalled by the appointment of a Minister for Metropolitan Affairs in 1998. To date the general attitude towards the social problems of urban areas has been constrained by the universalist philosophy of the Swedish welfare state. Traditionally the focus has been on achieving equal living conditions in all parts of the country and therefore attention focused on those areas that were below the norm, especially in Stockholm, Gothenburg and Malmö. There has been a long-term political emphasis on the equal distribution of infrastructure investments and political and organisational decentralisation policies. In effect inter- and intra-urban differences have addressed within the context of differences between regions and cities enabling the spatial dimension to be included in planing equal living conditions for all citizens. In a sense regional planning policies have foreshadowed the paradigmatic shift of the 1990s when spatial and social policies became linked to lay the basis of Swedish urban policies.

In the past cities have been seen as the object of social policies in general and as the Swedish welfare state has maintained a high level of social provision the neglect of special urban needs seemed to be justified. In particular, housing policies contributed to a view on the relationship between urban society and national social policies that sustained a non-area approach to local circumstances. The Social

Democrats saw housing policies as the backbone of Swedish social policy. In the post-war years the extension of the rental sector provided affordable housing offers for all, but during the 1990's the reduction of rent subsidies generated rising housing costs. The room to manoeuvre for housing companies shrunk as a consequence of de-regulation of the housing allocation system and the end to preferential special rules which prevented competition with private housing operators. Privatisation of housing estates owned by the communal housing companies has been a result of the new policies. The impact on the social cohesion effects of urban housing markets has been substantial, a considerable shortage of dwellings emerging since 1996.

The situation in Swedish cities, with their relative short history of urbanisation, is in some ways unique and thus different from other European countries. As there is a distinct gap between the north and the south of the country urbanisation has led to movement of population to the growing metropolitan areas around Sweden's three major cities. Migration from the less developed regions to these metropolitan agglomerations is an ongoing process. This was even more the case in the heyday of the `New Economy' of the early 1990s when internationally orientated IT-firms such as Ericson increasingly based their activities in the Stockholm region. Although the intention of the city to turn Stockholm into Europe's IT-centre has to be regarded with some scepticism, nevertheless the capital city and its periphery still exerts a strong influence on migration patterns.

Urban regeneration started in the early 1960s with the renovation and demolition of inner-city areas as a result the physical appearance of most urban centres has not been affected by social processes that were the object of heated debate during the 1990s. Deprivation, social exclusion and other issues surrounding social cohesion in urban societies mainly occur in areas outside the city centre. While inner city neighbourhoods have been socially upgraded and opened up for commercial use there is a growing need to house the remaining lower income groups. The state launched its Million Programme (MP) in 1965 and housing for one million Swedes was built over the next decade. These housing estates were placed at the edge of cities and the overall proportion of rented housing increased, although this programme also allowed forms of private ownership of houses in the periphery. There have been further investments in edge of town housing estates and new building in the following years, the so-called post-MP areas.

While the figures for unemployment and other indices of social deprivation for the central neighbourhoods are relatively low these peripheral housing areas have attracted most attention and this led to initiatives that finally resulted in urban regeneration policies. As mentioned above, Swedish cities are still the "powerhouse" of the Swedish economy and therefore the mirror of wider societal changes. The demographic structure of different groups in society shows a clear trend towards fragmented family life, more one-parent households, increasing rates of divorce and longer periods of pre-family life with an expanding housing demand by young single persons. This produced a polarised understanding of what the quality of urban life means for family and non-family households in the city (Nyström, 2003). This general trend toward a more individualised urban structure is accompanied by the influx of international migrants attracted by the excellent provisions of the Swedish labour market and welfare state. In reality immigrants are subject to the reduced benefits available for socially less favoured groups in which foreigners are over-represented. Moreover, the migration of the 1990s has been of a type that Swedish society has not previously experienced. The composition of the migratory population, and their settlement patterns, has been different from that of earlier "guestworkers". There is a now visible ethnic minority that is concentrated in those urban areas outside the centre of the big cities. Today over one in five of Stockholm's inhabitants belongs to these new migrant groups. The attitude of Swedish society towards these groups is an ambivalent one; the social environment in which they find themselves can be described in terms of inter-ethnic conflicts, discrimination, racism and disadvantages in the labour and housing markets. Reforms of the welfare state target these vulnerable social group the most; while the restructuring of the social security system continues to provide benefits for the "insiders" through pensions, unemployment allowances and other supportive budgets for those who are considered to be employable. But even then, the private care necessary to top-up state subsidies can only be afforded by the better-off (Andersson, 1999).

It is therefore no coincidence that areas with the greatest concentrations of immigrants have been the ones which area based approaches to socially problematic neighbourhoods have targeted first. The minister for ethnic minority integration, Leif Blomberg, pointed out that he intends the extra resources targeted at these areas to focus on increasing labour market integration. The so-called "Blomman" assistance programme was restricted to a few highly segregated neighbourhoods in Gothenburg and Stockholm. Running for a period of three years, the capacities of inhabitants had to be improved and supported by local initiatives and managed by the municipal authorities. State and municipality are equally responsible for providing the financial resources required. This programme has focused on the social sphere of the neighbourhood and did not invest in the physical environment of the area. There was considerable emphasis on participation by the targeted groups. Language courses, meeting places for immigrants and Swedes, training and other labour market oriented facilities have been financed to contribute to an anti-segregation policy. However, due to the way in which the projects were organised and managed control of the initiatives was placed the hands of the local district administration and the municipal actors. Critics have pointed to a lack of adequate support from the national government, arguing that it has not been consistent in its programme. Also the time-limited nature of the “Blomman” programme means there is a lack of long term support which has undermined its sustainability and de-motivated many actors. The future of the programme remains unclear, although with the “National Examples” there was a sort of extension of the area-based approach. In 1998, central government again took the initiative to target deprived neighbourhoods with a high rate of unemployed and ethnic minorities. Under this new, still ongoing, programme the focus of urban development was directed towards long-term and sustainable improvements. The selected areas have to function as “national examples” for other disadvantaged neighbourhoods. The list of intended actions includes the improvement of cultural, educational, professional, commercial and public parts of the supported areas (Elander, 1999).

Besides state organised urban development support policies, the two biggest cities, Stockholm and Gothenburg, have undertaken their own projects in line with the previous programmes. After an evaluation of the experiences of both “Blomman” and “National Example” programmes, these municipalities have continued an area-based approach. For a period of only two years, the two cities worked out agreements with 24 neighbourhoods and with the Ministry of Culture to further support the redirection of urban policies from a project to a process approach that gives priority to bottom-up strategies. Evaluation of the integrated projects is now a crucial aspect of the local learning process. This means more room for experiments that are becoming increasingly important for the whole planning process.

All these programmes can be seen as empowerment strategies oriented to improving the human potential of affected neighbourhoods, although only the “Stockholm Urban Fringe Programme” invested part of its financial resources in improving the physical environment of the areas.

The relevant municipal departments and the public housing companies contributed an equal share. The programme lasted for three years and was completed in 1998. The objectives of the investments have not only been focused on the built environment but also on integrated social aspects such as the reduction of unemployment levels. Participation by neighbourhood inhabitants has been emphasised as important and was supported in different projects. The physical infrastructure provided by this programme included new buildings and leisure opportunities and, in the long run, the physical side of the projects gained the most attention. The failure of the Stockholm specific programme lay in the mismanagement of financial resources and the lack of control exercised by local inhabitants (Andersson and Pallander, 2002).

Urban Policies in France

Urban regeneration programmes in France can be traced back to the 1970s thus there is a considerable depth of experience that has developed with renewal strategies and political attempts in different circumstances encapsulated within the "politique de la ville". Despite this it has not been possible to identify a political recognition of the need to develop an integrated approach to urban problems. This is the result of the particular situation of French cities and their role in the national political constitution. The position of Paris as not only the political capital but as the national educational, economic, cultural and social centre of the country has led to a complex centre-periphery debate that has shaped the contents of regional and spatial planning policies. The question of decentralisation of administrative responsibilities has appeared several times on the agenda of French politics over the last decades. After strenuous efforts the effects of decentralisation are seen as being important and the government elected in 2002 restated the importance of decentralised policy approaches. The problematic nature of this debate about devolving more rights to lower level institution highlights a significant obstacle that has limited the achievements of nearly 30 years of urban regeneration. In short, it points to the dominance of top-down approaches and the limited and sometimes symbolic nature of participatory governance (Blanc, 2002).

The long and difficult history of urban regeneration policies has, to some extent, to be understood as a consequence of the lack of interest in housing policies within the French welfare state. This is related to do the priority that has been given to other fields of social policy. The prioritorisation of infrastructure and employment related investments can be traced back to the 1920s when the principal decisions affecting urban inhabitants were taken. From the governmental side, the limitation on rental increases seemed to be sufficient provide social support to the lower class populations living in cities. This perception was not challenged even when it was clear that the effects of legislative restrictions on the housing market were contradictory. Housing became unattractive as a form of investment and the resulting de-investment led to serious overcrowding and under supply that threatened living conditions especially in the inner-cities. This did not change during the post-war years when the economic reconstruction of France absorbed most of the available resources. It was not until the 1960s that housing attracted political attention. In line with the *etatist* approach of the 5th Republic the demolition of housing in the central neighbourhoods of cities was undertaken on a huge scale. A massive gentrification of these areas followed that enabled upper middle-class and the better-off to return or stay in these "cleared" and now very attractive urban core areas. Accompanying the renewal programme the suburbanisation of other groups was instituted and partially enforced by the state. On the outskirts of the bigger cities nearly 3 million dwellings were constructed within one decade to house those households that could not afford the increased rents demanded in inner-city areas. As in other European countries the expectations of these new housing estates were informed by very simplistic assumptions about the quality of urban life. Drawing on the work of Le Corbusier and his colleagues the idea behind this policy was that the separation of different spheres of city life would improve the living conditions of all urban inhabitants which up-to-then were perceived as suffering from stress and unhealthy conditions. According to this vision high-rise building in the periphery offered better housing and would contribute to the development of a "modern" urban life.

Soon after the first inhabitants occupied the new apartments on the fringe the disadvantages of these estates became apparent. While the improved infrastructure (heating, sanitary facilities, etc) of these high-rise estates was widely recognised as being better than that of the old inner-city housing areas the distance of the estates from other parts of the city and to daily work places created major problems. It did not take long for these new housing areas to develop a negative image. This stigmatisation was made worse by the naive belief of urban planners that these areas would spontaneously develop a sense of community, something that clearly was not happening. Instead a feeling of not belonging and not being at home motivated many inhabitants to leave the estates as quickly as possible. When the national government redirected their housing policy and stopped financing new housing estates middle class tenants moved out into individual homes well away from the despised high-rise estates. As a consequence, the socially less favoured groups were left behind and so the process of inner-city clearance and re-housing led to a highly segregated urban landscape.

The decline of living conditions in the high-rise estates was accelerated by the conflicts that developed after ethnic minorities moved into flats vacated by the middle class. Stimulated by stricter immigration regulations introduced in 1974 the reunification of families of "guestworkers" predominantly took place in these estates on the periphery of cities. Algerian and other North African immigrant groups have since suffered an extra handicap as they were held responsible for the deterioration of these neighbourhoods and for their increasing crime rates.

With the launch of the "Habitat et Vie Sociale" (HVS) the national government recognised the need to react to the deteriorating situation in the peripheral neighbourhoods. The programme appeared to be innovative both in its selection of supported "areas of opportunity" and its emphasis on participative democracy. The HVS, however, was more or less a pure urban planning policy aiming to improve the physical environment. The inclusion of tenants was never clearly specified and largely discretionary, which left the form and the contents of participation subject to top-down decisions. Moreover, the lessons from the failure of this architecturally inspired approach to neighbourhood improvement were not learnt at this stage. It turned out that rents increased after the HVS regeneration was finished and this disadvantaged the inhabitants of the neighbourhood even more. A special housing benefit fund had to be introduced to reduce the negative impact of the programme. Furthermore, the programmes' more ambitious plans to attract middle class households back to these improved areas was a failure.

As a result of the difficulties with HVS, and following violent riots in the deprived areas, the Mitterrand government introduced the "Développement Social des Quartiers" (DSQ) - a more neighbourhood related regeneration programme. The politically determined priorities emphasised employment strategies rather than housing improvement. However, most financial support was directed at the later and the impact of job initiatives was limited. As result the general situation of the unemployed and ethnic minority youth has not improved much. It turned out that the approach was not targeting crucial issues of discrimination, such as their lack of inclusion in urban planning strategies on infrastructure, communication and transport. In terms of participation and the contract model adopted by DSQ it failed to bring about the necessary reform of meso-level institutions to allow bottom-up organisations an input into the decision-making process.

Following on from this failure the next urban regeneration programme, the "Développement Social Urbain" (DSL), explicitly recognised the need to integrate depressed neighbourhoods into urban society. The persistence of departmental divisions of responsibilities and limited project organisation were identified as one of the main reason for the ineffectiveness of previous programmes. In practice this recognition has resulted in only a modest review of urban governance and this has largely remained a rhetorical issue. The integration of formerly independent national agencies in the "Délégation Interministérielle à la Ville" represented a step forward, as it brought the DSQ development, crime policies, cultural affairs and urban design together. However, this cross-administrative unit lacks the authority to meaningfully influence powerful institutions such as the department for urban planning or the police. It has also been argued that inclusion of the disadvantaged areas has been undermined by other neighbourhoods, thus the integration of stigmatised areas into the general strategies of urban governance was also made more difficult by actors from outside these institutions.

In the 1990s the DSL programme was renamed, but the new "Contract de Ville" incorporates the same thinking (Blanc and Stébé, 2002). The programme now includes more than 200 cities with approximately 1300 neighbourhoods. The underlying philosophy of regeneration still retains the idea that the areas included in the programme should be more attractive to investment and the middle classes. New methods have been tried, such as the implementation of free enterprise zones to attract companies and in some highly stigmatised areas demolition of high-rise building is continuing. Participation of inhabitants from the affected neighbourhoods is still limited by the prevailing political frameworks, although two laws recently passed by parliament may help guarantee the active participation of residents. For the first time, the cities have the duty to set up neighbourhood councils. The negative aspect of this novelty lies in the subjection of this new body to the direct control of the city council.

Conclusion

The European Commission has sought to recognise and support many of the issues and initiatives outlined above in its various urban and spatial communications, but it finds its scope for action even more circumscribed than national governments. The need to respect subsidiarity places strong restrictions on what it can do. Moreover we need to remember that national government's are also limited by their particular historical, constitutional, political and institutional/ organisational traditions. Policies do not develop in a vacuum they are constrained by the particular circumstances from which they emerge which determines the limits of what is possible. For instance in Germany the Federal State cannot impose policies on the *Lander*, it too must respect their subsidiarity enshrined within law. Even an apparently highly centralised and unitary state such as that in France has had to 'negotiate' with sub-national government and find ways of 'winning' the co-operation of municipalities in urban initiatives. In Sweden, as in France and Germany, the dominant societal approach to social issues/problems has been to guarantee equal living conditions for all citizens regardless of where they live. Such an approach makes it difficult to adopt policies that target particular places as they appears to be discriminating in favour of those places compared to the rest of the nation. Nevertheless in these countries it has gradually been recognised that there are places ('excluded spaces') that contain concentrations of problems and that the living conditions of those who live there are significantly below what would be accepted as the societal norm and which also serve to severely constrain the life chances of those living there. Whereas in Britain, perhaps influenced by the United States, there has been a greater readiness to adopt area-based policies.

In other countries, particularly those from the former 'Soviet Bloc' such as Hungary, there is as yet no indication that such policies are being adopted, which reflects the very different history and circumstances of those societies. In Hungary there is still a debate over the extent to which urban areas as such merit special treatment vis-à-vis rural areas. Even with regard to the planning system there appears as yet to be no clear decision on how to proceed other than to seek a solution through the attraction of inward investment. Nor has the system of local governance had sufficient time in the post-socialist period to develop a new tradition of governance and establish a series of generally accepted norms of organisation and behaviour. All of which makes it difficult to begin experimenting with new approaches.

Moreover we should also bear in mind that the way(s) in which urban problems are defined and conceptualised has important implications for both the manner and means by which they are addressed. The conceptualisation and definition of urban problems frequently develops out of, often largely unstated, ideological and political positions (see Atkinson, 2000a). Once again the point to bear in mind is that policies do not develop in a vacuum.

Nevertheless it is possible to identify two general approaches to urban areas and their problems:

Traditional planning policies that are largely determined by the inherited approach embodied within planning systems and the professions and politicians that oversee those systems. These systems exist within particular politico-legal contexts that facilitate or limit their activities vis-à-vis urban areas.
Targeted (area-based) urban policies that seek to address the particular problems of urban areas. Increasingly there is a recognition that such policies need to be part of an integrated approach that is co-ordinated with wider social and economic policies.

These two basic approaches often exist side by side and may actually come into conflict with one another, although the particular mix varies from country to country.

At the same time there has also been a growing emphasis on the need to develop a partnership approach to urban problems. However, we need to recognise that partnerships can take many different forms. For instance in the 1980s in Britain the partnership approach largely referred to public private partnerships; in France it was largely seen in terms of a partnership between different levels of the state in both a vertical and horizontal sense whereas in Britain in the 1990s and 2000s urban regeneration partnership referred to multi-sectoral partnerships between public, private, voluntary and community sectors. It is this last sense that has tended to emerge in European Commission pronouncements in the latter part of the 1990s and early 2000s.

Finally we need to recognise that within Western Europe, supported by the European Commission (see Atkinson, 2001 and 2002), there has been an increasingly emphasis on the involvement of local citizens/residents and the `community' more generally in both traditional planned approaches and targeted urban policies. However, the roles assigned to these social forces vary considerably from country to country (see Atkinson, 1999b and 2000b). Once again this variation, in terms of both meaning and practice, has its roots in the different historical, social, political and legal traditions of each country which sometimes makes it difficult to accept that at local level citizens/residents/communities should be able to at least play a part, other than through elections, in determining how policies are developed and implemented.

However, given the current emphasis on the role of multi-sectoral partnerships and community participation in area-based urban regeneration initiatives, we once again need to be sensitive to the very different forms of thinking about, and attitudes towards, state-civil society relations across Europe. Thus terms such as partnership and community participation take their meaning from the different political, legal, social and cultural traditions of each country. As a result policies deploying these means often differ considerably between countries even when they operate under the same EU programme (e.g. URBAN and URBAN II). Nevertheless it is possible to recognise that broadly similar issues are being addressed by a range of policies that do share certain similarities and which increasingly appear to form the `new conventional wisdom' of urban regeneration across much of Europe.

References:

Andersson, R. (1999) "Divided cities" as a policy-based notion in Sweden. In: Housing Studies. Vol. 14, Nor. 5, pp601-624.

Andersson, R. and Pallander, C. (2001) The Swedish Background Report for the UGIS project. Uppsala.

Atkinson, R. (1999a) `Urban Crisis; New Policies for the Next Century', in M. Chapman, and P. Allmendinger. (eds) Planning in the Millennium, J Wiley, Chichester.

-, (1999b) `Countering Urban Social Exclusion: the Role of Community Participation in Urban Regeneration', in Haughton, G. (Ed) Community Economic Development, The Stationery Office: London.

-, (2000a) `Narratives of the Inner City: The Construction of Urban Problems and Urban Policy in the Official Discourse of British Government, 1968-1998' Critical Social Policy, Vol.20 (2), pp211-232.

-, (2000b) `Combating Social Exclusion in Europe: The New Urban Policy Challenge', Urban Studies, Vol. 37(5/6), pp 1037-1055.

-, (2001) `The Emerging `Urban Agenda' and the European Spatial Development Perspective: Towards and EU Urban Policy?', European Planning Studies, Vol. 9(3) pp385-406.

-, (2002) `The White Paper on *European Governance*: Implications for urban policy', European Planning Studies, Vol.10(6).

-, (2003) ` Urban Policy and Regeneration: bringing the fragments together?' for New Developments in British Social Policy (eds) N Ellison and C Pierson, Palgrave Press, London.

Atkinson, R. and Cope, S. (1997) `Community participation and urban regeneration in Britain', in Hoggett, P. (Ed) Contested Communities, Policy Press, Bristol.

Atkinson, R. and Moon, G. (1994) Urban Policy in Britain: The City, the State and the Market, Macmillan, London.

Bennett, R. J. (1998) Local government in postsocialist cities. In: Enyedi, G. (ed) Social change and urban restructuring in central Europe. Budapest.

Blanc, M. (2002) Strategies for the Social Regeneration of Disadvantaged Neighbourhoods in France (1977-2002). In: Walther, U.-J. (ed.) Soziale Stadt – Zwischenbilanzen. Opladen.
Blanc, M./Stébé, J.M. (2002) High-rise Social Housing in France: From Dreams to Disillusion.: Turkington, R./van Kempten, R./Wassenberg, F. (eds) Hgh-Rise Estates in Europe. Delft.
Commission of the European Communities (1997) Towards an urban agenda in the European Union, Communication from the Commission, COM(97) 197, final, 06.05.97, Commission of the European Communities, Brussels.
-, (1998) Sustainable Urban Development in the European Union: A Framework for Action, Communication from the Commission COM(1998) 605 final, 28.10.98, Commission of the European Communities, Brussels.
Cortie, C., Dijst, M. and Ostendorf, W. (1992) The Randstad a Metropolis? In: Tijdschift voor Econ. en Soc. Geographie, (83) (4), pp 278-28.
Dicken, P. and Öberg, S. (1996) `The Global Context. Europe in a world of dynamic economic and population change', European Urban and Regional Studies,vol.3(2), pp101-120.
Dieleman, F. M. (1996) The quiet revolution in Dutch Housing Policy. In: Tijdschift voor Econ. en Soc. Geographie, 87 (3),pp. 275-282.
Department of the Environment Transport and the Regions (2000) Our towns and cities: the future. Delivering an urban renaissance, Cm 4911, HMSO, London.
Eckardt, F. (2001) Rotterdam - Konturen einer globalisierten Stadt. Münster.
-, (2002) Eine periphere Gesellschaft. Marburg.
-, (2003a) Die soziale Stadt als Wunsch. Auswertung des Bundeswettbewerbs "Soziale Stadt". Berlin (forthcoming).
-, (2003b) Störkörper im Betrieb? Die organisatorische Anbindung der "Sozialen Stadt". Paper to the Conference on "The Social City" of the German Local Policy Research Forum, Stuttgart 4.May.
-, (2003c) Pim Fortuyn und die Niederlande. Populismus als Reaktion auf die Globalisierung. Wiesbaden.
Elander, I. (1999) National strategies for urban renewal and housing rehabilitation: the case of Sweden. In: Andersen, H.S. and Leather, P. (eds.) Housing renewal in Europe. Bristol.
European Spatial Development Perspective (1997) European Spatial Development Perspective. First official draft, Informal meeting of Ministers responsible for spatial planning of the Member States of the European Union, Noorwijk, June 1997, Commission of the European Communities, Luxembourg.
European Spatial Development Perspective (1998) European Spatial Development Perspective. Complete Draft, Department of the Environment, Transport and the Regions, London.
European Spatial Development Perspective (1999) European Spatial Development Perspective. Towards Balanced and Sustainable Development of the Territory of the EU, Committee on Spatial Development, Brussels.
Hall, P. (1993) `Forces Shaping Urban Europe', Urban Studies, vol.30(6), pp883-898.
-, (1195) `The future of cities in Western Europe', European Review, vol.3(2), pp161-169.
Harvey, D. (1989) `From Managerialism to Entrepreneurialism: The Transformation in Urban Governance in Late Capitalism', Geografiska Annaler, vol 71B, pp3-17.
Heidenheimer, A., Heclo, H. and Adams, C. (1990) Comparative Public Policy. The Politics of Social Choice in America, Europe, and Japan, Macmillan, London.

H M Treasury (2000) Government Interventions in Deprived Areas (GIDA) Cross-cutting Review, Spending Review 2000, H M Treasury, London.
Hirst, P. and Thompson, G. (1996) Globalization in Question, Polity Press, Cambridge.
Imrie, R. and Thomas, H. (eds) (1999) British Urban Policy. An evaluation of the Urban Development Corporations, Sage, London.
Imrie, R. & Thomas, H. (1993) 'The limits of property-led regeneration', Environment and Planning C: Government and Policy, vol.11, pp87-102.
Lever, W. (1993) `Competition within the European Urban System', Urban Studies, vol.30(6), pp935-948.
Lever, W. and Bailly, A. (eds) (1996) The Spatial Impact of Economic Changes in Europe, Avebury, Aldershot.
Lichtenberger, E. (1995) `The future of the European city in the West and the East', European Review, vol.3(2), pp183-193.
Meijer, M. (1993) `Growth and decline of European Cities: Changing position of cities in Europe', Urban Studies, vol.30(6), pp981-990.
Musterd, S. and Ostendorf, W. (1998) Segregation and social participation in the welfare state: the case of Amsterdam. In: Musterd, S. and Ostendorf, W.(eds) Urban Segregation and the Welfare State: Inequality and Exclusion in Western Cities. London.
Nyström, L. (2003) Quality of Urban Life in Europe in the 21st Century. With a Focus on Three Nordic Capitals. In: Eckardt, F./Hassenpflug, D. (eds.) Consumption and the Post-Industrial City. Frankfurt.
Ostendorf, W. (2002) Segregation and Urban Policies in the Netherlands. In: Schnell, I. and Ostendorf, W (eds.) Studies in Segregation and Desegregation. Aldershot.
Paddison, R. (1993) `City Marketing, Image Reconstruction and Urban Regeneration', Urban Studies, vol.30, pp339-350.
Social Exclusion Unit (1998) Bringing Britain together: a national strategy for neighbourhood renewal, Report by the Social Exclusion Unit, Cm 4045, HMSO, London.
Temesi, I. (2000) Local Government in Hungary. In: Horváth, T. M. (ed.) Decentralization, Experiments and Reforms. Budapest.
Tosics, I. (2001) The post-socialist Budapest: the invasion of market forces and the attempts of public leadership. In: Hamilton, F.E.I. and Dimitrowska-Andrews, K. (eds.) Globaliziaton and Transformations in Eastern and Central European Cities. Tokyo.
Turok, I. (1992) 'Property-led Urban Regeneration: Panacea or Placebo?', Environment and Planning A, vol.24, pp361-79.
Wegener, W. (1995) `The Changing Urban Hierarchy in Europe', in Brotchie, J., et al (eds) Cities in Competition. Productive and Sustainable Cities for the 21st Century, Longman, Melbourne.

A Coal Mine is not a Coal Mine:
Image Improvement and Symbolic Representation of the Ruhr Area, Germany

Achim Prossek

The Ruhr Area (Ruhrgebiet) is one of Europe's biggest agglomerations and one of the largest old-industrialized regions. The Ruhr Area has gone through an economic struggle for over four decades now, and it still has a problem with its bad image which has stuck to it ever since. Additionally, it has a disadvantage vis-a-vis other cities because of the general "prejudices towards its cityscape" (Sieverts 1996, 46). The question of image is also a question of regional identity, and to me there seems to be a need to develop both for further if the region is to make progress. This paper is about developments in image improvement. It analyses the Landmark-project by the Emscher Park International Building Exhibition (IBA), which was an important development program from 1989 to 1999. It describes the role of industrial heritage as well as the role of a new shopping mall by taking a closer look at the Gasometer and the CentrO-mall in the city of Oberhausen. As a tool for regional development - especially with regard to the symbolic level - and as a tool for enhancing regional identity the State North-Rhine-Westphalia set up a new cultural event, the heavily subsidized Ruhrtriennale, which commenced at the end of August 2002. One way of analysing the representational strategy behind the Triennale is by looking at its newspaper, folder and advertisements. One of the main questions that will be addressed in this paper is which region, which Ruhrgebiet is being represented by the Triennale and in which fashion this is done and to what effect.. Then the problem of regional identity will be discussed, taking into account the history and the structure of the region. Finally, an attempt is made at evaluating the described strategies and projects. The paper concentrates on the conference issues, therefore no overview of the historic development will be given. For a brief history of the development of the Ruhr region from the beginning in the 1850s until the 1970s see for example Petzina (1998), for the younger development and IBA background in short Shaw (2002), for a detailed description and discussion of the IBA Kilper and Wood (1995).

Gasometer and CentrO

Only one relict of the former Gute-Hoffnungs-Hütte steel mill remains in the city of Oberhausen: the Gasometer, with 117 meters the highest in Europe. Since 1994 its sole use is for cultural events, mainly exhibitions. The first one was a very successful exhibition about the history of the industrial development of the Ruhr Area. It was strategically a good idea to start with an exhibition of the regional history: Half a million people saw the exhibition during 1994 and 1995. The Gasometer, who was in great danger of being torn down before, had beenlaunched as a landmark for the city. A poster announced: "Welcome to the club" (Willkommen im Club), showing the Gasometer together with the Eiffel Tower, the Dome of Cologne and the Berlin Brandenburg-Gate. For the first time an industrial relict was seen as an icon for a city, cultural and historical equivalent to other well known iconic buildings of European Cities. The Gasometer as a landmark became a symbol for the structural change and a symbol of an awakening regional identity. It was adopted in the collective memory of the Ruhr Area, being a historical monument not only for the citizens of Oberhausen, but for the citizens of the other Ruhr Area cities too: The Gasometer became one of the most used illustrations in newspapers and magazines, with exhibitions like Christo & Jeanne Claude's installation "The Wall" in 1999, the year of the final presentation of the IBA spending, resulting in more attention for it.

There are only few things left from the former steel mill and works: a former casino and guest house, today part of the new environmental technology center, and a stock house from the architect and designer Peter Behrens from the 1920s, both monuments which have given the street the name "Alley of Industrial Culture". Together with the other sites of industrial culture, Zollverein Pit XII and Duisburg-Nord being in top-position of representative images of the new Ruhrgebiet, the Gasometer became a symbolic place, telling about the renewal of the old industrialized region. Telling about not so much of becoming a normal region (which has been a goal for a long time until the 1980s), but rather an exceptional one. The proximity of the Gasometer to the shopping center CentrO with its food and drink promenade had a special effect: Since 1998 it is officially marketed as a part of the CentrO. For the shopping and entertainment center this is an effective mechanism of image upgrading, because it integrates itself into the history of the region, and therefore also into the regional image and identity.

Shortly after the CentrO-opening in 1996 a journalist investigated the scenery. His observation was that people behaved as if they were visiting some alien object and not a shopping mall. The behavior that people displayed was more in tune with a holiday in a foreign country, in a place very different from home: modern, clean, stylish. He found the scenery too strong to live against and with it, everybody feeling and behaving like a stranger in his/her own town (Smoltczyk 1998).

Today two things have changed: The first is the surrounding of the CentrO and the second is the attitude of the inhabitants of Oberhausen and the rest of the Ruhr Region. The district New Centre Oberhausen is growing with office buildings and leisure opportunities, it is beginning to look more like a normal quarter than in the beginning.

Secondly, and more important is the perception of the CentrO as the heart of the New Centre Oberhausen by the people. First of all, it now is fairly universally accepted. The structural change, for which the CentrO is a symbol, is not just seen as a specific process happening in the Ruhr Region but as a general and typical change from an industrialized to a postindustrialized society (Wood 2002). This view is supported by the fact that CentrO catches high votes in two rankings: First as a destination for shopping. There are other big shopping centers in the region, which are similar in size but older, for example the Ruhr Park Centre in Bochum or the RhineRuhrCentre in Mülheim an der Ruhr. However, CentrO is the most famous among them, especially for young customers. Secondly, when the inhabitants of the Ruhr were asked what they would show to visitors from outside, the Centro was named as the favorite destination followed by old collieries in general and other objects of industrial heritage. So as a "Must see"-place the CentrO is on the same level with the most famous places of industrial culture, especially for the younger inhabitants (WAZ, Jan. 12th 2002). It is no longer an alien element to the city and the region. It is losing its character as a so called non-place. Instead it is becoming a place of identification like other places of collective history. There is a shift of representation: The CentrO has become one of the most famous sites of the new Ruhr Region, well known in the Netherlands, well known among city planners, architects and urbanists, well known to the general (shopping) public. It is part of "The city as an event-strategy" of modern city-marketing. It plays a big role in the story about the "New Ruhr Region", giving Oberhausen an image of a dynamic and changing city rather than a dying one. Oberhausen now has the image of a shopping and entertainment destination. Its website is mainly for tourists, which is still unusual in the region. And therefore one can say with some justification that this is the one of the most important stories of image recreation in the Ruhr Region, second only to the IBA and its preservation of industrial heritage. Other instances for this story of image recreation are the Ski Center or the Warner Brothers Movie World, both in Bottrop. There are plans for further developments: Dortmund wants an Urban Entertainment Center in the new central station, Essen a shopping center at the same place, and the city of Duisburg wishes to build a shopping and entertainment center bigger than the CentrO just beside the central station. In Castrop-Rauxel "X-scape" is a coming investment, a successful indoor-wintersport and entertainment facility, imported from Milton Keynes in Great Britain.

The shopping, leisure and entertainment facilities bring large numbers of visitors in the region. This means thousands of people get a (small) new look on the region: one of the first steps for a new image. But danger lies in the character of events: Events tend to be unfashionable very easily, they inherently need renewal and new attractions, surpassing the old one after a period. This effect is reinforced by competing projects in and outside the region.

The Landmarks
Over the 10-year lifespan of the IBA 19 landmark projects were realized. The decision on places and objects ignored local authority boundaries but had a look on the specific situation of the site. The projects can be divided in five types (with some overlap):

1. Tip arrangements
   Tip Haniel, Bottrop; Tip Rungenberg, Gelsenkirchen; Tip Schwerin, Castrop-Rauxel; Tip Rheinelbe, Gelsenkirchen; Tip Beckstreet, Bottrop; Tip Schurenbach, Essen

2. Industrial Heritage Sites/ Re-use of former brownfields and industrial buildings
   Hall of the Century, Bochum; North Duisburg Landscape Park; Gasometer, Oberhausen; Nordstern Park, Gelsenkirchen; Coking Plant Zollverein, Essen; Zollverein Pit XII, Essen; Garden of Remembrance, Duisburg Inner Harbour

3. Natural hill
   Mechtenberg, Gelsenkirchen/Bochum/Essen

4. New Buildings on brownfields
   Academy Mont-Cenis, Herne; Science Park Rheinelbe, Gelsenkirchen

5. Light-installations
   Westpol-Ostpol, Kamp-Lintfort/Boenen; North Duisburg Landscape Park, Academy Mont-Cenis; Tip Rungenberg; Tip Beckstreet; Coking Plant Zollverein; Science Park Rheinelbe;
   (Source: Pachnicke, Mensch (1999)

All landmark projects stand in close relationship with the place as well as the wider space around them. This leads to an altered quality of the place and to an improved aura of the objects. The place becomes specific in two ways: site specific and space specific. Through the landmark projects the IBA increased the complexity of the region. Complexity means creating places which are symbolic, scenic and historic. Here past, present and future meet, a manifestation of times, therefore of the regional development. But it needs to be stressed that not all landmarks work in the same way. They have different functions and a different use. Moreover, there are different ways in which visitors can utilize individual landmarks. This makes them suitable for different groups of the population in their respective day-to-day space of action as well as in their mental map of the region.

A landmark is an object easily recognizable, something which places emphasis on an important point. In a polycentric urban space with almost no topographical differences the landmarks are given the new role of orientation within the region. They offer new ways of orientation by overcoming the confused situation within the built environment. It is possible to look from one landmark to another, from the Tetrahedron in Bottrop to the Gasometer in Oberhausen, from Richard Serras "Slab for the Ruhrgebiet" in Essen to Zollverein coking plant in Essen to the Nordstern landscape park in Gelsenkirchen and so on. In this way, several city frontiers are overcome, but also mental ones: by the "commanding" views spectators obtain from the landmarks the region is experienced as one (continuous) space .

As the list above shows there are different types of landmarks: former industrial buildings like the Gasometer or the Zollverein colliery or coking plant, or art on former places of technology or industry. On some sites artists worked with the buildings, like Jonathan Park, who illuminated the iron and steel mill in Duisburg. The whole site is part of a new kind of landscape park today. It has to be emphasized that landmark art does not stand for itself. It is a kind of securing the evidence, of poetologic archiving. It is working as a medium. It is a tool for individual, social, historical and regional localization processes. The artistic landmarks embrace a site-specificity, they reflect and interpret the old-industrial landscape between the rivers Ruhr and Emscher. Their message is sometimes not clear. They do not have one specific message for every observer. But overall they tell a story of a region in a deep and permanent change, a region in crisis, but also a story of it's renewal and potential.

Thus, the landmarks have the function of signaling change, of regional development. In their use in the media for illustrations they become icons of the new Ruhrgebiet. And in daily life they are used as scenery for a variety of activities: sports, theater, concerts or just recreation. But as agents between past and present they are symbols of a collective memory. As technical monuments they are witnesses to the industrial period which is nearly over in the whole of (Western) Europe. Almost all chimney-stacks and gasometers, pithead towers and blast furnaces are gone, the industrial silhouette disappeared in the last decades. The landscape of the region has changed dramatically during this time. The landmark art is therefore part of the collective remembering. The illumination of the Tetrahedron in Bottrop for example stands for the former "1000 fires", which blazed the sky in the heydays of heavy industry night by night (for example from the blast furnaces).

However, I would maintain that the landmarks do not only have a function in space but also in time. They show the origin of the Ruhr region and they reflect and interpret the present. They are a sign to the future within their new context. They are spaces of meaning, an impulse for recollection. All this taken together means that they are a source for narratives about the region. These narratives – and myths – exist in peoples' head, but likewise they are represented in cultural artifacts or in the media.

The landmarks do not only reevaluate their respective sites. They exist in a regional context, they reply or react to the regional surroundings. They are Ruhrgebiet-specific. Therefore they also enhance the value and complexity of the whole region. They are one element to identify the region as "the Ruhrgebiet". For the region it is a process of getting self-aware. One example may be helpful to illustrate this: The Gasometer in Oberhausen commands a new look on the region. It is not just because of Christo & Jeanne Claude's exhibition "The Wall" in 1999 ore one of the other exhibition-events which have taken place there, but because of the huge empty interior which evokes feelings of sublimity. The interior which is publicly accessible embodies the absence of the former use and its context. Looking from the top of the roof then confirms the experience from inside. What you see is not only a typical landscape of the Ruhr Area with a net of motorways, railways, waterways, industry and housing settlements and even old palaces or castles or of small farms in between in the nearest surroundings. You also witness a number of changes: former collieries turned into parks, and, just beneath the Gasometer, the CentrO shopping mall and other leisure and entertainment facilities on the site of a former ironworks.

Zollverein pit XII

The Zollverein colliery in Essen with the pit XII and the coking plant as hearts of the area became a UNESCO World Heritage site on Dez. 14th 2001. Built in 1932 it was one of the biggest and most efficient pits in Europe until its closing-down in 1986. It became an IBA project and was developed as the central anchor point of the industrial heritage trail. Art, culture and design characterize the new use: offices, galleries, exhibitions and concerts. The Design Centre North-Rhine Westphalia found a new home here in a building reconverted by Sir Norman Foster. The Zollverein pit XII is regarded as the "Cathedral of the Ruhrgebiet", its pithead tower became one symbol for the structural change.

In 2001 the Dutch architect Rem Koolhaas developed a masterplan for the further development. The second phase of investment is coordinated by the development agency Zollverein, which was founded in May 2001. It is a joint project by the City of Essen and the Project Ruhr, an agency owned by the state of North-Rhine-Westphalia to enhance structural change in the Region. Until 2001 almost 50 million Euro had been invested, for the next phase until 2006, the end of EU-sponsoring, the EU will give 40 million Euro, the State another 40 million Euro and Essen 10 million Euro. Four main projects are planned: First a "platform design" with a university and research institutes, second a commercial design enterprise park, third the so called "Metaform", a design world exhibition which is due to start in 2005 and then being held every five years, and fourth the Ruhrmuseum, a new museum for the natural and cultural history of the region. The Ruhrmuseum should play the role of a visitor centre for the whole Zollverein area with an estimated 150.000 visitors or more per year. For a critical appreciation of the plan see FAZ from Sept. 3rd 2002.

Zollverein became one of the main attractions of the new Ruhrgebiet. It is one of the most famous industrial monuments in the region and it is the only industrial World Heritage Site in the region (there are only three industrial World Heritage Sites in Germany). Its pithead tower symbolizes the new era of culture and design. But on a picture or photograph the pit looks like a pit. The architecture says something about architectural and industrial history, but nothing about the new use. At a World Heritage Site the architecture can't be changed without the risk of losing the title, therefore all the plans for combining the old with modern architecture failed so far. Thus, if the picture can't inform of the new use, there has to be an accompanying narration. Even the worth of the architecture has to be told because industrial buildings usually do not have the same acceptance like other representational ones. The

UNESCO-label is a great help in changing the perception of the colliery in particular and of the industrial history of the region in general. Only those who know of these (highly symbolic) changes and of the new design center are aware that the pithead tower symbolizes the new Ruhrgebiet, all the others see what there is on the "surface": a pit, old industry, not clear if still in use or not.

The development strategy for Zollverein is important for Essen as well as the whole region, but it nonetheless with an exclusive character. The area is located in the North of Essen, one of the poorest districts of the city. The development plan excludes the local inhabitants, it is not a program for them to benefit from. Only a few of the locals participate, for instance through bed and breakfast, which is most likely a growing sector (see Die Zeit, Aug. 29th 2002), the others have the option of feeling proud of Zollverein when watching the tourist busses, students, art visitors and academics visiting the area.

Wanted: Curiosity. The first Ruhrtriennale

"A festival of courious for courious (people)" ("Ein Festival von Neugierigen für Neugierige"). This slogan, taken from advertisements in the national newspapers and magazines in August 2002 marks the start of the first Ruhrtriennale on September 1st 2002, a new festival of culture, with a three-year budget of 41 million Euro, endowed by the state of North-Rhine-Westphalia. Gerard Mortier is the director, after having been in charge of the "Salzburger Festspiele" before. The Triennale is understood as a tool for development of the Ruhr Area. Almost all locations of the event are places of industrial heritage: former coal mines, steel mills all over the region are being used. It is intended to let the arts communicate with these buildings, with their esthetics, with their past. The Ruhrtriennale promotes itself as being different from other festivals held in normal cultural venues, such as concert halls, opera houses and theaters. In order to convey that this difference is not seen as something wanting but as a chance, curiosity is needed, an openness for the constructed "nature" of the new festival. Using former industrial sites as cultural venues has a history of almost 20 years now in the Ruhr (from subcultural/ alternative venues like Zeche Carl to commercial musical halls like the Collosseum, both located in Essen). This is why the target group of the slogan are people living outside the region, who in the main know little about the long history of development the region has undergone and who are also not familiar with cultural events taking place in old industrial buildings, or at least: not familiar with buildings of this size.

However, there is a deep truth to the above quoted slogan about the Ruhr Area. It offers to explore cultural events as well as the region, and it requests curiousity and open-mindedness. One recurring finding of image-studies about the Ruhr is that the image of the region is based on strong prejudices. Consequently, the best way to change images of the region is to let people see it for themselves. This is why the IBA invited thousands of people in a special host-program. But the old image is not the only reason for the difficulties in telling the story of structural change of the region. Others lie in the structure of the Ruhr Area itself: it denies the "usual" impression of the classic European City because most cities here are founded on industrial development. One does not find large ensembles of interesting architecture, except for workers' housing schemes, nor does one find one centre of the region, because of its polycentric structure with eleven cites and four districts (within the boundaries of the Kommunalverband Ruhrgebiet, the Association of Local Authorities).

The Ruhrtriennale plays with the old image of the region. Put bluntly, old image means the predominance of a proletarian culture and lifestyle, non-academic, people with no or little sense for design and art but for kitsch, being rough but direct and honest. In other words: simple and backwards. The Triennale newspaper tries to show a representation of this image. The pictures show interior design as it is estimated to illustrate the image of the region. It has some ironic touch, but, as always with irony, not everybody will get the point. The reason why the newspaper and folder, which are similar, have a touch of pop culture-strategy may be the agency that designed it: Boros from Wuppertal, which became famous for its scandalous campaign for the launch of Viva 2 Music Television. This design has to be read ironically to be understood. Because it illustrates a Ruhrgebiet which does not exist any more – and which probably never existed anyhow. It represents the old industrial region. A quotation in the Triennale-newspaper from a Ralf Rothmann book, an author who grew up in a city of the Ruhrgebiet in the 1960s then quickly moved to Berlin, describes the region in the way shown above, but it gives the region singularity and a kind of special ethos. An ethos of the working class milieu of the 1960s, one has to add.

The question then is as to why this image is used by a cultural festival which elaborates and stands for high culture. The link may be the locations. The vast majority of them are former industrial sites. Some will be used for events for years to come, some were renovated for the festival like the Hall of the Century in Bochum. Both, the play with the (old) image and the industrial relics-locations, give the festival a uniqueness it can't get just with the programme. The locations are used to create a special regional atmosphere, an atmosphere which allows the visitor to identify the festival as a cultural event within and of the Ruhrgebiet. This is why this strategy mainly addresses people from outside the region, a thought which is highlighted by an illustration in the Triennale-folder, where the Ruhrgebiet is located in the centre of Europe, with lines illustrating the flight distance from several important cultural cities of Europe: Edingburgh, Prague, Salzburg, Bruxelles, Paris, Copenhagen and so on. The intention is to place the region on the cultural map of Europe, to get it into people's list of cultural 'places to be'. For the inhabitants of the region it is less novel to go to the theater or to hear classical concerts in former industrial buildings. As was pointed out before, there exists a history of showing "high-culture" in these buildings and to set art in relation to the site, the region and its transformation. One example of a long list may be the World Music Days in 1995, a festival of Modern Music all around the region.

The first Ruhrtriennale has just started, therefore it is too early to judge its success. However, at the moment one can say that the goal to "put in place a functioning regional identity" (director Gerard Mortier in: die tageszeitung, Sept. 19th 2002) is somehow difficult to accomplish h with a communication strategy mainly addressing people from outside. However, one could maintain that positive reactions from the outside may be instrumental in creating a positive knock-on effect in the region, thus helping to boost regional identity in the Ruhr). Another, more general criticism would be that identity does not only come about by discussing it but also through taking it as a matter of course. This is a cautious criticism not aimed at the artistic program but rather at the Ruhrtriennale as an instrument for regional development. The positive effects of investment in buildings and infrastructure are easy to name, but taking effect on the level of image and symbolic representation needs sensibility – and probably (much) more time.

As a side-effect of marketing the area touristically there is some development in the merchandising and souvenir trade of the Ruhrgebiet. Until fairly recently only local markets existed selling city souvenirs and city postcards, but no regional products. In Gelsenkirchen, for instance, a first souvenir shop has opened a short while ago which concentrates not on the city but on the whole region. But the majority of the customers live within the region, searching for products which represent the or, more precise: *their* region, with the history of coal and steel playing a key role. It is similar to the visitors of the heritage trail: most of them come from within the region or from the near surroundings. This shows that there is deep interest in the history of the region from within.

The opposite of this more traditional understanding of the region is the merchandising which set in after the IBA. Industrial heritage and architecture as well as the landmark art projects were widely published as posters or exclusive postcard series. Obviously they have a different target group. Here we don't find scarves with "Ruhrpott" (that is a common slang word for "Ruhrgebiet") printed in a traditional typeset. This market has grown after the end of the IBA in 1999, the outlets being concentrated i at the sites of industrial heritage, tourist information centres and selected book stores.

The regional renewal, the discussion of regional identity and the work on the image of the region showed some effect on regional merchandising. The product range and the demand can't be compared with "classic" tourist destinations, but for an old industrialized region it is something new and a good beginning. As yet it is too early for typical geographical analyzes like the representation of the region on postcards or in travel guides: There simply is not enough material to analyse. However, there seems to be a changed consciousness which can be made out in the first products that have come on the market so far .

Regional Identity

One interesting and helpful way to analyze the identity of the region is to focus on its structure, on its character of being a polycentric urban region (PUR), as Van Houtum and Lagendijk did. They defined three types of identities, all being interdependent: the strategic, the cultural and the functional. The central conclusion of their case study on the Ruhr is the observation that, "In sum, the Ruhr has been presented as an example of a PUR where [...] only a weak form of geo-strategy has emerged." And they close their paper with open questions: "At present, it is still uncertain what the identity of the Ruhr area is. Is it an industrial region, a region with an industrial heritage, or a post-industrial region? And to what extend is it (still) a region?" (Van Houtum/ Lagendijk 2001, 760/761)

Economists analyzing the structural change claim that the Ruhrgebiet as a region stopped to exist when the dominance of the coal and steel industry was over. With the economic decline the social situation changed. From this perspective the Ruhrgebiet indeed is historic and obsolete nowadays. This paper however maintains that the Ruhrgebiet still exists, that it is reconstructed through its industrial heritage, through the landmark project and through a changed perception of the region, especially by younger people. This is indeed less geo-strategic but rather a change in the perception and the image of the region, it is a question of growing regional identity. But if regional identity can be used as "a collective mobilizing force and a tool for planning", as Raagmaa suggests, to "enhance" regional identity, (still) remains a problematic issue (Raagmaa 2002, 55/60). Although there has been a progress in constituting regional identity it is still in strong competition with local identities, which are historically grown and strong. The city has always been the level of identification for the inhabitants, and for most politicians the local are(n)a is the most important one of course. Additionally, there are other questions that also remain open: Who then, should use regional identity as a planning tool, and what could be the goal? Just economic development? In a polycentric region like the Ruhr Region regional identity is difficult to instrumentalize. One problem of the perennial "Ruhr-City"-debate ("Ruhrstadt") – i.e a permanent discussion of a new strong authority with responsibilities for the whole region – is that on the regional level it is difficult to mobilize people into political action, and that the instrumental element of regional identity is difficult to control.

An advantage of regional identity may be that it is less exclusive than other concepts of collective identity. Exclusion of the other is an inherent part of identity. But a not-at-all-defined identity of a not-at-all-defined region could offer multiple choices for the inhabitants. This regional identity of the Ruhrgebiet is strongly based on history. It delimits itself from the neighbors at the Rhine for example by defining itself as the Other, because it adopts the image ascribed, which, in sum, sees the region just as being "different" from the rest of Germany. In the words of city and regional marketing this defined singularity has another name: Unique Selling Proposition. The Masterplan for tourism in the Ruhr region, developed with the help of the IBA in 1997, was the first paper which tried to build a marketing and planning strategy upon the own and unique history and the evolved landscape. (MWMTV 1997) As Paassi points out, regions and regional identities "are social facts even if people do not actively think about them", but they "can generate action as long as people believe in them". (Paassi 2002, 139). The Tourism Masterplan, the work of the IBA in general, gave this belief a basis by suggesting turning the feeling of inferiority into uniqueness.

Conclusion

As the examples industrial heritage, landmarks and in particular the Zollverein pit XII have shown the strategy of improving the image of the Ruhrgebiet mainly builds upon the relics of the past. It was shown that this is not only done in order to cater for special interest tourism. This, I would argue, cannot be the sole motor of development anyhow. As Hospers maintains it "is unlikely that in practice the effects of industrial heritage tourism will be large enough to rejuvenate an entire industrial region in decline." (Hospers 2002, 402) Because more than 80% of the tourists come out of professional interest and the Ruhr region "does not have the mass appeal of places such as Berlin", "tourism should only be considered a minor part of the region's economy". (Shaw 2002, 88). But the important fact of the development of industrial heritage in the Ruhr region is the inward effect for the collective memory and therefore for regional identity. One could call this a necessary strategy, because the region suffered from the loss of its pride derived from industrial manufacturing (which has been very different from the pride of the British working class), the loss of the important role as the "heart German industry" and the ensuing problematic image of a region in decline. Maybe it is too much to say that there is now a new pride. But was has risen is a new awareness, a consciousness for the past, for the own history and the right to remember the industrial history just as others remember their past. "Importantly, the beginnings of a change in mentality can be seen, and will continue to be seen, in relation to politicians, local authorities and the people." (Shaw 2002, 89)

Because every city in the region share (almost) the same history it was possible to develop symbolic places for the whole region, not only for the city. This is why the region is defined through a common past. But this means, consequently, that the region is associated with a common present and future. This has to be understood as a general development. Also, it needs to be noted that inner-regional disparities exist, both economically and socially. The North, the Emscher sub-region, is weaker than the south which has undergone the transformation much earlier. As a result the IBA was only implemented in the North of the Ruhr, the part of the region which has been responsible for the persistence of the coal and steel image. Its image stood for the whole region, and therefore - vice versa - the renewal also stands for the entire region. Now, after the phasing out of the IBA, the Ruhr has got its specific symbols of renewal. As Salet points out, "the true sense of urban identity first and foremost demands cultural envolvement", particularly on the regional level (Salet 2001, 293) Salet considers the IBA as a good example for this mechanism, but he warns that the cultural transformation needs more time than the physical transformation did. This can be seen in the Ruhr Area where the economic decline began in the early 1960s, but the cultural transformation towards a more positive regional identity devoid of feelings of inferiority did not commence before the 1990s.

The Association of Local Authorities (KVR) had an image campaign running from 1998 until 2001, heading the slogan "Der Pott kocht" (a play upon words with slang name for the Ruhrgebiet). It followed a campaign which ran for over 13-years in which the strength of the region was demonstrated, mainly the economic strength, and in which the image of the region was portrayed in an emotionalized fashion. The majority of the younger inhabitants strictly supported the slogan of the recent campaign. Within the region it expresses a feeling of life and lifestyle. And to those outside the region it suggested that by using the word "Pott", which some find negative and dated, the people of the Ruhr were decided to determine the image of the region, the "Ruhrpott", themselves. This campaign can be seen as an apt support of the IBA strategy. They are both instrumental in fostering a new feeling of regional identity.

As was shown earlier on, in an old industrialized region cultural involvement is necessary for improving the image of the area as well as for nurturing regional identity, both aspects being interrelated in various ways. Of course this is not enough. One of the best ways to improve the image of a region in economic struggle may be the success in this sector – and selling that success as part of a PR-strategy which does not rely upon the (economic) evidence speaking for itself. A story of an economic rebirth would create a strong image. It would get new architectural symbols and a visible change in the cityscape. This is, despite some exceptions, still missing in the Ruhr. The region has undertaken various steps of (economic) change with some success, but it still has a long way to go. Maybe in the not too far distant future the answer to the question that Sieverts (1996) raised can be a positive one, "Is the Emscher Region a model for the City of the 21st Century?" Today it has taken one step away from the old image. The new "Merian" traveler-magazine about the Ruhrgebiet, for instance, has the official title "The New Ruhrgebiet", so had a supplement in the national newspaper Frankfurter Allgemeine Zeitung (FAZ). The new exists and yet the old still lingers on. But ever since the last big demonstrations of workers were over, the "new Ruhrgebiet" is gradually becoming the dominant representation of the region.

References:

Danielzyk, R./ Wood G. (2001) On the Relationship Between Cultural and Economic Aspects of Regional Development: Some Evidence from Germany and Britain. In: European Planning Studies, Vol. 9, No. 1, pp. 69-83.

Hospers, G. (2002) Industrial Heritage Tourism and Regional Restructuring in the European Union. In: European Planning Studies, Vo. 10, No. 3, pp. 397-404.

Kilper, H. / Wood G. (1995): Restructuring policies: the Emscher Park International Building Exhibition. In: Philip Cooke (ed.): The Rise of the Rustbelt. London, pp. 208-230.

Kommunalverband Ruhrgebiet (ed 2001) The Ruhrgebiet. Facts and Figures. Essen.

Ministerium für Wirtschaft und Mittelstand, Technologie und Verkehr des Landes Nordrhein-Westfalen (MWMTV) (Ed.)(1997): Masterplan für Reisen ins Revier. Düsseldorf.

Paasi, A. (2002) Bounded spaces in the mobile world: Deconstructing 'Regional Identity'. In: Tijdschrift voor Economische en Sociale Geografie, Vol. 93, No. 2, pp. 137-148.

Pachnicke, P./ Mensch B. (Ed.) Kunst setzt Zeichen. Landmarken-Kunst. Ausstellung vom 1. Mai bis 3. Oktober 1999 in der Ludwig Galerie Schloß Oberhausen. (Exhibition cataloque), Oberhausen.

Petzina, D. (1998) The Ruhr Area: Historical Development. In: Hesse, Joachim Jens (Ed.): Regional Structural Change and Industrial Policy in International Perspective: United States, Great Britain, France, Federal Republic of Germany. Baden-Baden, pp. 467-509.

Raagmaa, G. (2002) Regional Identity in Regional Development and Planning. In: European Planning Studies, Vol. 10, No. 1, pp. 55-76.

Salet, W. (2001): The Quest for the Regional City. New identities and institutional conditions in a context of metropolitan fragmentation. In: Geographica Helvetica, Vol. 56, No. 4, pp. 289-295.

Shaw, R. (2002) The International Building Exhibition (IBA) Emscher Park, Germany: A Model for Sustainable Restructuring? In: European Planning Studies, Vol. 10, No. 1, pp. 77-97.

Sieverts, T. (1996) Urban Network and Townscape. Is the Emscher Region a Model for the City of the 21st century? In: Wachten, K. (ed.): Change without growth? Sustainable urban development for the 21st century. Cataloque of the VI. Architecture Biennale Venice 1996, pp. 46-53.

Smoltczyk, A. (1998) Oberhausen liegt am Meer. In: Kursbuch 131 "Neue Landschaften", pp. 81-89.

Van Houtum, H. / Lagendijk A. (2001) Contextualising Regional Identity and Imagination in the Construction of Polycentric Urban Regions: The Cases of the Ruhr Area and the Basque Country. In: Urban Studies, Vol. 38, No. 4, pp. 747-767.

Wood, G. (2002) Wahrnehmung und Bewertung städtischen Wandels in der Postmoderne. Eine theoretische Untersuchung zum Strukturwandel in Oberhausen. Opladen (forthcoming).

Newspapers:

Frankfurter Allgemeine Zeitung (FAZ) from Sept. 3rd 2002

Die tageszeitung from Sept. 19th 2002

Westdeutsche Allgemeine Zeitung (WAZ) from Jan. 12th 2002

Die Zeit from Aug. 29th 2002

Marketing the North:
Place Marketing to attract In-migrants to the Northern Parts of Sweden

Thomas Niedomys and Lars-Erik Borgegård

The competition between places trying to attract different forms of capital seems to be increasing and adopting new modes and targets (Brotchie et al. 1995; Jensen-Butler et al. 1997). In the present paper we address a recent trend in northern Sweden: place marketing to attract in-migrants. While neither place marketing nor attempts to attract in-migrants are new phenomena, the combination of the two has been paid little attention by researchers, when compared to other forms, e.g. place marketing to attract business and tourism. We argue that this is a pressing lacunae in research since place marketing currently seems to have a very high priority among the local authorities in northern Sweden, but very little is known of these efforts.

The reason for the increased interest in these issues is assumed to be the population development of northern Sweden and stiffer competition for government support to municipalities. Many of the places in this region have experienced a high rate of out-migration and the already ageing population structure is further accelerated by low birth rates. This has meant a greater tax burden and difficulties with maintaining the standards of service levels - probably the same experiences are shared by many other European cities. The social problem that is focussed on in this paper could thus be seen as a matter of survival or prosperity for many cities; the local authorities are trying to maintain and, at best, augment their populations and local economic development by most means available.

The *aim* of this paper is to explore the promotional activities of local actors and their efforts in trying to attract in-migrants to the northern municipalities of Sweden. We specifically address the following questions: (1) how are the municipalities marketing themselves and how important is this marketing? (2) Do the marketers believe that they have been successful in their efforts? (3) What images are put forward in the municipalities´ marketing and how important are these images deemed to be in attracting in-migrants?

While the scope of these questions may seem modest, we argue that they will provide important information on the place marketing efforts of local authorities to attract new residents, as well as a foundation for other, more evaluative, pressing questions such as whether it is at all possible to attract inter-regional migrants by place marketing and how the potential in-migrants percieve such marketing. These questions will be addressed in forthcoming studies, but we emphasize that it is essential to have a solid knowledge of the basic facts when further research issues are explored. We agree with Barke (1999) and Millington et. al. (1997) that much of the earlier research on place marketing has been confined to a few, and mostly very populous, places whose experiences may be very different from the Swedish context.

Before venturing any further, a few clarifications are in order. Place marketing is an extensive area of scholarly interest, ranging from studies of urban renewal and hosting major events, like the Olympics, to the use of slogans. While the former is clearly beyond the scope of this paper, the latter is well within its brief. Thus we restrict our study to deal with what some would argue is more selling or promotion than marketing (other Swedish examples of the outer fringes of place marketing are provided by Ek (2001) and Hallin (1991)). Also note that the terms 'city' and 'municipality' are used interchangeably in the text.

Place marketing

Place marketing is an important aspect of attempts to create or promote attractive environments (Gold/Ward 1994), and for a long time places have been marketed in order to attract tourists, business and in-migrants (Ward 1998). However, it was in the beginning of the 1970s, when waves of de-industrialisation generally affected large parts of the western world, that a general interest in place marketing occurred (Hall 2001), and it continues to be important in times of economic recession - especially as regards attracting industries (Gold/Ward 1994). Most of the work on place marketing has focused on tourism or the industries and the area of marketing directed towards attracting in-migrants has largely been neglected. In fact, and to the best of our knowledge, there have been very few major studies on the topic of marketing and migration, which encompasses a wider geographical perspective.

The narrowness of city marketing has also been criticized by Millington et al. (1997), who have argued that the research has too often focused on a small number of case studies, mainly large urban and former industrial locations who may be exceptional in their experience (see also Barke 1999; Millington 2002). Furthermore, they argue that the theoretical perspectives and generalisations have been based on this small number of case studies, which need to be investigated further through a range of case studies: 'Research has indicated, for example, that it is extremely difficult to apply generalisations based on the US experience to the UK, and the UK is probably a special case in Europe because of the nature of its local government'. However, as Ashworth and Voogd (1994) note, this does not detract from the fact that researchers have generated much useful information on the characteristics of place images, and place marketing is still a lively area of research (for some recent examples see for instance Fox Gotham 2002; Gospodini 2002; Healy 2002; Millington 2002).

The promotion of places is often assumed to be directed at different target groups, stressing different attractions in particular places for different persons, but how far this is actually carried out is questionable. Krantz and Schätzl (1997) argue that cities so far have used an undifferentiated approach, but emphasize that 'the segmentation criteria in city marketing depend on the context in each situation'. This eventually leads to the question of why places are marketing themselves, but the apparent lack of evaluation of marketing results has been noted (see for instance Hall/Hubbard 1996; Young/Lever 1997; Barke 1999; Holcomb 1999; Hall 2001; Bradley et al. 2002). Barke and Harrop (1994) have suggest that some of the actors involved more or less do it because everyone else does it, or as Millington et al. (1997) puts it, the competition is 'fuelled by the fears of local policy makers that by failing to play the game they will become losers in the global economy'.

Migration and the importance of attractiveness

The new forms of mobility are increasingly the focus of migration studies and scholars´ investigations (King 2002). One key aspect of this process has been the seemingly greater and greater importance of places, regions and nations in attracting highly skilled in-migrants to enhance their competitiveness (Dziembowska-Kowalska/Funck 2000; Fotheringham et al. 2000; Rohr-Zänker 2001; Simmie 2001; Bradley et al. 2002). Traditionally, migration studies have emphasized economic factors as driving forces behind migration (Ravenstein 1889; Boyle et al. 1998), which for some time has led policymakers to focus on attracting business in order to enhance economic development and simultaneously attract in-migrants. This may be undergoing a slight change since traditional economic motives behind migration seem to be losing some of their validity to the advantage of soft factors such as quality of life (Rogerson et al. 1989; Garvill et al. 2000) as a consequence of changes in production and consumption (Hall/Williams 2002). It should be noted however, that the extent of this trend is highly uncertain, at least when it comes to inter-regional migration in Sweden.

In order to attract the desired in-migrants, place marketing, which in Sweden seems to have been more focused on attracting industries and tourists, may have had a recent shift and become more directed towards attracting in-migrants. This is in accord with Findlay and Rogerson (1993), who some years ago anticipated that migration patterns in the future will reflect, to some degree, the perceived advantages of localities as they are portrayed through place imagery. As discussed earlier there are no known evaluations or studies of place promotion to attract in-migrants. However, in a study of in-migration to the north coast of New South Wales in Australia, Walmsley et al. (1998) found that many of the migrants had not visited the destination area prior to their in-migration, suggesting that it was the overall image of life that was important to them (see also Saunders 1985; Müller 1999). This gives indirect support to the relevance of place marketing as a means of attracting in-migrants.

The Swedish experience

When trying to understand and contextualize the marketing efforts of the northern municipalities, a brief historical description of the migration flows in Sweden is in order. Starting with the 1960s, the migration flows from the rural areas, especially in northern Sweden, were strong towards urban areas with a high labour force demand in central and southern Sweden. In order to compensate for the losses of population the Government, which was the main planning actor at that time, initiated a regional policy aimed at remote areas (Westlund 2001). In the 1970s the net migration wave changed and the 'green wave', as the counter-urbanisation process was called, took place, built up by a strong growth in the service sector combined with a decentralisation of workplaces and a desire to live in the countryside (Borgegård et al. 1993).

The next decade was characterised by weak urbanisation (Öberg 1991), with a net gain of population due to the so-called 'Whole of Sweden' strategy of refugee reception, in which large refugee flows to large municipalities were channelled into most municipalities throughout the country (Andersson 1996). The negative net internal migration flows of many municipalities were then in a way 'hidden' for the superficial observer. Up to this point the competition between the municipalities was not that explicit. In the early 1990s, however, a strong urbanisation process meant gains for the three metropolitan regions and the university towns, i.e. regional centres. During the 90s the regional policy impact lessened substantially (SOU 2000:87), and an increasing number of municipalities struggled to keep up service levels. Hence getting more taxpayers, or at least people to be included as a receiver in the 'national adjustment system' (designed to balance and even out the economic differences between rich and poor municipalities) is essential in place competition and has given rise to new strategies.

Method

The municipality is the geographical research unit that is the focus of our study. In most studies the city is the unit of place marketing etc. In the Swedish case, any focus on 'cities' is almost impossible for administrative reasons. The cities and towns are centres of a territory that most often also includes the outskirts of a city. Statistical data on economy, taxation etc. are based on these units that are governed by local government, which also has responsibility for the citizens in the area. We do not make a case for a distinction between cities and municipalities. In general terms, the urban centre of the municipality normally makes up 50-70 per cent of the population - in metropolitan areas and university municipalities even more. For our present purposes we regard municipalities as the logical unit to use, also because marketing is usually aimed at the main urban centre as well as at the smaller urban centres and countryside environments. In this study we employ the following three categories: very small municipalities (up to 10,000 inhabitants), small municipalities (10,000 to 50,000 inhabitants) and medium-sized municipalities (from 50,000 to 130,000 inhabitants).

The major part of the empirical data used in this paper is gathered from a survey sent out to all 85 municipalities in the northern parts of Sweden during the autumn 2002 (see figure 1 below). The total number of municipalities in Sweden is 290. The survey method was chosen in order to obtain an overall view of the marketing activities of the local authorities, using a mixture of open ended and closed questions in the postal questionnaire. The response rate is 80 per cent, which is very high, and there is no pattern in the non-response questionnaire.

Other sources of information about the images used by the municipalities in marketing themselves come from the brochures, letters, documents etc. that the local authorities used in their campaigns. Naturally, since not all municipalities were conducting campaigns at the time of this study, information was also gathered from elsewhere such as the information available via the municipalities websites', which is a major source of information about the municipalities in Sweden. In some cases the survey information and the printed material did not give sufficient information for our purposes, so, a few telephone interviews were conducted to handle these deficiencies. We also discovered when comparing our sources of information that in some cases the given numbers in marketing budgets did not seem to be correct. There is a suspicion that some respondents may have underestimated, to say the least, how much money they spend on marketing, but equally the marketing budgets may be dispersed amongst a number of administrative units and the actual total costs may be difficult to estimate. Caution is therefore important when analysing some parts of the collected material.

In this paper we have focused on the marketing activities of northern Sweden (Norrland and the forest regions, which also include mid-Sweden). This is a vast part of the country that has in general experienced the most negative population development in Sweden during the last decade. Thus the local authorities in this region are expected to have exerted themselves more than in other regions in trying to attract in-migrants. There are approximately 1.4 million inhabitants in the region, which is about 15 per cent of the total Swedish population. Most of the region is, by European standards, very sparsely populated. In figure 1 below, a map of Sweden shows the municipality borders outlined and the study area in grey. The black circles represent the central places in the municipalities that responded to the questionnaire.

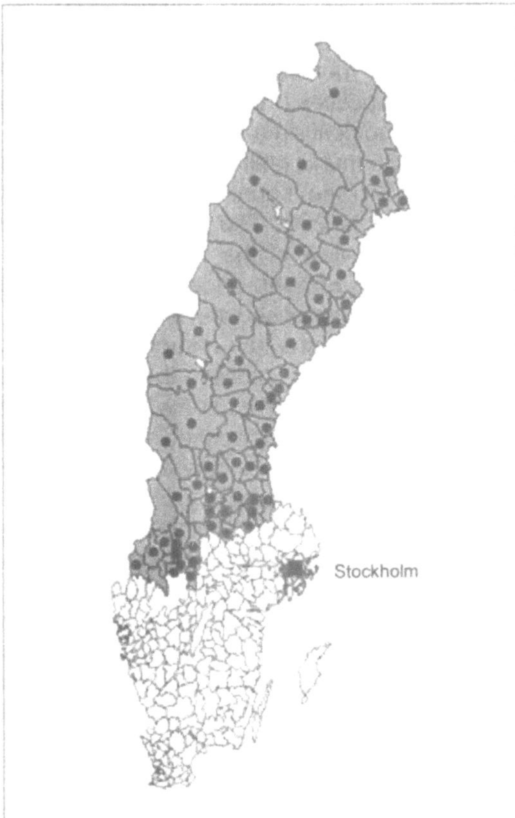

Figure 1: Map of Sweden. Study area outlined in grey and municipalities responding to the questionnaire marked with black circles.

The importance of attracting in-migrants

As discussed in the introduction, the marketing of municipalities in Sweden seems to have become a matter of high priority, at least by the occurrence of campaigns over the last few years. Our survey results indicate that these campaigns in fact are more frequent nowadays. In the late 1990s, only six of the municipalities in the studied region had carried out marketing campaigns to attract in-migrants. This number increased to 14 in 2000, and almost doubled to 27 by September 2002, which means that almost half of the municipalities responding to our questionnaire had carried out some form of marketing campaign to attract in-migrants.

However, it may also be the case that marketing to attract industries and tourists has become more important. Table 1 below, does not tell whether this type of market has become more important over time, but it does tell us the weight given to each of the targets as the respondent has perceived how politicians prioritize each of the targets on a scale from 1 to 4 (from totally unimportant to very important). The conclusion to be drawn is that there are no major differences among the municipalities and marketing seems to give much the same priority to all three groups - business being the most important (especially to very small municipalities) followed by in-migrants and lastly, tourists.

Target group	All municipalities	Very small municipalities	Small municipalities	Medium-sized municipalities
	n = 68	n = 23	n = 37	n = 8
In-migrants	3.50	3.39	3.54	3.63
Tourists	3.40	3.30	3.46	3.38
Business	3.59	3.61	3.57	3.63

Table 1: The importance given to marketing in-migrants, tourists and industries.

Another way of measuring the importance given to marketing is money spent, which is shown in table 2 below. However, as discussed earlier, these figures should be treated with some caution. There are indications that some of the cities have spent a lot more on marketing than the survey shows. With this in mind, the spending on marketing, on average per capita in 2002 was 5.5 Euro for the total marketing and 1.1 Euro per capita for marketing to attract in-migrants. Table 2 also reveals that the spending on marketing to attract in-migrants is increasing at a faster rate than the total spendings on

Year	2000	2001	2002	Relative change 2000-2002
Marketing total	5,678,000 Euro	6,825,000 Euro	7,406,000 Euro	+ 23 %
Marketing to attract in-migrants	988,000 Euro	1,331,000 Euro	1,595,000 Euro	+ 38 %

Note: The rates were calculated at 1 Euro = 9.09 SEK (2002-10-29)

Table 2: Money spent on marketing.

However, it may be the case that for places having experienced a loss of population it is more important to attract in-migrants than for those experiencing an increase. This raised the question of how important it was for the municipality to attract in-migrants (on a scale ranging from 10, very important, to 1, completely unimportant). As expected, those municipalities whose population had increased during the last decade were less eager than average to attract in-migrants.

Pop.development last ten years	All municipalities	Pop. increase	Pop. decrease less than 10%	Pop.Decrease more than 10%
	n = 67	n = 11	n = 34	n = 22
Mean value	8.45	8.36	8.53	8.40

Table 3: The importance given to attracting in-migrants compared with the municipalities population development 1990-200

Contrary to what was expected, the municipalities experiencing the highest rate of population decrease had a lower emphasis on the importance given to attracting in-migrants of the two groups with a population decrease. From this we may ask whether these municipalities are increasingly 'giving up' or have other, more pressing, issues to deal with, like attracting industries? It is important to remember, however, that there are no major differences among the three groups which suggests that the population is generally of great importance to the municipalities in this region.

Ways of attracting in-migrants

Much of the work on marketing places has emphasized the use of slogans and symbols in the marketing campaigns (see, for instance, Ward 1998). Slogans and symbols are also frequently used by the municipalities in northern Sweden (about 71 per cent use slogans, 81 per cent use symbols or logos to market themselves), but interestingly there are disagreements about how important they are. About 25 per cent of the municipalities say that slogans and symbols are of little or no importance, while 75 per cent say that they are very or rather important in marketing the municipality.

Marketing through...	Share using	Marketing through...	Share using
Exhibitions	73 %	Present inhabitants	38 %
Website	63 %	Industry and business	38 %
Brochures	58 %	Other	31 %
Letters to potential in-migrants	56 %	Radio and television	19 %
Advertising in the press	54 %	Schools and universities	17 %
Homecoming days	48 %	Offers	13 %

Table 4: Ways of attracting in-migrants (n = 52).

In Table 4 above it is shown how, or by which means, the municipalities market themselves. Marketing the municipality at exhibitions and using the websites seem to be most common, followed by brochures and advertising in the press. Interesting to note is the variety of marketing methods used to attract in-migrants. If we compare our data with the findings of Millington (2002), we see that newspapers/magazines and brochures/leaflets is the most frequent media used by local authorities in the U.K. and events/exhibitions only make up 8 per cent.

Factors of importance to attract in-migrants

In order to find out what factors were believed by the marketers to be of importance in attracting in-migrants, a total of 38 alternatives were given in the questionnaire (with three of them left blank to fill in freely if there were other significant factors not taken up as alternatives in the survey). The municipalities were asked to rate each of the factors of potential importance to attract in-migrants on a scale from 1 to 10 (from unimportant to very important). In Table 5 below fifteen of the most important factors from the survey are presented.

The results show that, in general, the foremost factors in attracting in-migrants are of a kind that might be expected in smaller municipalities. It is hard to distinguish any clear differences between the very small and small municipalities. The 'soft' values such as quality of life are ranked very high, while service, childcare, education and labour opportunities are ranked lower - although they are still very important. The medium-sized municipalities have, in general, lower values even on other factors not shown in Table 5. This may be a result of attempts to attract in-migrants from Stockholm and perhaps being unsure of what they as municipalities have to offer that will distinguish them from their competitors. For instance, because career opportunities are probably fewer in a medium-sized municipality than in the capital city, they then emphasize the somewhat ambiguous 'quality of life'.

Table 5 below shows how the different factors have been ranked by the three groups of municipalities. Clearly the medium-sized municipalities have different 'priorities' than the smaller municipalities. Higher education, entertainment- and culture, and communications are ranked very high among the medium-sized municipalities, but low among the other groups. However, this group only consists of six municipalities and the next section will show that these differences among the three groups of municipalities are not that explicit.

Factor of importance	All municipalities		Very small municipalities		Small municipalities		Medium-sized municip.	
	n = 66	(rank)	n = 23	(rank)	n = 36	(rank)	n = 7	(rank)
Quality of life	9.31	(1)	9.07	(5)	9.40	(2)	9.60	(1)
Living environment	9.30	(2)	9.56	(1)	9.45	(1)	8.29	(7)
The built environment	8.93	(3)	9.27	(2)	8.88	(3)	8.50	(5)
Outdoor life	8.63	(4)	9.07	(6)	8.63	(8)	7.83	(12)
Child-care	8.62	(5)	9.13	(4)	8.80	(4)	6.40	(26)
Outdoor life opportunities	8.62	(6)	8.93	(8)	8.70	(7)	7.67	(14)
Costs of living	8.56	(7)	8.88	(10)	8.61	(9)	7.60	(15)
Of great natural beauty	8.55	(8)	8.85	(11)	8.74	(5)	7.00	(21)
The 'spirit' of the place	8.52	(9)	9.00	(7)	8.71	(6)	6.83	(23)
Quality of schools	8.44	(10)	9.13	(3)	8.50	(10)	6.40	(27)
Labour market opportunit.	8.37	(11)	8.93	(9)	8.10	(15)	8.17	(10)
Future prospects	8.31	(12)	8.08	(17)	8.50	(11)	8.00	(11)
Education opportunities	8.26	(13)	8.64	(12)	8.17	(14)	8.25	(9)
Trade and industry	8.15	(14)	8.08	(18)	8.08	(16)	9.00	(3)
Close to water	7.98	(15)	7.50	(25)	8.44	(12)	7.25	(18)

Table 5: Factors put forward in marketing and how important they are believed to be when attracting in-migrants.

The questionnaire also included one question to give some notion of whether the respondents believed that they had been successful in their marketing campaigns to attract in-migrants. Obviously such a question is problematic since, in some cases, it could be seen as a matter of self-evaluation of the marketer. Still, it is an interesting question and the results show that a clear majority (73 per cent) did think that they had been successful and only 3 per cent believed that they had not. In relation to this self-estimated success it is perhaps more interesting that the majority of the municipalities had made no evaluations of their campaigns (59 per cent). The success claimed by many of the respondents might thus be questioned.

Therefore, we may well ask why the municipalities are not doing evaluation studies when they are spending quite a lot of money on marketing campaigns? One positive interpretation is that they 'know' the outcome intuitively, so there is no real need for a (costly) evaluation. It may also be the case that they lack knowledge or skills for undertaking evaluations. From a political standpoint, it could be better/safer not to know the outcome of an evaluation. Maybe a positive image is in the nature of a marketing campaign and that 'good results' are necessary to get 'good publicity', but in the long term it also runs the risk of spending a lot of money on something whose outcome is unknown. An evaluation puts the finger on a number of questions, formal and as regards content, important considerations in improving forthcoming campaigns.

Analysis of brochures and website information

Of the 85 municipalities, 15 were chosen to study more thoroughly. To see how they were marketing themselves; three groups of five municipalities in each group were chosen based on their number of inhabitants – the same division as used earlier in this paper. Some of these were selected because they had carried out marketing campaigns recently and the others were chosen randomly, but with some consideration of their geographical location. The focus of attention has been the local authorities' websites, which have become a major source of information and the material produced in connection with marketing campaigns (see also Urban 2002). The aim was to establish what kind of images are presented and whether they focus on certain segments of potential in-migrants.

Very small municipalities

This group does not have much information on their websites that directly could be regarded as marketing to attract in-migrants. Instead the websites work as descriptions of the local authorities' activities and services. What could be interpreted as marketing is somewhat diffuse, but most of the websites describe their beautiful surroundings and their communications with other places, which seems to be more directed towards visitors. Some of the very small municipalities do market themselves with a view to potential in-migrants directly through brochures to specific population segments. Factors that are put forward are cheap housing in exclusive rural settings, nature, a safe environment and good childcare and schools. Communications are also important, perhaps due to the peripheral locations of these municipalities. Families with children are the prime population segment targeted and thus activities that are thought to address the whole family are highlighted.

Small municipalities

In this group both websites and brochures are used as means to attract in-migrants. The 'small-town idyll' is prominent with cheap housing, mostly in attractive houses and rural environments, but at the same time "close to everything". As with the very small municipalities, good schools are frequently mentioned. However, the small municipalities do not seem to direct their marketing efforts to any particular population segment since the variety of factors put forward may work as possible attractions to anyone. Another difference from the group of very small places is that the small municipalities seem to have put much more effort into their websites and that these are seen as tools to attract in-migrants. This could presumably be explained by the fact that they have more resources in terms of staff than the very small municipalities.

Medium-sized municipalities

To some extent the medium-sized municipalities market the same things as the others. Cheap housing costs, but now more explicitly compared with the capital Stockholm. Being close to nature but at the same time within easy reach of the city's supply of entertainment and culture is also promoted. This group of places also has the most homogeneous marketing compared to the very small and small municipalities (apart from one municipality which markets palm trees and beaches not to be found in the northern hemisphere and certainly not in Sweden). Among the more realistic factors marketed are the highly developed industry and the opportunities for higher education found in these municipalities. If any population segment is to be identified it is students and highly skilled professionals that are most sought after. Other target groups are difficult to identify, probably since marketing aimed at them as potential in-migrants might sometimes be mistaken for promoting tourism. The medium-sized municipalities do differ in one respect: the efforts made and the money invested in marketing to attract in-migrants. Some of the local authorities have made their marketing easily accessible via their websites, and well adopted to potential in-migrants, while others have put their efforts elsewhere. Some of these places have also adopted slogans more implicitly than others in their marketing campaigns.

Type of municipality	Very small municipalities	Small municipalities	Medium-sized municipalit.
Images put forward in brochures and websites	*Cheap housing in exclusive rural settings *Nature *Good communications *Good childcare and schools	*Cheap housing in exclusive houses *Rural environments *'Close to everything' *'Small-town idyll' *The labour market	*Cheaper living than in the larger cities (e.g. Stockholm) *'Close to everything' *Close to nature *The labour market *Higher education *Pleasure and Culture

Note: The findings are not ranked.

Table 6: A summary of findings in the brochures and websites

In the summary above, it is rather striking how similarly the cities market themselves. This may partly be explained by the fact the most municipalities aim at Stockholm region and try to put forward factors that speak in their favour. Since many of the places try to attract families with children their images are also likely to be similar, stressing what they believe is important to attract this group. However, if marketing has any effects on migration, it may be difficult for the potential in-migrants to choose a destination, since they all seem to be alike. In marketing terms, however, 'unique selling points' (USP) are very important for successful marketing (Krantz/Schätzl 1997). But what is the situation when it comes to attracting in-migrants? Judging from the findings of this study it is hard to say whether municipalities actively try to be 'unique' or just fail to put forward a 'unique' marketing image. It may also be the case that a 'unique' image as regards a municipality is not that important when it comes to attracting in-migrants.

Conclusions

In this paper we have addressed the following questions: How do municipalities market themselves and how important is marketing? Do they believe that they have been successful in their marketing efforts? What images are put forward in the municipalities' marketing and how important do they believe these images are when attracting in-migrants?
First of all, the municipalities of northern Sweden market themselves in a variety of ways, using everything from offers to exhibitions. However, many of the marketing approaches used are similar among the municipalities. The survey shows that, for most of the municipalities, attracting in-migrants is very important. This is largely independent of their earlier population development. In general there are no major differences in the importance of attracting in-migrants, tourists or industry.

Secondly, a clear majority of the respondents estimate that their efforts towards attracting in-migrants have been successful. However, rather few had made any evaluations of their marketing results. This is important to look into for further studies.
Thirdly, with a few exceptions, there are no major differences in terms of images in the marketing campaigns. The impression is that they all try to sell more or less the same place. It is likely that this is so because of the focus on attracting in-migrants from the Stockholm region. Then, factors such as comparatively low housing costs and a high level of 'quality of life' are put forward. Stockholm seems to be 'setting the norm' for the design of the marketing campaigns of municipalities in northern Sweden. However, the marketers could also be seeing the potential in-migrants as a homogeneous group with similar preferences.

Acknowledgments:
The authors wishes to thank Bruno Jansson, Lena Magnusson and Karin Tillberg Mattsson for useful comments and to Jan Teeland for linguistic improvements. This study was supported by The Swedish Research Council.

References:
Andersson, R. (1996) The Geographical and Social Mobility of Immigrants: Escalator Regions in Sweden from an Ethnic Perspective. Geografiska Annaler 78 B(1): 3-25. Ashworth, G.J./Voogd, H. (1994) Marketing and place promotion. In: Gold,
J.R./Ward, S.V. (eds) Place Promotion. The Use of Publicity and Marketing to Sell Towns and Regions. West Sussex.
Barke, M. (1999) City marketing as a planning tool. In: M. Pacione. (ed) Applied geography: principles and practice. London.
-, /Harrop, K. (1994) Selling the industrial town: identity, image and illusion. In: Gold, J.R./Ward, S.V. (eds) Place Promotion. The Use of Publicity and Marketing to Sell Towns and Regions. West Sussex.
Borgegård L-E., Fransson, U./Lundin, L. (1993) Work. In: Viking Abrahamsson, K. (ed) National atlas of Sweden: Work and leisure, Stockholm.
Boyle, P., Halfacree, K./Robinson, V. (1998) Exploring Contemporary Migration. Harlow.
Bradley, A., Hall, T./Harrison, M. (2002) Selling Cities: Promoting New Images For Meetings Tourism. Cities 19(1): 61-70.
Brotchie, J., Batty, M., Blakely, E., Hall, P./Newton, P. (eds) (1995) Cities in competition. Productive and sustainable cities for the 21st century. Melbourne.
Dziembowska-Kowalska, J./Funck, R.H. (2000) Cultural activities as a location. factor in European competition between regions: Concepts and some evidence. Annals of Regional Science. 34(1): 1-12
Ek, R. (2001) Stadens marknadsföring och dess geografiska visioner. In: Pacheco, J. (ed) Stadskultur. Research Report Research Report in Sociology 2001:2, Sociologiska institutionen, Lunds universitet.
Findlay, A./Rogerson, R. (1993) Migration, places and quality of life: voting with their feet? In: Champion, T. (ed) Population matters. The local dimension. London.

Fotheringham, A.S., Champion, T., Wymer, C./Coombes, M. (2000) Measuring Destination Attractivity: A Migration Example. International Journal of Population Geography. 6(6): 391-421.
Fox Gotham, K. (2002) Marketing Mardi Gras: Commodification, Spectacle and the Political Economy of Tourism in New Orleans. Urban Studies. 39(10): 1735-1756.
Garvill, J., Malmberg, G./Westin, K. (2000) Värdet av att flytta och att stanna – om flyttningsbeslut, platsanknytning och livsvärden. Rapport 2 från Regionalpolitiska utredningen (SOU 2000:36), Stockholm.
Gold, J.R./Ward, S.V. (eds) (1994) Place Promotion. The Use of Publicity and Marketing to Sell Towns and Regions. West Sussex.
Gospodini, A. (1999) European Cities in Competition and the New 'Uses' of Urban Design. Journal of Urban Design. 7(1): 59-73.
Hall, M. C./Williams, A. M. (eds) (2002) Tourism and Migration: New Relationships between Production and Consumption. Dordrecht.
Hall, T. (2001) Urban Geography. Second ed, London.
-, /Hubbard, P. (1996) The entrepreneurial city: new urban politics, new urban geographies? Progress in Human Geography 20(2): 153-174.
Hallin, G. (1991) Slogan, image och lokal utveckling. In: Berger, S. (ed) Samhällets geografi. Uppsala.
Harvey, D. (1989) From Managerialism to Entrepreneurialism: The Transformation in Urban Governance in Late Capitalism. Geografiska Annaler 71(1 B): 3-17.
Healy, P. (2002) On Creating the 'City' as a Collective Resource. Urban Studies 39(10): 1777-1792.
Holcomb, B. (1999) Marketing Cities for Tourism. In: Judd, D. R./Fainstein, S. S. (eds) The Tourist City. London
Jensen-Butler, C., Shachar, A./van Weesep, J. (eds) (1997) European Cities in Competition. Aldershot.
King, R. (2002) Towards a New Map of European Migration. International Journal of Population Geography 8(2): 89-106.
Krantz, M./Schätzl, L. (1997) Marketing the city. In: Jensen-Butler, C., Shachar, A./van Weesep, J. (eds) European Cities in Competition. Aldershot.
Millington, S., Young, C./Lever, J. (1997) A Bibliography of City Marketing. Journal of Regional and Local Studies. Vol. 17: 16-42.
-, (2002) An assessment of city marketing strategies and urban entrepreneurialism in UK local authorities. PhD-thesis, Manchester Metropolitan University, Manchester.
Müller, D. K. (1999) German Second Home Owners in the Swedish Countryside. Department of Social and Economic Geography. Umeå, Umeå University.
Young, C./Lever, J. (1997) Place promotion, economic location and the consumption of city image. Tijdschrift voor economische en sociale geografie. Vol. 88: 332-341.
Ravenstein, E. G. (1889) The laws of migration. Journal of the Royal Statistical Society 52: 214-301.
Rogerson, R. J., Findlay, A. M., Morris, A.S./Coombes, M.G. (1989) Indicators of quality of life: some methodological issues. Environment and Planning A 21(12): 1655-1666.
Rohr-Zänker, R. (2001) How to Attract Managers and Professionals to Peripheral Regions? Recruitment Strategies in the Weser-Ems Region, Germany. European Planning Studies. 9(1): 47-68.

Saunders, M. N. K. (1985) The influence of job-vacancy advertising upon migration: some empirical evidence. Environment and Planning A 17(12): 1581-1589.
Simmie, J. (ed) (2001) Innovative Cities. London.
SOU 2000:87 (2000) Den regionalpolitiska utredningens slutbetänkande. Näringsdepartementet.
Stevenson, D. (1999) Reflections of a 'great port city': the case of Newcastle, Australia. Environment and Planning D: Society and Space 17(1): 105-119.
Urban, F. (2002) Small Town, Big Website? Cities and their Representation on the Internet. Cities 19(1): 49-59.
Walmsley, D.J., Epps, W.R./Duncan, C.J. (1998) Migration to the New South Wales North Coast 1986-1991: Lifestyle Motivated Counterurbanisation. Geoforum 29: 105-118.
-, /Lewis, G. J. (1993) People & Environment. Behavioural Approaches in Human Geography. Second ed. Malaysia.
Ward, S. V. (1998) Selling Places: The marketing and promotion of towns and cities 1850-2000. London.
Westlund, H. (2001) Spatial Policy for Sparsely Populated Areas: A Forlorn Hope? Swedish Experiences. In: Johansson, B., Karlsson, C./Stough, R. R. (eds). Theories of Endogenous Regional Growth: Lessons for Regional Policies. Heidelberg.
Öberg, S. (ed) (1991) National Atlas of Sweden: The Population. Stockholm.

Images in Action.

City-Image Making in Processes of Urban Transformations

Antonella Bruzzese

Having a good image, strong and well-defined image, seems to have become in recent times a sort of "guarantee of success", however one might articulate such a concept. In today's increasingly *image-conscious* (Jukes, 1990), appearance-oriented society of finely-edited communication, the image, by virtue of its potential as a medium for the experience of reality, has taken on the qualities of an object that can be acted on and manipulated, and therefore designed and built. Images of cities are no exception.
The need expressed by municipalities to define a stronger image for a city finds its realisation in a multiplicity of policies and strategies that involve the transformation of urban space. Many recent urban development and redevelopment projects implemented by European cities in the past twenty years are explicitly aimed at building, enhancing or even overturning the image of a city, becoming a recurring theme that ever more frequently redefines priorities and the way choices are made in urban interventions.
Well-defined image for cities is today a key point to reach different aims: to promote cities in the international scene, to attract firms and tourism, to recreate a sort of inner coherence for different projects of specific local context, to represent urban identity. But even though these goals were always present in urban history, the importance of the informational dimension, the condition of growing competition between cities and the use of urban marketing strategies have changed the *nature* and the *role* and also the *content* of the city images.

New contexts

The issue of the image of cities is not new. It has been the object of attention of a diverse range of disciplines, leading to a variety of declinations of the concept of the "image".
As one is aware, already during the sixties, Kevin Lynch (1954,1960) brought it to the attention of architects and urban planners, highlighting the relevance of the immaterial dimension in the field of urban studies. The image of a city as perceived by its inhabitants was the object to be analysed, with the aim of translating the resulting knowledge into an aid to be used directly in interventions on the physicality of anthropocised space: the understanding of the perceived image was thus instrumental

in the process of defining the means of intervening on the physical form of the city.
On the other hand, reflections upon the subject of the wide-reaching effects of the mass-media and more generally on economic transformations occurring in consumer society led into the centre of the debate upon the transformation of contemporary society (and the contemporary city) the issue of the image and visibility, considered as priorities in consumer-oriented production (Harvey, 1990), which in particular anchored onto the issue of the role of images (of any kind) as the centerpoint of economy and communication.
But it is in the eighties that a new interest in this topic is born, that further conjugates and reinterprets in operational terms both the aspect of the immaterial dimension of urban transformations and the central role of market forces and the communicational dimension. Within a profoundly altered context affected by physical, social, economic and administrative mutations, the first examples of marketing strategies applied to cities acknowledge the image both in terms of an *"immaterial resource"* that contributes to the defining of the *"product-city"* and as a *instrumental element* in the reaching of developmental targets (Ashworth, Voogd, 1990)
Urban marketing, this "new" discipline (Casella, 1997), attempts to contextualise from a theoretical point of view and in a broader picture an issue as ephemeral as that of a city's image, in an attempt to define it *role* with respect to the practical aims of this discipline; from an operational point of view, by presenting itself as "a group of techniques and instruments" (Salone, 1994), it attempts to designate *operational strategies* that governments and local administrations can adopt to satisfy their "need" for a strong and well-defined image.
From this point of view, *competition* and *"self awareness"* in particular can be read as keywords to understand many processes occurring to contemporary city. Competition thus, being a direct confrontation between geographical areas, ever more imply a process of exploration of the specificity of each individual location, a sort of *"self-analysis"* necessary to identify which elements can work as motors of development (Caroli,1999). The resulting knowledge, centred around criteria of economic attractivity, leads to reinterpretate the elements that constitute the city and its territory in function of the degree of competitivity that the city itself can achieve on the market: image of the city is just one of these elements.

City image declinations

In such context, the image of the city is not only and not simply a visual representation of the city itself, rather a city's *fame*, or reputation. As "the simple notion of a city" (Belli, 1995) or an "image facilitating synthesis" (Amendola, 1995), the city image shares with the visual image the immediacy of perception, but it is based not upon objective values, rather on values that lie between the *real* and the *imaginary*" (Bailly, 1994). In this way city image takes on the role of an "immaterial asset", which contributes to the definition of the "supply of cities" or, to use another marketing term, the "urban product", which is as equivalent in value to other aspects such as physical conformation, functions, level of activity as well as atmosphere and symbolic value of the city itself (Ashworth and Voogd, 1990).

Assuming this point of view, above all city image is the *outcome of a voluntary process of construction of a multilayered project* that operates upon a given territory on a number of different levels (physical interventions, urban policies, the promotion of attractions and communication strategies). So it has become an object that can be acted on, manipulated, and therefore designed and built and that has to answer to different characteristics.

City image "must be"

More often within the context of the *city=product* analogy, the image of the city, seen as an "autonomous" object that can be acted upon, is as subjected to the same rules and processes employed in the development of any other marketing or mass communication strategy. So ever more frequently city images, despite having been marked by history, respond to the tactics of the world of advertising; the historical and architectural heritage of cities is lined up side by side with product-like representations (Bailly, 1994).

The importance of a relational dimension of territory, manifest in the increment of the factors and actors contributing to the process of territorial production and in the level of economic interdependency with the surroundings, underlines that, for a city, is not enough, simply "being" or having "know-how"; rather cities "must" communicate to make visible and accessible "what they are, what they can do, their qualities and their value" (Ostillio, 2000) in order to earn recognition for capabilities and distinctive features that distinguish one location from others.

To this goal a city's image "must be positive so as to maximise the city's opportunities" (Bailly, 1994), and especially must satisfy prerequisites of "efficient layout".

According urban marketing strategies (Caroli, 1999) the characteristics to *efficiently define an image* of the city should be:

- sufficient integration within the context of the region's "vocation" and its productive activities;
- a foundation of credibility and, to some extent, verifiability;
- a sharp focus on a small number of key elements that successfully reflect the multifaceted nature of a location;
- an emphasis on aspects that differentiate a place from others, so as to make it unique or at least sufficiently distinct from competing locations;
- finally, an adequate emotional appeal.

City images role

Inside the logic that the image of the city is a *project* and a *product* the action of translating a location's assets into terms of economic potential elevating the perceived value in internal and external markets of such assets can have the effect of enhancing economic processes capable of generating wealth and further development.

The city's image, in this case, assumes the role of a *strategic resource* "that can be counted upon in the achieving of objectives of value-generation and development in the long run" (Ostillio, 2000), or is better configured as a sort of "intermediate" product: the outcome of a project, but at the same time an element capable of having specific effects on processes of urban transformation. The growing production of slogans, metaphors, advertising campaigns and in general the production of the images of cities show how they are not marginal in schemes of urban transformation, but can have a big influence on economic and urban growth - both to deter and enhance.

But if urban images must answer to the need of comprehensibility, synthesis and communicative efficiency, and have to be able to lead further processes of development and sense of belonging by inhabitants, the processes of image-making, cannot be made only by communication and advertising to be effective, but have to deal with different levels. In which way? What local governments work on, to reach this goal?

How cities deal with image-making: four approaches

It is possible to recognise different manners to work on city-image in a complex way, focusing on different aspects and problems related. Four examples can help to describe them: the realisation of flagship projects, which became the new icons of the city as happened to the Guggenheim Museum in Bilbao; the use of events and cultural planning which can create a temporary visibility to the city as in Glasgow when it was Capital

of Culture 1990; the functional specialization as marketing strategies in Montpellier tried to build during the '80 with the "technopole"; the reinterpretation and translation in economic value of local traditions as happened in Cremona where the musical tradition was the core of a project of urban regeneration.
Each approach is of course not an example of exclusive implementation of one mode rather than another. It can be better interpreted as an example of one taking more importance than another, since these interventions on the city's image (the flagship project, the temporary event and so on) often occur side by side, interact and build upon each other within a single area.

"Insertion"
Instances of cities that identify themselves with architectural artefacts with strong "personalities" are a recurring theme in urban history: in the language of urban marketing they are called "flagship projects", projects of a strong visual impact that are often the work of architects who have become part of the international "star system", sometimes standing out considerably from their context and thus implicitly attempting to impose themselves as the new icons of the city, icons of a multiplicity of processes of renewal.
A case to point is the Guggenheim Museum built in Bilbao in 1997, although this building is in fact one of the more recent projects in a twenty-year regeneration project for the city. Frank Gehry's museum, strongly supported by the greater part of Bilbao's population[1], perfectly embodied the answer to Basque society's need for a new symbol capable of displaying the power that the museum itself, in terms of financial return, has generated – thus becoming the most powerful, internationally recognised and heavily publicised emblem of "new" Bilbao.

---

[1] *First feasibility studies for museum realisation and management thought necessary a number of 400.000 visitors per annum, to cover the investment of 132,22 million of Euro. In the first year visitors were 1.360.000 (113.000 on average per month), more than three times the initial hypothesis. In the second period –from October 1998 to December 1999 – visitors were 1.265.000. 79% and 87% respectively went to Bilbao just to see the museum, or – arrived for other reasons- stayed more in Bilbao to visit the museum itself. Nowadays the average number of visitors is assumed one million per year. This success made the Guggenheim Museum the second museum of Spain after Prado in Madrid. An interesting elaboration of data collected by Peat Marwick company is Solima L. (1999) L'impatto economico del musei: l'esperienza del Guggenheim Museum di Bilbao, in "Economia della Cultura"*

The museum gave huge visibility to an extremely complex and articulated process of regeneration of the city[2] that had been implemented following the industrial and occupational crisis, and is the physical embodiment of the administration's awareness for the need to act upon the image of the city. So on the one hand the general logic of the urban regeneration programme was aimed at solving structural problems (the provision of infrastructures, improvement of accessibility, creation of new skills), and on the other the need to act on the way the city was perceived from the outside called for the creation of a symbolic economy, based on both the production of spaces and "symbols" (Zukin, 1995), that is so well reflected in the "spectacular" architecture of the museum, capable of attracting national and international attention even more as a message than as a functional container.

"Temporary lighting"

The building/transformation of the image of a city is not, however, necessarily entirely based on the realisation of "stable" elements: ever more frequently, public administrations put their efforts towards making their city the host of international events, counting on the potential of cultural initiatives to enhance the image of the city. The image and cultural wealth of cities have been shown to be mutually influential and complementary, justifying the role of recent strategies aimed at increasing the importance of cultural issues in overall urban policies and demonstrating their validity in terms of influence on the city's image.

The role of cultural production as a driving force behind the economic development of the city has for some years been of primary importance on the agendas of administrations dealing with urban regeneration on a number of different scales, from the local to the pan-European. Rotterdam, Glasgow, Barcelona, Lisbon are examples of cities that have seen the production - and consumption - of culture have played a central role in the "revitalisation" of the city.

On the other hand the large event does not just act as a showcase for a location as product; it has an intrinsic aspect of communication of place. So as well as *adding to the location's wealth of assets, it succeeds in communicating them as well.* (Caroli, 1999, p243). Not only do such events periodically showcase what a city has to offer thus strengthening its image (see Glasgow), but they act as channels of communication through which a city and its territory can express themselves (F.Bianchini & M.Parkinson, 1993; M. Boyle and G. Hughes,1994).

---

[2] *Strategic Project for Metropolitan Bilbao is inside the Territorial Partial Plan for Metropolitan Bilbao (PTP) started in 1989, ordered by Basque Government and by Forenses Deputation of Vizcaya. It was directed by Eduardo Leira and José Luis Burgos.*

Glasgow is a particularly interesting example in terms of the administration's strategic use of a process of incrementation of the role of culture in the city's activities. The city's strategic outlines from 1982 to today contain direct references to the promotion of cultural activities as a pivotal areas for the development of the city, and this is especially true in 1990 when considerable effort was made to take advantage of the city's status as Cultural Capital. "*Glasgow's miles better* " was the slogan that summed up a series of images (the city of culture, the city of events, the renewed city, the city that regenerated itself etc) that were becoming accepted in common perception. It therefore fed and at the same time enhanced a phenomenon that was already occurring. The public administration's need to find a linguistic emblem for these changes, based on the language of advertising, underlines the intention to conjure up an image that would increase this particular kind of consumption.
Despite the *limited breadth* of the results, concentrated in particular sectors - the main criticism aimed at the council's strategies, along with that of temporary effectiveness - this process was seen by both public and private bodies firstly as a good opportunity to concentrate on a particular field to be used as an *engine for the regeneration* of an urban economy long in crisis and secondly a *chance to alter the negative perception* of the city, tied to its occupational and financial difficulties.

"New specialisation"
Another approach, which is more inclined to build images aimed at specific user-groups, concentrate on reinforcing and giving greater visibility to the *specialist knowledge* of a location, based on particular field that the location is identified with from the outside.
The example of Montpellier is an emblematic of an administration consciously choosing a specific role (the technopolis) and building it up in the image of the city until it almost becomes synonymous with the city itself[3]. In a context of rapid administrational as well as economic, demographic and social change that the city lived through since the end

[3] *After left socialist wing won the election in 1977, with the major George Frêches- still holding office and main reference man in politics of city renovation- the government of Montpellier managed an industrial strategy strongly orientated to innovation, based on the realisation of Technopolis, each of them characterised by only one function (Euromedicine, Agropolis, Antenna, Heliopolis, for example). In 1984 Technopolis was settled down, and it became a sort of synonymous of the city itself. First technological park were made during seventies: their appeal and the role they played in the region economy showed a way which was further enhanced with incentives and tax relieves, counting on European facilities and integration between public and private investments. (At this regards see M.Parkinson, The rise of the entrepreneurial European city: Strategic responses to economic changes in the 1980s, in " Ekistics", n. 58(350/351), 1991, 299-307)*

of the seventies, the implementation of "market-oriented" urban policies meant for the city of Montpellier the adoption of a number of operational instruments (incentives, tax breaks, promotional activities, etc) aimed at promoting the "image de marque" (Salone, 1994) of its specialisation as a technology park, in the belief that this would improve the city's potential presence both on the national and international markets, the latter being made increasingly accessible through a growth in international competition.

In Montpellier the issue of the image of the city was consciously addressed by the public administration since the early eighties, with a specific view to optimise the urban economy through the use of a number of channels and approaches: from economic programming to cultural policy, from targeted projects to promotional campaigns - all of which, however, rotated around the city's technical specialisation as a driving force. The role of the image of the city was in this instance double: it was a *tool* used to promote economic development as defined by the municipality itself, but it was also an *outcome*, in that the perception of the city on the part of inhabitants and outsiders was totally redefined.

" Re-examining tradition"

Besides opting for urban development in a particular direction and therefore the promotion of particular sectors, there is the opportunity to view a location's assets in terms of historic, artistic and cultural traditions as unique characteristics worthy of promotion.

In the case of Cremona musical tradition is deeply rooted in the history of the city and especially in the memory and activities of its inhabitants, and represents a resource that can be interpreted in terms of economic potential. The recent "Prusst[4]" promoted by the Council of Cremona, "Un Po di Musica. Il parco musicale del Po e dell'Arda" ("A bit of music. The musical park of the Po and Arda") plays on a pun that goes beyond the specific intention to make a musical park: the general contents of this programme refer to the recognised importance of music for the city and are a declaration of intention on the part of the Concil to use as a driving force behind the regeneration and transformation of the area the musical tradition and the many businesses operating in this field in the area. A

---

[4] *PRUSST stands for Programmi di Recupero Urbano e di Sviluppo Sostenibile del Territorio, (Urban Requalification and Sustainable Territory Development Programs) Ministerial Decree n.1169 of 8/10/1998 and Ministerial Decree n.1169 of 28/05/1999- The PRUSST was promoted in September by Municipality of Cremona and realised by the Territorial Management Office of Municipality (Settore Gestione del Territorio del Comune). Italian architect Lamberto Rossi coordinated the Program.*

field which, from the viewpoint of planners and administrators, can become the city's distinguishing feature, the short image, clear and easily communicated, with which Cremona identifies itself both internally and externally and while of course not being the only one represents a main "strategic" resource, capable of sparking off a developmental process.
In this sense "music" becomes a project itself, the central axis of a whole series of policies and initiatives aimed at promoting the city of Cremona and giving it autonomy and visibility, which is distilled into a number of planning processes (the Prusst, and the Variante PRG) in terms both of proposed physical transformations (the building of a theme park, the promotion of certain routes) and also the communication and promotion of the city itself. Cremona "city of music" the outcome of a deeply-rooted tradition based on historical fact, but also of an intentional and well-coordinated process, an example of another mode of intervention on a territory and on one's image.

Marginal notes: which images for which action?
From these examples, that can be considered, from one point of view, "successful examples", some considerations can be pointed out about the nature of the image and the role of its building up inside the process of urban transformations

Not only communication
Firstly it is evident that each case cannot be reduced to a simple issue of communication or promotion neither to a set of homogenised practices. The image transformation is never the product of isolated operations and especially is not an action only image based, but rather is the result of strategies carried out *over time* that aim to complete and enhance a broader process of transformation of a territory in all its aspects, aimed at summing it up in the construction of an image. Image making process rather, intersects, supports and often redirects multiple and very diverse processes of urban transformation; as we could see in the different cases selected where the work on the image of the city was inserted in a strategic plan plus an architectural project (Bilbao); in cultural programs (Glasgow); in economic and financial programs (Montpellier); in promotional and urban development program (Cremona).

Sectoriality vs synthesis
Then if we consider the images emerging form the image making processes presented (the new icon, the cultural and event character, the idea to promote the city as tecnopole or city of music), despite their

differences they shows two opposite tensions which can be defined as sectoriality vs synthesis attempt.

Infact from one hand, to be efficiently defined according marketing strategies, city images are *sector-based*, showing the *partial nature* of the resulting images and the choices of action that these both determine and represent. Often the highly-distilled nature of the resulting images is accompanied by a ruthless selection of *content* and *target category*, according to indications generated by an accurate analysis of demand carried out according to marketing procedures that leads not only to a very *sector-specific* and *forcedly positive result* but also to a definition of the image of the city based largely on the *consumer potential* and almost always an *absence of space* in the resulting representations. This results in a number of choices (the precedence given to architecture most oriented to increase international visibility, such as the Guggenheim; or the selection of a particular type of event able of upholding a city's role on an international level at the expense of the involvement of local resources, as someone's accusation to Glasgow cultural strategies) that produce images of cities aimed at serving the needs of certain categories of the population, reduced to "targeted" buyers. A condition that generates high levels of exclusion the moment it becomes the main criterion for the choice of urban interventions.

From another hand, despite the sectoriality that distinguishes them, ever more frequently these images tend to *embody a process of synthesis,* seeking in this way to hold together an overall view of the city, with parameters different from the past. A synthetic image which express the implicit will to overcome the fragmentation of the urban picture (Secchi, 2000) and the difficulty in bringing a territory together in a defined concept.

This was traditionally the duty of the masterplan, but today greater effectiveness better concise communication and a longer-lasting result seem to be achieved by images built through advertising and marketing techniques. Paradoxically, some such images can end up replacing those produced by the masterplan: especially for this reason they must be investigated at the stages in which they are built, spread and appropriated by the inhabitants.

Another time it would be reductive to continue to consider a image making process as an accessory and a purely promotional aspect of urban planning and therefore not strictly part of the field of design. Rather, its position should be critically reconsidered within the processes and tools that act upon the transformation of the territory.

Effectiveness

Finally I would like to point out another issue. One of the main critics aimed to these image making processes is the partial nature of their effects, even if the more interesting cases are complex and try to act at different levels. So questions that emerge concern which kind of effects are generated by such practices, and more general how to define what the *effectiveness* of the image making processes is, in order to understand how one can *evaluate* it.

Simply measuring the effectiveness in terms of economic incomes (growth in tourism, increase in investment) tends to give a partial view that does not adequately describe the complexity of the factors involved. City images are not simply projects, but they are more complex if we think about them as "qualitative representation based on real and imaginary" (Baily,1994) so image making processes should have the capacity to root the proposed images in the collective imagination to work as new conceptualisations of the city capable of becoming "images for action". Goal not easy to reach neither to evaluate.

From this point of view better would be to interpretate effectiveness as a project's capacity to spark off "further development" over time. So the criteria for measuring the effectiveness could be considered the *degree of involvement* of individuals in the local system, to testify the strategic nature of the choices that such images promote.

Common vs convincing

Observing different cases it is possible to see two complementary and opposite way the image making process try to reach local involvement.

From one hand we can see city images thus built and communicated, that succeeded in being metaphors of new vocations and "identities" that a city chooses to promote when they function as catalysers or ***guidelines***, that different projects (and actors) can use as reference systems within a general picture (Glasgow is an example of this). In this case the involvement of other actors, and projects is a result of a "convincing" image. The question at this point is which devices of appropriation by inhabitants of these images top-down built can be used.

From the other hand, there are examples of cities that, from the outset, attempt to build up images as broadly shared as possible, through operations that seek to involve local forces at the stage of definition of the new "plan for the city". In this case the *involvement* is the starting point to build a "common" image of the city. In this case instead the question is if it is still possible in the contemporary city, characterised by social and physical fragmentation, to have a city image which can be shared, as many politics and projects want to build.

These questions are still open and represent issues worthwhile to investigate, in particular in a context like ours, where the construction of images is an integral part not only of the experience of the city and its territory, but also – and especially – of its processes of transformation.

References

Amendola, G. (1997) La città postmoderna. Magie e paure della metropoli contemporanea, Laterza, Roma-Bari

Ashworth, G.J., Voogd, H. (1990) Selling the city: marketing approaches in public sector urban planning, Belhaven Press, London New York

Ave, G. and Corsico, F. (eds)(1994), Marketing urbano in Europa, Torino Incontra, Torino

Bailly, A. (1994) Urban representations: the imaginary at the service of the economy, in Ave, G. e Corsico, F. (eds), Marketing urbano in Europa, Torino Incontra, Torino

Belli, A. (1995) Immagini e linguaggio. Tracce per una ricerca, in "CRU" n.3

Bianchetti, C. (1998) Città, politiche e piani, in "Rassegna", n.75,

Bianchini F.& Parkinson M. (1993) Cultural policy and urban regeneration: The West European experience, Manchester

Boyle M. and Hughes G. (1994) The politics of urban entrepreneurialism in Glasgow, in "Geoforum" 425.4

Caroli, M. G. (1999) Il marketing territoriale, Franco Angeli, Milano

Casella, A. (1997) Marketing della città: premesse alla definizione di una "nuova"disciplina in "Commercio" n. 60

Castells, M., (1989) The informational city, Blackwell, Oxford (UK) e Cambridge (USA)

Dematteis, G. (1999) Non basta una forte identità, la città vive solo se è un "nodo", in: "Telèma", n. 15, Attualità e futuro della società multimediale, Il futuro della città nel mondo telematico, winter 1998/99, Fondazione Ugo Bordoni, pp. 65-68

-, (1995) Immagine e identità urbana metafore spaziali ed agire sociale in "CRU" n.3

-, (1994) Il marketing urbano: cooperare per competere in Ave G. and Corsico F. (eds) Marketing urbano in Europa, Torino Incontra, Torino

Golfetto, F. (1996) Un marketing per le città? Riflessioni sulla nascita di una disciplina, in "Economia e Management" n.5

Guerin, J.P. (1994) Marketing urbano e identità territoriale, in Ave, G. e Corsico, F. (eds.), Marketing urbano in Europa, Torino Incontra, Torino

Harvey, D., (1990)The condition of Postmodernity, Basil Blackwell

Knight,R.V.(1995) Knowledge-based Developement: Policy and Planning Implications for cities, in "Urban Studies" n. 32

Kotler, P., Haider, D.H., Rein, I. (1993) Marketing places: attracting investiment, industry, and tourism to cities, states, nations, The Free Press, New York

Lynch, K., (1954) Perceptual form of the city, MIT Press

-, (1960)The image of the city, MIT Press

Ostillio, M.C. (2000) La comunicazione territoriale, in E. Valdani e F. Ancarani (eds) Strategie di marketing del territorio, EGEA, Milano

Paddison, R.,(1993) City Marketing, Image Reconstruction, and Urban Regeneration, in "Urban Studies"., vol. 30, n.2, pp. 339-350

Jukes, P. (1990) A shout in the street, University California Press, Berkley
Salone, C. (1994) Strumenti di piano e competizione internazionale: il marketing urbano come alternativa "strategica" ai modelli deregolativi degli anni ottanta, in Ave, G. e Corsico, F. (eds), Marketing urbano in Europa, Torino Incontra, Torino
Secchi, B. (2000) Prima lezione di urbanistica, Laterza, Roma-Bari
Zukin, S., (1995) The culture of cities, Blackwell, London

Changes in the Management of Urban Space in the Eyes of the Inhabitants of Warsaw

Mikołaj Madurowicz and Marek Pieniążek

Contents in outline
The following article shows the results of a research on how city dwellers perceive a process of changes in the development of urban space. It also attempts to find relation between this perception and spatial management policy. The research was carried out upon the example of skwer Prusa – a small square near Krakowskie Przedmieście Street in Warsaw. (The term "skwer" means a part of a square or a street garnished with lawns, flowerbeds, shrubs and other plants; a small city park, usually encircled by buildings.)
The interviews were conducted in the latter part of March and in the beginning of April 2002 among all occupants of the neighbouring buildings (28 people) and were compared with the results of interviews conducted simultaneously with people passing by the skwer (175 people).
The analysis of the results is preceded by a short presentation of historical conditions of spatial changes in the city and in the skwer as well.

Introduction

Spatial changes in Warsaw are to a high degree determined historically. The developing process of Warsaw as a capital city for more than 400 years had been uninterrupted until the Second World War. This continuity was broken in the years 1939 and 1944. These years mark both the subsequent phases of physical devastation of the considerable parts of the city and the degradation of its cultural message, legal relations, as well as the destruction of what is presently called "city's climate" – something that creates its unique atmosphere.
In the first post-war years Warsaw, or rather its ruins, witnessed an enormous inflow of people from other regions of Poland. Their spontaneous behaviour forced the decision to rebuild the city, however, such mass migration toward the capital combined with heavy losses during the wartime resulted in significant changes in urban society.
In the time of private and municipal property being nationalized and city authorities reduced to regulatory and executive bodies, a centrally controlled campaign to rebuild the war-torn Warsaw was launched. A propaganda slogan was spread that the capital was being reconstructed by the whole nation. The guidelines on urban management changed

completely under the influence of the new ideology. For the in-coming population, the city was only just arising.

Selected historical conditions of spatial changes in the city

In the time of rapid city reconstruction it was a common practice to fill the bombsites between the buildings with greenery. At this minimal cost, the effect of ostensible continuity of frontages was obtained. Warsaw is dotted with areas of old buildings, now in various condition. One can still come across the rentable tenements, for instance in the modernist quarters dating back to the 1960s and 1970s. The neighbouring houses are not there anymore because where the war damages were too serious the buildings were rarely reconstructed. The remaining tenements were kept unchanged as the quickly growing city was constantly lacking housing space. Besides, open spaces in the city centre, streets widened at the expense of the already un-built-up parcels were not contradictory to the then urban planning doctrine. Since the second half of the 1950s, after a short period of socialism-realism, a search for implementing the assumptions of the Athens Charter in the field of urban planning was more and more evident.

Stare Miasto (the Old Town) is the only pre-war district of Warsaw which was to a certain degree accurately recreated. Trakt Królewski (the Royal Route) with the streets leading to the distant royal summer palace in Wilanów constitutes its natural extension. By the 1920s a centre of the city had spread along these streets, and especially along Krakowskie Przedmieście Street and Nowy Świat Street (see: figure 1).

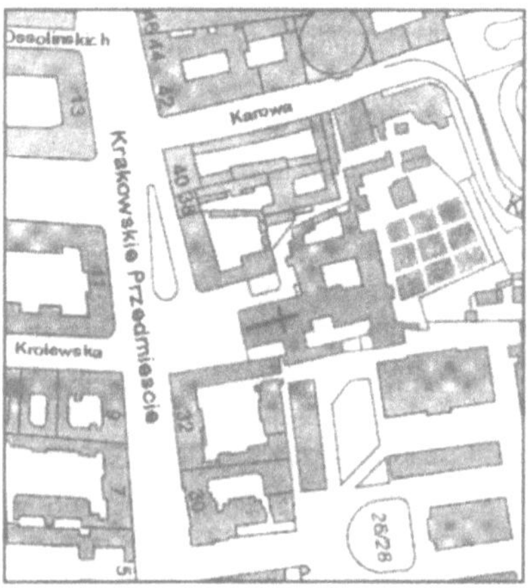

Figure 1: Neighbourhood of skwer Prusa (1937)

After the war the Old Town and the Royal Route lost their meaning. The Old Town was to symbolize city's durability and certify to its centuries-old tradition. The Royal Route with its bourgeois buildings and the 19th century palaces did not match the capital of the socialist country; it could not be more than just another tourist attraction. Therefore, it was not something unusual to leave a gap between the buildings, such as the discussed skwer Prusa. The new centre of Warsaw with its new symbols such as the gift of the Soviet people – Pałac Kultury i Nauki (the Palace of Culture and Science) – was to be developed southwest from its historic predecessor. And so it happened.
Nowadays only a few fragments of Warsaw remind one to a lesser or greater degree of spatial architecture of the city before 1939. But in consciousness of the majority of the contemporary Warsavians, who are very often descendants of the post-war migrants, Warsaw in its present shape has existed "for ever".

Skwer Prusa situated at the corner of Karowa Street and Krakowskie Przedmieście Street, in the vicinity of the University of Warsaw, has not always been a peaceful place and it became skwer only after the war. Today, it is one of the nooks of the capital's inner-city and this is how the Warsavians know it (see: figure 2).

Figure 2: Today's Skwer Prusa

The square is a characteristic fragment of the Warsaw's urban fabric: it changed its appearance, function, role and names. Until the end of the 18th century, it was a part of the Visitants' jurisdiction, until 1916 – a part of the inner-city concentrated around the royal castle, since 1916 – a part of the Krakowskie Przedmieście district, then a part of the city's historic quarter and presently, it belongs to the Śródmieście district encompassed by the Warsaw's Centrum-borough. And despite the unstable administrative position, the place has always been a city's landmark (see: figures 3-4)

Figure 3: Krakowskie Przedmieście Street. On the right side in the background - Bristol Hotel - about 1930…

Figure 4:…and nowadays…

In the first half of the 17th century the present skwer was occupied by two mansions, one of them being a possession of starost of the różański district and the other of the Radziejowscy family, surrounded by the stables and farm buildings. At that time, mansions were usually located near the edge of Skarpa Warszawska (the Warsaw's Escarpment), in a certain distance from the street. Hence it is highly probable that the area in question constituted the back of the aforesaid mansions – between the royal stables (today's numbers 30-32) and wąwóz Piekło (today's Karowa Street).

More or less where Karowa Street is now, on the north side of the skwer, one could possibly still find the remnants of the 17th century fortification

bastion and the sanitary-defensive embankment raised around the city in order to protect it against the menacing Turkish assault (1621) and against the plague (1624). A brick wall surrounding skwer Prusa may have been built upon these fortifications.
100 years later, in the twenties of the 18th century, the space at number 38 was occupied by a wooden manor, at number 40 on the Karowa side – by a short annexe and two other buildings behind: a residential annexe and the stables. By the half of the 18th century these will be replaced by two tenements and a wooden manor in-between belonging to the Nuns of the Visitation and situated on the premises of their convent (which had been just an inconspicuous wooden church back in 1653).
At the same time Krakowskie Przedmieście Street was widened at the level of the left flank of the convent, where (in front of the today's church) a cemetery was located. The cemetery was closed and eliminated only in 1784 when the surface was cobbled.
According to the historic documents, in 1820s, at number 38 there was the first property in Warsaw leased to a private person – a wine merchant Mikołaj Pszenny, while at number 40 (in the Visitants' residence), there was a trading centre dealing in furniture, china, watches and decorative accessories manufactured by the deaf-mute.
Starting from 1825 the history of skwer Prusa takes a big-city colouring. This is where a famous and commonly known wine shop "Simon I Stecki" was situated, visited both by the Warsavians and the visitors throughout the whole 19th century. Before the outbreak of the World War II the following businesses operated on this area: a *Schraider's* factory of silver products, WŁ. Podgórski's factory of paraffin lamps, a photographer's studio "J. *Kostka I Mulert* and last but not least, the editor's office of an extremely popular newspaper entitled "Kurier Warszawski." Shortly before the outbreak of the war, in the 1930s, a famous restaurant "Fukier" hosted its guests at number 38, and in 1945 an inn called "Karczma Rzym" made an ephemeral appearance in the remaining fragment of the building at number 40.
Vitality of this place was violently disrupted in 1944 when the Nazis set fire to the tenements at numbers 36, 38 and 40. The ruins were pulled down after the war and a small skwer was arranged instead. Taking advantage of the fact that the chaplaincy and the west annexe of the Visitants' convent were knocked down, Karowa Street was widened at the expense of the convent's territory. Since then, the place has been filled with various plants, at first in a very chaotic manner, but with time, it began to look more and more like a park with trees and flowerbeds (see: figures 5-6). Then, a statue of Bolesław Prus, the most warsavian of all Polish writers, was erected in the skwer and in front of the Visitants'

church stood the monument of the Primate of the Millennium – Cardinal Stefan Wyszyński (Zieliński 2001).

Figure 5: Bristol Hotel during Russian occupation (before 1918)

Figure 6: Bristol Hotel today

Spatial changes and their perception

The conducted interviews were divided into two sections. The first one investigated inhabitants' awareness of the former state of the place in question. The interviewees were asked to assess the aesthetics of the skwer and then justify their opinion. The second section of the interview aimed at verifying whether the respondents felt the need for a change, what should such a change apply to and whether the interviewees were ready to participate in the process of planning the change.

Over 80% of the interviewed occupants of the neighbouring buildings were able to provide information about the previous architecture of the place in question. 40% of these answers included details about the buildings, a little more than 20% of all answers contained subjective remarks – "neglected, not safe" were the most frequent epithets used to refer to the condition of the place a few years earlier. The passers-by would mainly point to the lack of monuments – 15% of all answers (see: figures 7-8).

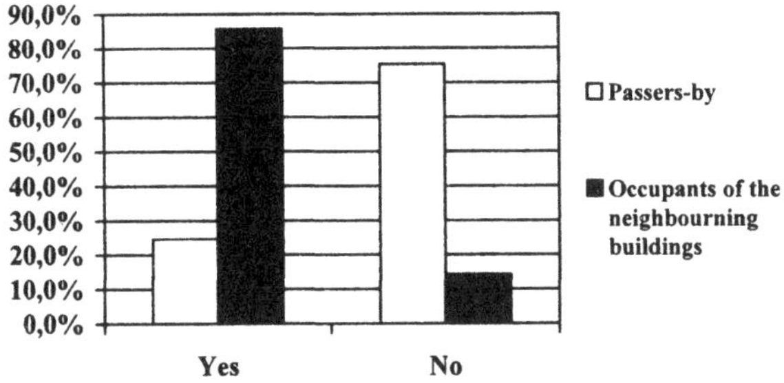

Figure 7: Do you know how the skwer Prusa looked in the past?

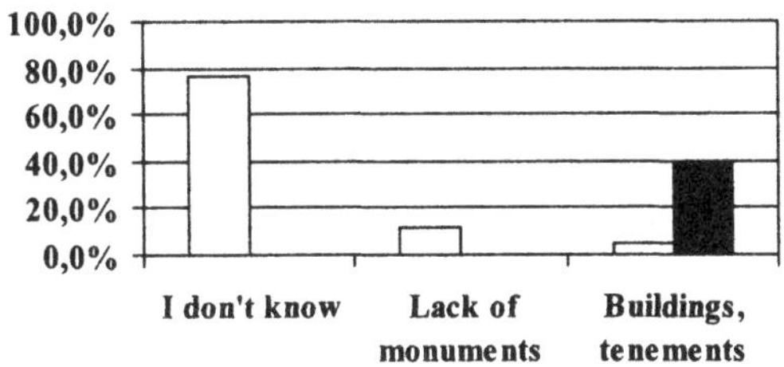

Figure 8: Do you know how the skwer Prusa looked in the past?

The interviewees when asked whether they liked the present appearance of the skwer responded in unison – yes – around 80% of all answers. They justified their answers mentioning the presence of plants allowing for a moment of relaxation in the centre of the city. Whereas the respondents dissatisfied with the present state of the skwer commented that there was not enough greenery and that it was impossible to relax there considering the unfading noise around – opinion of 10% of the interviewees.

Despite the general contentment about the appearance of the park, 60% of the interviewees wanted change. The question asked included optional answers, it also allowed for individual suggestions. The most popular response was to arrange outdoor coffee bars – almost 20% of the passers-by. The inhabitants wished for more plants and park benches – a little more than 20% among them. Individual respondents forwarded a proposition to build a state-of-art construction, or to extend the Visitants' convent (see: figure 9).

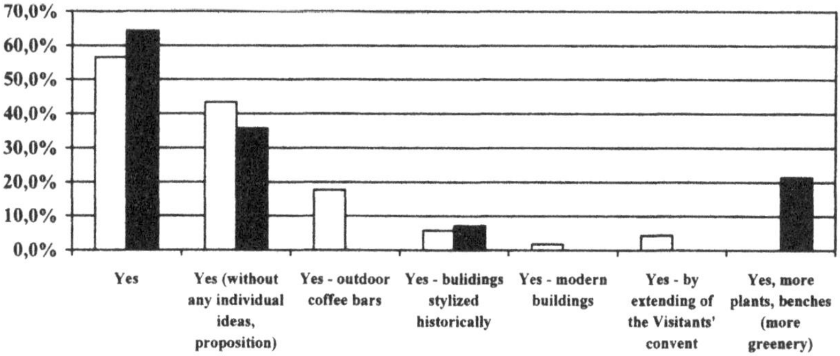

Figure 9: Would you like to change the present appearance of the skwer Prusa (if yes - in what way?)

More than 60% of the occupants of the neighbouring houses and more than 40% of the passers-by would like to have a say about changes in the development of the skwer. Surprisingly, the respondents were generally reluctant about offering their private time to participate in the process of change planning. Nearly 80% of the occupants refused to take part even in one short meeting concerning this issue. Reactions of the passers-by were similar. Only about 20% of the occupants expressed their willingness to participate in many meetings, declaring their determination to deal with the matter to the bitter end. It is puzzling that about 20% of the passers-by were ready to take part in one or a few one-hour meetings (see: figure 10).

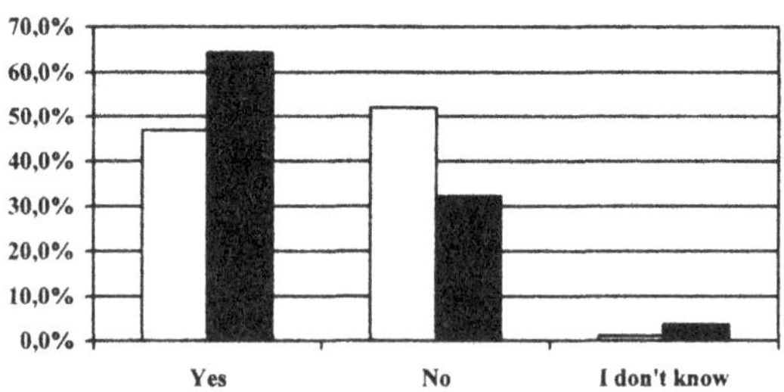

Figure 10: Would you like to have a say about changes in the development of the skwer?

Almost 65% of the occupants declared to be aware of the projects to change the appearance of skwer Prusa. But only 20% of the respondents among passers-by admitted to have such knowledge. Nearly all occupants of the neighbouring houses talked about using the space for new constructions; only 10% of the passers-by gave a similar answer (see: figure 11).

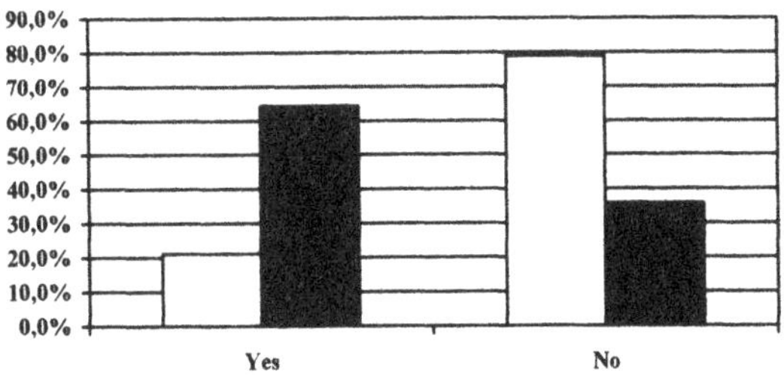

Figure 11: Do you know any new urban projects concerning the management of the skwer Prusa?

It is interesting to look at the results of cross-analyses which did not take into consideration the opinions of the occupants of the houses neighbouring the skwer. The results are as follows:

- It is mainly people who have lived in Warsaw for more than 30 years that were able to describe a previous appearance of skwer Prusa and these were not only the inhabitants of the Centrum borough, but also of peripheral boroughs like Ursynów.
- Skwer Prusa appeals mainly to the people who have lived in Warsaw for more than 30 years. At present, many of them own houses situated in peripheral districts of the city!
- It is generally the elderly people living in Ursynów (!) who are most accustomed to the present appearance of the skwer. The inhabitants of the Centrum borough come only after.
- However, it is mainly the inhabitants of the Centrum borough who wish to have influence on the changing management of the skwer. At the same time no more than 40% among them were willing to take active part in this process.
- Any new development plans for the area were known mainly by the Warsavians from the Centrum borough and to those who have lived in Warsaw for more than 30 years.
- The most willing group to co-decide about the changes concerning the management of the area are the Warsavians who have lived in

Warsaw from birth. Moreover, 60% of them would dedicate their private time to this cause.

Therefore, the inhabitants' awareness constitutes the first problem faced by urban planners and investors. The questions are whether the act of defending the existing state of affairs is just an attempt to preserve a commonly known appearance of the place and whether the opinions expressed by the inhabitants can have any influence on how a given place will be developed.

A public discussion about the future of skwer Prusa was commenced by "Gazeta Stołeczna," a Warsaw's local supplement to one of the biggest Polish newspapers. Its readers generally expressed their regret that this place, so deeply rooted in the consciousness of the inhabitants of Warsaw, meaning especially the post-war generations, visited by the students of the University of Warsaw, by occupants of the neighbouring houses, mothers with children, and tourists, should be different again. This is one of the readers' opinion:

> "The park with a statue of Prus. I cannot imagine Krakowskie Przedmieście without it. It's savagery! It's the place where you can rest while strolling along the Royal Route. It's a beautiful frame for the Visitants' Church. Save this little skwer! Can't we really do without another impersonal office building there?" or "The idea to build this place up is at least stupid!" ("Gazeta Stołeczna" 25.01.2002).

Jan Rutkiewicz, urban planner and author of the Spatial Development Plan for the Capital City of Warsaw, responded in the columns of the same newspaper providing the following arguments:

> "The plan was not designed to gain the maximum territory for private investment, but to construct the largest possible urban frontages. It's a conservative plan which attempts to recreate city's density using a method of delicate embroidery. No more than 1% of the capital is a traditional city. This kind of area needs to be enlarged." ("Gazeta Stołeczna" 25.01.2002).

The journalists were of a different opinion. One of them wrote:

> "We consider the green areas, open spaces and parks as Warsaw's treasures. They should be kept unchanged and better managed." ("Gazeta Stołeczna" 15.10.2001).

When interrogated by the press the president of Warsaw said he was amazed to hear that the matter had caused such a stir. It does not surprise anyone that before the war the whole area was built up. ("Gazeta Stołeczna" 25.03.2002).

Public awareness of the previous appearance of the place and emotional attachment to it collides with yet another reality – the one of legal and economic relations in the time of transition to market economy. Open spaces in the centre of the city are extremely attractive for private investors. Very often the city as the administrator of the space and investors meet with an obstacle in the form of claims set up by the owners deprived of their properties by the communist authorities. When both parties, expecting to obtain maximal profits, fail to reach an agreement, the lawyers enter the stage. The situation is even worse when a temporary profit collides with the development plans. In consequence, it is the legal institutions that decide about the shape of the city, undoubtedly to the detriment of the city itself.

The city's spatial policy is meant to prevent such practices. The document which regulates this problem is the Spatial Development Plan for the Capital City of Warsaw. According to this Plan the biggest investing areas are naturally located near the city boundaries. The skwer in question is situated near the limits of the Warsaw-Centrum borough, treated in the Plan as one of the strategic areas in the city. It is where the greatest concentration of offices, banks, and trading centres with accompanying services is anticipated. The system of strategic areas is to be enriched with squares and streets within the limits of the Warsaw's "Stary Salon" and "Nowy Salon". Warsaw's "Stary Salon" (literally: the Old Lounge) encompasses the historic part of the city from the Citadel through the Royal Route – hence skwer Prusa – to Łazienki park and Belweder (the Belvedere). Warsaw's "Nowy Salon" (literally: the New Lounge) encloses the areas in the centre of the city situated near the Vistula. It needs to be mentioned that "Stary Salon" is excluded from intensive investments even though it is a part of a big-city zone. A special role in forming the city's identity is attached to "unusual places," easily identified both by permanent inhabitants of Warsaw and by visitors. Is skwer Prusa one of these places? The conducted research seems to confirm it. However, it is hard to predict whether this place will not be built up in the future. The Detailed Plan for Developing the Śródmieście District, with the Royal Route as its part, presupposes that the gap between the buildings, i.e. the discussed skwer, will be built up. The plan mentions a building not higher than 18 metres.

Recapitulation

The discussed example of skwer Prusa allows one to identify the present tendencies in the process of space modelling in Warsaw and in inhabitants' perception of this process. Undoubtedly, inhabitants' emotional attachment to the characteristic places in their town should be positively received. Nevertheless, one should remember that the places often considered as traditionally "warsavian", have their origins in a very recent past. Perceiving them as "something that has been there for ever" results from discontinuity of mass memory, disrupted by the war. Only the oldest city dwellers can remember how the city looked before. This memory is likely to fade with the young generations, to which point the results of the research.

It is worth to emphasize that Warsavians are strongly attached to the places of recreation, one of which is skwer Prusa. Nonetheless, it is possible that the defensive attitude toward the present state of the skwer is a direct consequence of the lack of ideas on how to change it. Reluctant attitude, especially among the young people, toward participation in the process of urban planning only confirms the last argument. The conducted research has not discovered the reasons for such a stance. Scepticism among the young generation could derive from their life goals; it could be a manifestation of strong egocentrism of the modern man, but also of the conviction inherited from the time of socialism about pointlessness of having a private opinion about the matters of the community.

Also, trust in the purity of the designer's intentions is violated by economic aspect of the plan, inborn with market economy. Despite the persuasive assurance about a non-commercial character of the Royal Route's development plans, it is obvious that investments in this area are closely connected with big profits as for the city as for the developer. And this must trigger off conflicts (Jałowiecki 1992).

The role of the press in the process of shaping of the urban space is also interesting. Strong media are powerful, indeed. They inspire people to express their opinions. They provoke "verbal participation." Lively discussions in "Gazeta Stołeczna" and on its Internet portal page can have some influence on spatial future of the city. After all, such action brought effect in the case of the discussed skwer Prusa – for the time being, the urban planners have withdrawn their projects to build the place up.

(translated by Anna Kozdój)

References:

Jałowiecki, B. (1992) Gra o miasto w sytuacji transformacji ustroju. In: Biuletyn KPZK PAN, 157. Warsaw: PWN

Martyn, P. J. (1999) Przedwojenny układ zabudowy Śródmieścia Warszawy. Warsaw: Zamek Królewski

Zieliński, J. (2001) Atlas dawnej architektury ulic i placów Warszawy. Krakowskie Przedmieście. v.7. Warsaw: TOnZ

"Gazeta Wyborcza": daily issues: "Gazeta Stołeczna" 09.10.2001, 15.10.2001, 25.01.2002, 25.03.2002. Warsaw

"Plan Zagospodarowania m.st. Warszawy". In: "Krajobraz Warszawski" (52). Warsaw: WPPiA BZ m.st. Warszawy

Icons and myths of future urban districts

Philippe Fayeton

In the 19th century social utopias, ranging from Hygeia to Familistère de Guise and from Icarie to Harmony, the representation of "utopia" took the form of an iconographic, limited space. The new spatial arrangement was to create a new social order. But it was precisely this utopia, this "nowhere", which needed a real site to exist.

Yet as a contrast, contemporary newly developed urban quarters are imprinted by a morphology and architectonic "handwriting". Myths and iconographic representations are used to "communicate and promote" the new quarters which lead to a threefold question:

- Do these icons and myths belong to a possible (real) utopia?
- What do these utopias consist of?
- And finally, how do you get part of this utopian community?

Presently, the two large (20 hectares) city districts, "Sextius-Mirabeau" in Aix-en-Provence und "Französisches Viertel" (French quarter) in Tübingen, are in the state of development and provide a good subject for analysis.

Both, Aix-en-Provence and Tübingen are university cities, actually twin towns and satellites of their metropolises, Marseille and Stuttgart. Moreover, both cities cover similar dimensions (120.000 and 85.000 inhabitants) and both new districts have been placed next to the city centre. Furthermore, the two projects have developed strangely symmetrical:

- In 1989 the French state railway (SNCF) allocated 20 hectares of land to the City of Aix-en-Provence
- Similarly, the retreat of the former French occupying forces from Germany in 1990 left a 20 hectares area in Tübingen to reallocation

Chronological development		
	"Sextius-Mirabeau", Aix-en-Provence	**"Französisches Viertel" Tübingen**
1989	The SNCF announces reallocation	
1990	International competition for "city economy" ("économie urbaine")	The retreat of the former French occupying forces is announced ; first considerations for replanning of the area
1991	Rough draft of a master plan (PAZ / plan d'aménagement de zone)	The French forces leave Tübingen ; start of the urban development competition
1992	The master plan (PAZ) is passed	Rough draft of a master plan (Rahmenplan)
1993	Public tendering of property for sale.	The district council passes the master plan
1994		The city acquires the entire federal area
1995	First ground breaking	Public tendering of buildings and property for sale.
1996		First ground breaking

Publications		
Editors	**"Sextius-Mirabeau"**	**"Französisches Viertel"**
Local administration	*Aix suit son cours* (Aix follows its course)	*Stadt mit Eigenschaften* (A City with Features) *Private Baugemeinschaften* (Private Building Societies) "*Südstadt* " / magazine ("Southern City") *Rahmenplan* (master plan)
Builders (Promotion leaflet)	*Etoile-Mirabeau* *Les Toits de l'Olympe* *Le Square* *Résidence La Duranne*	

As both quarters are still under construction, it is too early to evaluate their urban character. However, we can analyse the publications presenting the various steps of development. These documents differ strongly in terms of content, editors, authors and methods used.

Local administration's documents

The documents are very similar in terms of their editors, authors, addressees as well as dates but differ considerably in material, flair, content and discourse.

Title	*Aix suit son cours* (Aix follows its course)	*Stadt mit Eigenschaften* (A City of Characteristics)
Name of the district	Sextius-Mirabeau	Französisches Viertel
Dimensions Dimensions (opened) support	21,5 x 30,5 cm 3 wings + filed supplements 64 x 30,5 cm high-gloss print paper, four colour print (4C)	21 x 29,7 cm 32 pages 42 x 29,7 cm recycled paper two colour print (black, bistre)
Speaker	Municipal Public Relations Office	Municipal Office for Urban Redevelopment
Enunciator	The Mayor The Secretary of urban development The Architect (prize winner)	The Mayor The Project manager / Chairman The world-renowned urban planner The Vice-mayor The famous urban design critic The Historian The Journalist The master plan The first city inhabitants
Addressee	The people of Aix (voters) Potential inhabitants Potential investors	The people of Tübingen (voters) Potential inhabitants Potential investors
Dates	1994? (without date)	1995 – 3rd Edition June, 1999
Content	The mayor's "masterpiece" The missing district of Aix An "exemplary" urban development project Spatial Programme, Overview	The "compact" city concept Chronology 1990 -1997 The Project (Projects) 1992 – 2010 Budget The project management team

The site managers' promotion brochures (Aix-en-Provence)
The four site managers reside permanently in on-site bungalows. Plans and models are shown there as well as promotion leaflets are handed out. All brochures resemble each other in size, material and content and form a complete unity.

Initiative for (private) investment in Tübingen
The brochure *"Private Gemeinschaften, kostengünstig und individuell"* (Private co-operatives, inexpensive and individual) supports people who want to join building co-operatives. Based on previous experience, it explains the main steps, the advantages and dangers of similar projects. Aside: the magazine "Südstadt" (South City) is mentioned here as a means primarily of promoting internal communication between co-operative members. This magazine also makes the information accessible to migrant workers (through articles in Greek and Turkish).

1. Icons and Myths

1.1 The local authorities' brochures

Sextius-Mirabeau: "Aix suit son Cours" *(Aix follows its course)*
The elaborate design of the brochure in triptych form presents three icons and three postulates. The aerial photo of Cours Mirabeau (Main Street) which recurs as a leitmotif throughout the brochure is followed by the motif of the Holy Trinity:

• Father God in the person of the mayor Jean François Picheral (as Peponne at his desk, the Lord's face), photo 50 x 50mm

• God the Son, embodied by the vice-mayor for urban development, Alexandre Medvedowsky (as a young technocrat in light jacket and dark necktie), photo 40 x 40mm

• And the Holy Spirit, represented by the architect Oriol Bohigas (the artist himself, in a pink shirt with open collar), photo 40 x 40mm

The reverse side of the brochure offers directions to the information centre for the construction project Sextius Mirabeau, the location of several public events, where everyone is invited to admire the model of the award-winning project as along with the other design entries for the international competition. Each of the mentioned patron saint speaks the commemorative words according to his role.
The mayor explains his decision to build *"the district Aix has been lacking" (le quartier qu'il manquait à Aix")*, the anxiously awaited district, which will transform the city: *"an enterprise which will bestow to the city the face of a modernity fit to it's image."* (*"une opération qui donnera à la ville un visage d'une modernité adaptée à son image"*).

It is to be an *“exemplary enterprise in urban development”* according to the vice-mayor for urban planning. An international competition *“for city economy”* for ten selected teams of architects was organized. The best draft was selected by means of a *“rational”* process by a committee of technicians.

The composition of the jury (representatives and technicians of the city administration, the architect of Bureau of Historical Preservation, representatives of various clubs) guaranteed the transparent and democratic procedure (which was reinforced).
The competition prize-winner, architect Oriol Bohigas, well aware that *“the city is made of public spaces”*, thus he clearly describes the function of his plan: *“This is why the public space - streets, squares, paths, façades, living space - has been given absolute priority.” (“C’est pourquoi nous avons fait de l’espace public - rues, places, itinéraires, façades, lieux de vie - notre priorité absolue.”)* Referring back to the urban design of the 1970s he emphasizes that he did not forget to draw these elements (bridges, footbridges, fountains, public facilities) with particular care and to select the various materials (paving-stones, edge stones and street surfaces) that are in this context of particular importance.

The programme of the quarter and the spatial design follow a somewhat mythical spatial organizational principle à la Vitruvius: the new district is composed out of a spacious street scheme that sets everything accordingly in its place. In the west there are the middle class accommodations (*“halfway between welfare housing and great luxury” ("à mi-chemin entre logement social et grand standing")*, in the east luxury apartments (*“close to the Cours Mirabeau”)* and student accommodations (close to the main station and universities). And, as it should be, a large parking lot, a casino and a concert hall complete the ensemble.

The district “Französisches Viertel“: “A City of Characteristics”
There are no allusions to the Creator in this presentation, but rather images which, as in a family photo album, present children, families, craftsman and “common” citizens. In various articles, inhabitants, architects and lawyers are requested to confirm the advantages of the functional heterogeneity. This unique proposal, called *“the City of Short Paths”*, can be summarized by the following 5 points:
- *“The plan joins four areas to form the “spine” of the Südstadt” (Stadt mit Eigenschaften, p. 18)*

- *"to once again situate the larger part of the workplaces within the more functionally heterogeneous districts"* (12)
- *"public space is designed as a place of habitation"* (16)
- to create *"... space for the unfolding of a vivid city life" (19)*
- *"to provide the inhabitants and merchants in the south of Tübingen with a self-planned urban infrastructure, capable of being adapted to their varying needs"* (14)

An intermediate evaluation (1999) acknowledges the first successfully established trades in the district.

As can be read in "objective" literary contributions, the plan is endorsed by a number of "neutral" celebrities (journalist Ulrike Pfeil, historian and Südstadt native Johanna Petersmann, the art- and architecture critic Christian Marquart from Stuttgart and the internationally renowned architect and urban designer, Rem Koolhaas).

The building programm does not simply present a list of building-density figures, but is also organized around a set of urban-political intentions, meant to encourage personal and financial interest. The focus lies on aid in the acquisition of residential property, in establishing companies, as well as to grant subsidies to socially-involved, private clubs for their work in such institutions as community day-care centres.

2.2 Developer's discurs

Sextius-Mirabeau

All four brochures open like a postcard triptych that shows famous places and buildings of Aix.

Few of the apartments for sale are shown (only 2 out of 4). Only in one case are the façades of the future buildings shown.

Instead, the leaflets offer "elegant" perspective drawings (3 out of 4):

Presented objects	Number of mentioned objects / Number of documents mentioned in
Simplified map of the location/ plan (in relation to Place de la Rotonde)	4/4
Fountains at Place de la Rotonde	4/4
Provencal greengrocers' stores in the Old Town	4/4
Trademark of the developers	4/4
Perspective view of the building	3/4
Elements of classical architecture	3/4
Café terrace in the Cours Mirabeau (main street)	3/4
Cité du Livre (large extended library and communication centre)	2/4
Interior plans of the apartments	2/4
View on façades	1/4

The main aspects are:
- link between tradition and modernity
- prominent location
- maximum of sunlight in the housing units
- quads and terraces

The tying link of the 4 brochures is expressed in a single virtue: "extraordinariness". The purpose of the *extraordinary* blend of modern and traditional building materials is, after all, to realize an *extraordinary* building at a glamorous site in the *extraordinary* city of Aix-en-Provence, which promises an *extraordinary* standard of living reserved for an *extraordinary* elite.

The district Französisches Viertel
"The aim of the urban development management [...] is to open the market for residential property to a broader class-spectrum of the population."(2)
One step towards this goal is to integrate the people in the development process of the residential areas of a district. In this case there are no developers "à la française" here (with the exception of three apartment houses). Nor are there promotion leaflets. From time to time building co-operatives advertise in the local newspapers for additional interested parties to join.

The brochure "Private Gemeinschaften, kostengünstig und individuell" (Private co-operatives, inexpensive and individual) has no other purpose than to dispel the fears of possible private investors facing the adventure of a self-funded apartment unit.

"In an private building co-operative, the members assume the responsibilities usually shouldered by the developer, an effort that can pay off :

- *a building-cost reduction of up to 25%*
- *no mass-produced architecture [...], but individual and group needs can be accommodated*
- *...the freedom to select your own partners"* (2-3)

2. Utopemes

Despite obvious differences, both building projects share four requirements of utopia known as "utopemes":

- Island
- Mutually Otherness
- Historic Confusion
- Happiness

2.1 Utopeme: Island

According to Thomas More is utopia an island. It is interesting to notice that both projects that are being compared here, can be seen as a "somewhere-else / beyond" with regard to the existing city, although they, at the same time, seek to complete, perfect and be integrated into that city.

Sextius-Mirabeau: "the missing quarter"

Even though Sextius-Mirabeau is located in the middle of the city of Aix-en-Provence, the district is presented of as being "outside". Sextius-Mirabeau is always thought of in relation to the Place de la Rotonde (next to the Old City), the Cours Mirabeau (Main Street) and the Old City. As a result of this way of thinking, the city of Aix-en-Provence is, in a curious way, reduced to merely its historic core.

Sextius-Mirabeau, the protected utopian island, is situated just a stone's throw away from "the heart of the historic city", yet still in the middle of an ocean called "Provence":

- Etoile-Mirabeau *"on the border of the historic core" ("à l'orée du cœur historique"),*
- Whereas La Résidence La Duranne in fact represents *"the city in the countryside"* (*"c'est vraiment la ville à la campagne"*).
- Les Toits de l'Olympe is *"next to the heart of the city"* (*"à deux pas du cœur de la cité")*

• While Le Square floats *"between heaven and earth"* (*"Entre ciel et terre"*)
The central aim is, then, to invest in a new island set at the far end of Cours Mirabeau. The developers of the island praise the diverse fortress-like elements, such as the barred windows, doors and security systems: *"solid apartment doors with high-security locks" ("porte palière à âme pleine...et serrure 3 points"*) (Etoile-Mirabeau), *"intercom system and coded access"* (Les Toits de l'Olympe).

Französisches Viertel: "Chance of the Century"
In the case of Tübingen the aim is to recapture an island, which had been occupied and then later abandoned by an "intruder". The intruder (the French army) has been well known since the Thirty Year War and has proved to be a "decent" intruder whose cultural value is well recognised. Since then, the intruder has become a friend, coining names for the new district and several streets (Allee des Chasseurs, Provenceweg, Aixerstraße).
There is no attempt here to refer to the Old City itself, but rather to the "good, old quality of life" thereof. The conception of the new district follows the principle of the compact city, imitating the pioneer spirit of the new settlements of the 1970's. The idea is characterized by the insular self-sufficiency of the daily routine: The "City of Short Distances" means, having all of the necessary everyday amenities close at hand, be it a daycare centre, a bakery, a doctor, a hairdresser, a plumber, an architect or an attorney.

2.2 Utopeme: mutually otherness

The utopians of the two cities follow the same lines of argumentation, which culminate with the new city districts. Their identity is formed through a process of mutual reflection. The utopians in Aix, as do those in Tübingen, desire to be "different" and to prove this to each other by their modes of habitation.

Splendor and Prestige in the district Sextius-Mirabeau
The address "Aix-en-Provence" is prestigious (Les Toits de l'Olympe) because it is surrounded by "prestigious" buildings:
• *"There is the Cité du Livre nearby, the new community centre, the future marketplace"*
• *"Next to the city [...] half way to the city centre and to the university"* (*"à deux pas de la Cité du Livre, de la nouvelle salle de spectacles, du futur marché"*.)
• *"Just a few yards away from the Rotonde and the Cours Mirabeau" ("à quelques pas seulement de la Rotonde et du Cours Mirabeau")*.

The contact to these prestigious places and to people of influence seems to spread prestige like a virus. The seat of "infection" is located in the Old City, in Cours Mirabeau, Place de la Rotonde and Quartier Mazarin, where formerly, aristocrats, respected legal personalities and the academia of the university lived and spent their time.
The utopians of the Sextius-Mirabeau district profit from the historical prestige of this address, and it is in this prestige that its elitist consciousness is rooted: it's just different here. The following is said about the residential area Le Square: *"Le Square is offered to a few privileged... Le Square asserts its unique character [...] and highlight its exclusiveness"* (*"L'édification du Square offre...à quelques privilégiés [...] Le Square s'érige... et revendique son caractère unique. Il marque sa différence"*). And this about the Résidence La Duranne: *"for outdoor sport fans, whether it is with family or with friends there is the Clubhouse."*
Such a glamorous and elitist attitude requires a spectacular building: although average in size, the apartments are said *"large"* , the windows are no ordinary windows but *"broad full-height glazing"*; the construction is described as being of *"high-quality"* and the interior design portrayed as *"intelligent"*.

Intelligentsia in the district Französisches Viertel
The intellectuals and "green-alternatives" meet in the district Französisches Viertel: to them the new address serves to highlight their alternative way of living (open-minded and environmentally aware) and to express their desire for individualism. Those renting here embark on an "adventure" and for this adventure, they get a double award: they receive a "custom designed" accommodation and save up to 25%.
The group "Projekt 14" decided to build several communal rooms (a sauna, a fitness studio, a home workshop, a bicycle cellar and a common room):
"In this project individuality is of prime importance. No two apartments are alike and even the variety of the people behind the windows can be read on the façade [...] It is a great advantage that everyone involved carefully considers each constructive element of his or her apartment." (Andreas Stahl, Architekt, in *Private Baugemeinschaften*, p. 6.)
This individualism is of course, reserved for small elite, for *"without doubt: the planning project of the Tübingen Südstadt does not for every individual lifestyle"*, it has been specially conceived for *"people who have deliberately chosen and continue to choose an urban lifestyle."* (Christian Marquart, in *Stadt mit Eigenschaften*, p. 23.)
The close interaction of the inhabitants incited a fear (according to several articles printed in the local daily Schwäbisches Tageblatt) that a

"ghetto" for architects or lawyers might develop, or in the words of the historian Johanna Petersmann, that the district will become, "a mecca of urban designers and literarians." (*„Es ist zu hoffen, daß die verschiedenen Südstadtquartiere nicht nur zum Mekka von Stadtplanern und Feuilletonisten werden.*" Johanna Petersmann, in *Stadt mit Eigenschaften*, p. 11.)

2.3 Utopeme: Historic Confusion

Time is in no hurry in utopia. The state of perfection of this (Christian) rebirth can only be attained within eternity. Aix and Tübingen show that there is more than one way to blend characteristics of yesterday, today and tomorrow and thereby scorn the fleetingness of the time.

An Alliance of Tradition and Modernism

The character of the district Sextius-Mirabeau is defined by its name, which is a historical reference. Not by chance the name of the Roman Consul Sextius is reapplied and combined with the one of Mirabeau (Honoré Gabriel Riquetti, Comte de Mirabeau. Born 1749 in Aix-en-Provence, well-known popular speaker and dull politician died 1791 in Paris.) In the name lingers the "Tradition of Aix", a historic reminiscence starting with Roman times right to the aristocrats' 17th and 18th centuries and their so-called "Hotels particuliers".

Thus the status of Aix-en-Provence as the capital of the district Provence, the residence of the court and host for the international song festival (Festival International d'Art Lyrique) was strengthened.

As a consequence, the Le Square complex is the *"perfect expression of the union of exquisite materials and modern convenience"* (*"est l'expression parfaitement réussie d'une union entre la noblesse des matériaux et le confort de la modernité")*, while Etoile-Mirabeau *"unites tradition and modernity"*. Here it is possible to *"live within an extraordinary project* (Les Toits de l'Olympe) *which restores the connection to the Old City"* (*"vivre au sein d'un fantastique projet qui renoue les liens avec la ville ancienne")*, or if one prefers, to *"combine the modern with the Art of Living [...] youth and the Art of Living"* *("conjugue à merveille modernité et art de vivre...conjugue jeunesse et art de vivre")* as in Résidence la Duranne.

exquisite materials	And	modern conveniences
Old City	And	extraordinary project
The traditional	And	the modern
Art of Living	And	modernity
Art of Living	And	youth

“Tradition” refers to a (glorious, glamorous and mighty) past one inherits. As one’s own birth is part of history, one integrates oneself into an (apparent) historical logic.It suffices to allude to such simple symbols to “summon” the knowledge of tradition (wrought-iron craftsmanship, solid-wood doors, and stone façades).
Modernity brings progress in association with the future. Because of a modernity, which accomplishes today what was planned for tomorrow, the recluse is placed above those who are “not-modern”. The symbols of the modernity which are embodied by the seal of approval represent the minimum construction standards. This standardized modernity has become dated.
It is not a modernity of discontinuity within an adventurous avantgardism, but rather a modernity that came into its own right through science and law; a modernity that was ennobled by tastefulness (“de bon goût”).
The discontinuity that modernity supposes is immediately revalued as the normative rule. Was this not the modernity, of which Henri Lefèbvre spoke, when he referred to the *“shadow of the missed revolution, its own parody”. (" l’ombre de la révolution manquée, sa parodie".)*
The alliance of tradition and modernity makes the recluse the centre of a historic deconstructed space, removing all traces of time: time becomes contracted as is in a black hole. The syntax of tradition and modernity shall take the fear out of the death: The utopians of Sextius-Mirabeau shall enjoy eternal youth.

The Next World
Only once the Tübingen project calls upon “tradition”. It is then the tradition of the Old City. Nevertheless, in the brochure of the city administration reference to the past is made in particular in the contribution by Johanna Petersmann, the “Südstadt born” historian. In her article she uses the (the city’s) history as a basis to explain the new districts impact on future. But the article does not glorify an apparently glamorous past, but uses the stormy historic evolution to point to a forward-looking idea.

2.4 Utopeme: Happiness

Both projects take very different “paths to happiness”, which correspond to the diametrical needs.
2.4.1 Individuality in the district Sextius-Mirabeau
The utopians in the district Sextius-Mirabeau are new hedonistic patricians who want to be enchanted by the dolce vita.
Le Square invites future inhabitants offering them *“to profit daily from advantages of a city in the midst of a revival [...] to be persuaded by [...] the Le Square complex, without much ado, shall quench the thirst of*

desires." (*"profiter au quotidien des attraits d'une Cité en plein renouveau ... laissez-vous séduire... le Square saura assouvir toutes vos envies, sans contraintes").*
Résidence La Duranne offers *"true comfort and quality of life [...] to make life easier."* (*"un véritable confort et une qualité de vie... pour vous faciliter la vie.")*
Could you resist the pleasures of this "God's estate?"
Les Toits de l'Olympe promises: *"surroundings designed to win you over; [...] a lawn for you pleasure in an inner courtyard, [...] isn't it wonderful when one is heard?"("des espaces de vie qui sauront vous séduire ...vous permettront de profiter d'un cadre verdoyant à l'abri d'un patio intérieur... c'est bon d'être écouté").*
This *"ideal of a life" (" douceur de vivre").*, which is realised in the Etoile-Mirabeau residence, can also be called the quintessence of *"Provençal life"* according to the brochure for the Résidence Port-Royal.
It is understood that the perfect individual privacy in this quarter will not be ruined by the noise of children : in this quarter with as many as 2000 planned apartments there is neither space for a kindergarten, nor an elementary or secondary school.

2.4.2 Mutual Happiness in the district Französisches Viertel

The theme of a perfect, happy future is easily seen in the photos: smiling married couples with the model of their future house, a couple with a child, craftsmen, a group of children at play. The happiness portrayed here is that of a world free of unnecessary cars, where work and private life intermingle easily, within the scope of rational urban development:
"The opportunities for a rich diversity of contacts, [...] the advantage of short distances, [...] of varied [...] sensibly designed surroundings." (Christian Marquart, in *Stadt mit Eigenschaften*, p. 23.) This mutual happiness is an individual happiness that one shares with enthusiasm, particularly in the form of numerous social facilities (such as nursery schools, daycare centres, kindergartens, elementary schools, gymnasiums and dance halls).

3. Connivance vs. Consent

Both projects, Sextius-Mirabeau and the Französisches Viertel, seem to inherit an utopian dimension, or appear at least wrapped in "utopian ideas". A new question is obviously: how does one become a member of this utopian community?
In any case a new code is necessary in order to join the utopian community. In Tübingen the code is called "consent of the settlers", in Aix "connivance (complicity) of the investors (Up to 70% apartments in Sextius-Mirabeau belong to investors).

3.1 The Consent of the Settlers

The consent is carefully worded in articles written by residents, who express themselves with words and smiles. This consent derives from the common will to invest in a location formerly outside the city and thus to take part in the "beyond" exclaimed by Johanna Petersmann. It focuses on the concept of "the constant development" which has maintained itself in Germany and in particular in the university city of Tübingen (Tübingen is the city with the highest density of libraries as well as opticians in Germany. Even two shops for ecological construction materials can exist.), where the Green alternative party have a strong political mandate. The enthusiasm of the green pioneers is partly to be seen in the context of the lack of building sites in Germany and in particular in the area around Stuttgart. This consent is based upon the participation of the clubs in the individual planning phases, on the manner of implementation and on the participation of building collectives. The search for the consent bears, in itself, utopian tendencies, with its attitude of denial toward those conflicts, which could affect the apparent unity of the building collectives.

3.2 The connivance of the investors

The arguments used to promote the district Sextius-Mirabeau (extraordinary construction, glamorous address, unique city of Aix, extraordinary quality of life, elitist milieu) do not all stand up under closer examination.

In truth, the "exquisite traditional building materials" consist of nothing more than simple lime plaster and the "exquisite natural stone facades", a mere 2,5 cm of stone facing. The qualitative solid wooden doors of the "Hôtels Particuliers" of Quartier Mazarin are in the end fire resistant industrial doors.Moreover, the proclaimed "extraordinary" comfort elements are for the most part standard required elements, anyways; indoor courtyards are often just planted roof gardens over underground garages; supposed sunlight terraces, for the most part, merely east-facing balconies.

In short: The presented arguments fail under examination. Nevertheless, there is no deception. Because everyone, with the help of the plans and models, is able to plainly see, that the claims aren't true; everyone knows what is meant by "sensible exposure" *("l'ensoleillement judicieux")* of a north-facing room. And there is also no fraud, when it is said that the Etoile-Mirabeau residences is "steps away from the Rotonde", but still lies 750m distant. There is no deception, because it must be assumed that the elitist clientele of the residence are capable of decoding the discourse of advertising, and in the end is content with the "glamorous" address. There is no deception, because they have connivance with regard to the reading of the urban- and architectural code.

4. Conclusions

In general, the two promotion leaflets are quite very different: On one hand, the patrician hedonism of investors is emphasized (Aix-en-Provence), on the other hand the co-operative pioneers' sprit is praised. However, both leaflets convey the same "Utopemes" and use them as Significants.

Let us remember Umberto Eco's strongly didactic example of the significant 'horse' which refers to concrete animal, while his 'unicorn' significant refers to the mythological animal (Eco 1973).

The question is now: what do the district Französisches Viertel and the district Sextius-Mirabeau refer to? Are they meant to be the animal 'horse', the 'unicorn', Don Quichottes' Rosinante or a rocking-horse?

In both new districts the island 'utopia' is no longer the progressive island, isolated from the reactionary mainland, but instead symbolises more a marina or a harbour. The one can say that every boat (building) floats independently, but with the same rhythm as the others. And every boat stays, quite wisely, connected with the mainland through its energy, telecommunication and water supply.

For the materialized island utopia, it more or less sufficies to simply be a decent address. In the end, the new district seems to be *"the only decent"* place, as was *"Quartier de la Sous-préfecture"* in Aix-en-Provence represented for Emile Zola in its own time:

"*Plassans est divisé en trois quartiers absolument distincts : le vieux quartier où vous n'aurez que des consolations et des aumônes à porter ; le quartier St Marc, habité par la noblesse du pays, un lieu d'ennui et de rancune dont vous ne sauriez trop vous méfier ; et la ville neuve, le quartier qui se bâtit en ce moment autour de la Sous-Préfecture, le seul possible, le seul convenable*". Emile Zola, *la conquête de Plassans.*

This code system works, because the concept of urbanity is founded on symbolic qualities rather than on material ones, as Mondada pointed out: "Urbanism is less defined in termes of material qualities (as for example, denistiy of population, transport, exchanges) as in symbolic ones." ("*L'urbanité est moins définie en termes de propriétés matérielles (p.ex. en termes de densité de population, de transports, de flux, d'échanges) qu'en termes de propriétés symboliques".(Mondada 2000, p. 38)*

Utopia needs architecture and the city and a place to become a reality. In contrast, architecture and cities do not necessarily need utopia. Both are quite content with symbols or even just marketing strategies. *"Because the atmosphere and charm of the quarter is ultimately born in the minds of its inhabitants – to the chagrin of all the."* (Ulrike Pfeil, *Schwäbisches Tagblatt* on the 29.8.91, quote in: *Stadt mit Eigenschaften*, p. 20.)

"Fun-shopping" may be used as one example to illustrate the aforementioned aspect: it is the most recent and successful concept for shopping malls (Carré Sénart and Val d'Europe near Paris, or Sainsbury's near Manchester, or the West Edmondton Mall in Alberta (or CenrO Oberhausen)). In the words of the Sénart county district president, Jean-Jacques Fournier, that concept "elevates shops to the level of cities". We will most likely need yet another key to decode this postulate, which seems to mistake rocking-horses for thoroughbreds.

Reference:

Eco, U. (1973), *Le signe*. biblio essais, Livre de poche, 1993.

Mondada, L. (2000). *Décrire la ville, la construction des savoirs urbains dans l'interaction et dans le texte*. Paris: Ed. Economica.

Images, Memory and Urban Regeneration

Leonel Fadigas

Cities are made of stones, bricks, iron, sand, light and memories. City history is the result and the expression of a long story of relationship between men and landscape: Between individual and collective stories, experiences and ways to use and transform the natural and artificial resources. In a certain way cities are made more by culture than by construction materials. Urban fabrics result as a special type of landscape where time passes through and adds identity, authenticity and the cement that links generations.

In fact cities are one of the expressions that landscapes assume as the materialisation of the human habitat. They express in its form, in the organisation and in the diversity of its spatial relationships, the times, the types and the intensity of its human cultural, economic and technological occupation. And they also express the visual and physical dimension of multiples realities and memories.

Visual material, such as photographs, paintings, engravings, maps, urban plans and drawings record along the time images, scenaries and memories. At the same time they show the evolution and the changes in different moments of urban social, technological and cultural history and its impact on the image of the city. Ideas about the appearance of a city change at different rhythms and speed raising the question of knowing if these changes are the result of deliberate choices in urban management or if they are autonomous developments in the townscape resistant to interventions (Alkoven, 1993).

The image we built about a city is made by what we see and by what we understand, by the reality and by the imagination. This image, this way to see and to understand cities, is the recreation of the reality and an enlargement of the comprehensive field of what we have in face or in mind.

As a human product, cities represent a way to use land, soil and resources. Its construction and development are always the result of a prolonged and continuous recycling process of uses, materials, forms, concepts, ideas and memories.

Each epoch is expressed, as image, urban scenary and global landscape by structures and morphologies that are associated to its most representative economical, social and cultural aspects and characteristics.

In the European framework, and in the mediaeval period, the relationship of the cities with its rural surroundings is merely functional.

By reasons imposed by its internal organisation and by the way as defensive preoccupations have imposed them a limit area surrounded by walls. In the global landscape mediaeval cities are seen as well defined dots in surrounded by extensive rural fields. Its aspect is the aspect of a compact organisation from where only relevant buildings assume themselves as landmarks: a castle or a cathedral. Power and faith are the mental references associated to that scenery.

Renaissance urban development, in its different forms and expressions, is associated to new relationship between city and its surrounding area. An embrionnary dialog has started a dialog that transformed itself in an opening relationship where built units and urban fragments appeared outside walls. More active commercial changes and economic activities and the reduced defensive importance of the walls explain that new urban forms. Less defined, more ambiguous in its contours.

City opening to its exterior landscape is followed, in a visual and scenic aspect, by changes in life styles, ways of life and the recognition of the country as a privileged space to live. With which architecture explored the possibility and the interest in building palaces and gardens in the countryside, as new monuments. Walls, when they remained as urban fragments, stayed as cultural marks, historical references or as support of new utility buildings that have profit its existence as part of its construction.

City image have changed at the same time that society and the surrounding landscape has discovered that the surrounding landscape was not the exterior space but a new dimension of the urban scenery: The understanding of landscape as something of global.

Industrial revolution with its collection of technological, economic and social changes and innovative development processes increased the relationship between city and the surroundings. With new expressions, new urban concepts and forms, where *city and progress*, *city and welfare*, *city and survival conditions* were leitmotiv of discussion, preoccupation and engines of social, land use and urban transformations.As well He place became a synonimous of security and space special way to feel freedom (Tuan, 2001).

The increasing physical and populational dimention of the cities in this period made not only new urban scenerys but also new mwntal concepts and understanding of what a city was, as geographical, functional and social entity and as social and cultural source of ideas and innovation. Contemporary cities stil are the direct result of these urban concepts and understandings. What is however changing?

If city is memory and stone is at the same time a modelling system of society and mentalities. The abused way of using natural resources reduced the rural landscape diversity, imposed violent urban changes,

built new fragmentary environments and disrupted balances appeared to show real effective and strong environmental and social crisis. City image also became something of strange and apart of the usual linkage between man and its geographical, physical, cultural, and social surroundings. The new urban environment started to impose the need of rediscover and regain memories, heritage and cultural links; and, of course, mystery, factor of preference and interest in landscape quality.
In a word, cities are made of solids, voids, memories and landmarks and space and objects perception changes itself according to urban and rural landscapes evolution.
The improvement of acessibilty systems has helped to create and to develop new landscapes and new ways to see to interpretate and to understand them. Faster displacements allow wider but less detailed landscape views, while the observer see more images than in lower displacements.
Space-time relationship converts in a flutuable scale. Landscapes are seen differently if we are producers of that landscape or if we are merely consumers. Acting on the space to use it or to modify it gives a sensation of property that is a process of seeing and interpretating landscape differently from when we only content ourselves with its contemplation (Fourneau, 1989).
The image we have of a city is not the real one but our interpretation of what that specific city is. As an interpretation, city representation by drawing, by photo, by film, is a mental interpretation, a cultural way to identify patterns, buildings, materials, solids and voids, colours, topography, people, traffic, light and shadows.
With all this we capture identities (or what we think it is a city identity) and create a special and private relationship with a city and particularly with our city. The result is that cities may belong to anyone by different reasons, be seen by different eyes in different ways, have different forms, colours, souls and smells.
Urban scenaries are not mathematic expressions. They are changed by mind and the mind changes the eyes. City image is, for that, the result of a complex pattern of views, different and similar, that is captured by mind and eyes. The phenomenon known as landscape only exists as a cultural creation resultant of an emotional projection on the environment and of an aesthetic and disinterested understanding of the values that produce us pleasure or repulse (Carbo, 1996).
In fact, city image is not one and it is not unique. It is, perhaps, each one image, each one own image, and each one interpretation of what each one see and feels. And its richness is its compatibility with all the different images that its inhabitants and its visitors have.

If the multiplicity of all those views allows having a common sense of identification, a common understanding of what the city is we can assure that a real, unique image is possible and an identity is clear and possible of transmission between generations.
City image, as a mind construction, is a memory; a memory of the past and a memory of the future.
Because these image, as a collective and common image, represents a tool, a rule and a parameter for its transformation and evolution.
Urban changes are, for that, more than changes of scenery, of architectural models and of economic and social patterns. The technological potential at our disposition has significant impacts on the strong and fast processes of territorial and landscape transformations.
Contemporary cities and metropolitan areas are the example of this relationship between technology and urban changes.
This process of urban evolution is not only a contemporary reality. All the urban history has been made by that relationship. Technologies made the tools for the urban transformations in all the times. Its intensity, being proportional with the technological development of each development moment of the society, gives an adequate expression to urban landscape transformation. In fact, acting as a complex ecosystem, cities develop and transform themselves presenting, in each moment, an own, individual and characteristic expression and image (Lynch, 1973)
As far as urban transformations increase city image transformations conflicts and problems may appear as the result of an unbalanced development process. Human communities living in a special place, having between them and the physical and cultural urban structure itself a close complicity and a own identity may react against those transformations if they occur against its needs, wills, expectations, memories and identity.
In this case cultural and social resistances are the result of a lack of complicity and understanding of what a city is -in its complexity and its immaterial nature. To be attentive to this is understand that landscapes, city images, urban scenaries, are also memory, spaces of affections and culture, life and future territories, where past is always present.
And the collective heritage enlist as memories the moments, the facts, the landmarks, the forms, the fabrics, the colours that in each moment are the most representative and authentic image of a city as its inhabitants and visitors live and love it.
Memories are the result of cultures that in each time are the expression of forms and technologies that are manifestations of the presence and the cultural and social evolution of its populations and communities. At the same time memories also are marks of the human capacity of learning and adaptation to the environment and the reflex of the fact that

cities don't exist without their inhabitants, those who live and work in and have a particular relationship with its urban fabric, identity and image. A relationship that is essential to get the close complicity that controls the urban evolution and make it possible in a cultural continuity.

> "Landscape is memory. But beyond its limits, landscape shows the marks of the past, rebuilt memories, projects in the look the shadows of other time that only exists as reflex of itself in the traveller's memory" (Llamazares, 1990).

In this sense landscape assumes an importance that surpasses the simple description of a place where things happen or a place where projects are built to create a world to be liveable, qualified and sustainable for life and pleasure.

For that, cities and change are indistinguishable synonyms. Its continuous process of doing and undoing urban fabric gives sense to the idea of city as a space of continuity and future. In this way change also is synonym of innovation and future, giving structure and modernity to the contemporary urban redevelopment and architectural proposals: Building today the cultural and architectural heritage of tomorrow.

And making cities with architecture made not to settle the places but to make them sacred. That's to say to give them the meaning of "*made for the men in communion and balance with nature*".

Landscape, city image and urban scenery transformations are the result and the reason of new urban life demands and the emergent changeable character of contemporary cities. Architects and town planners are, in this new floating process of urban evolution and human needs and demands, obliged to adapt the traditional processes of designing and making the urban territories and the urban projects (Wall, 1999).

This attitude is now a central question for urban planning specially when the subject of that planning is the urban fringe or the old brown fields and territories and the degraded inner city quarters and places. Planning is not an abstract exercise but a way to make liveable the places made for people live, work, relax, progress and be happy.

Looking to the urban fringes landscapes we understand very well how, in those territories, the challenges of the future times are challenges of landscape organisation where urban and residual rural spaces must be regenerated in order to make them urban territories with references, quality, memories and human dimensions.

In a word, to make them a city.

Environment has nowadays an increasing presence at urban scene and in the interests of urban people. Much of this interest results from a need

and a search of quality that could change and balance the unqualified urban and architectural organisation of urban and peri-urban landscapes.
This means that environmentally qualified landscapes allows the creation of “natural” scenaries not only with environmental functions of biodiversity protection, clima conditioning, recreation facilities or landscape and architectural integration. Many times they represent the maintenance of rural fragments inside urban expansion areas and a strong referential for memories and cultural heritage of the local people or of those who recently came from the rural areas to the main city.
These rural fragments may be used as green spaces, greenways, recreational facilities and landmarks in the relationship between people and his cultural environment. A way to keep common references and identities is, when we pass from a rural cultural society to an urban cultural society and keeping a balanced and healthy relationship inside the community.
Landscape is an ecological, aesthetic and geographical unity created by the human action and by the reaction of nature. This means that what we see is transformed by the sensibility and the emotions and by an anthropological background made by a long and continuous history of relationship with the environment and other communities. Quality of life is, in this sense, a concept associated with the habitat, the culture, the emotions and the way of life of people who use it.
However, the definition of quality standards to measure quality of life must be supported by parameters without which we can not define levels and situations of reference to apply in the urban qualification programs and projects.
The quality of life parameters related to bio-physical aspects represent relatively stable criteria but those related to human comfort, psychological perception and aesthetic, cultural and emotional aspects are difficult to establish. Subjectivity is always present and introduces other kind of standards to establish common and usual criteria to define and to compare comprehension, quality, interest and identity levels.
The landscape image and the landscape quality are complex to define and to evaluate. But its role has an identity factor is nuclear for the concept of quality of life. Subjectivity introduces in the understanding of this concept others units to measure quality and emotional relationship. Because identity and comprehension are essential parts of what we understand as a landscape: scenery, landform, and homeland.
Natural elements have an own expression in the urban morphology, texture and fabric. Its identification and dimensioning as values expressing environmental quality levels are not possible through a unique physical measure unit. Comfort, quality and identity are

expressed in different ways and felt by people through sensibility, emotions and culture. The quality of a space or scenery is the final result of a complex melting pot of emotions, sensations and culture. It is possible to describe it but very difficult, if no impossible, to evaluate or to compare perception two persons have about it.

The creation of environmental indicators becomes an essential contribution for urban management, urban planning and urban design; not only to prepare more comfortable spaces but mainly to design spaces, where we could feel the sense of continuity that reinforces social cohesion and identity. It will contribute to the living spaces the character of a real human habitat. In fact the psychological well being sensation is based on a group of situations and conditions that includes physical, mental, environmental and cultural factors and that must be present in all planning decisions and acts affecting human life and environment.

Man has perception and sensitivity, is active and able to act and to transform his environment and his social being. For that, environmental indicators to evaluate landscape quality must refer themselves to those dominions: sensitive experience of the space, urban or rural; uses and action plans for people, people's and groups capacity of action and transformation and the possibilities of social participation (Corraliza, 2001).

The scenic value of natural landscapes, the effective value they represent to the people who lives there or who relates with them also is a natural resource (Schauman,1988). Not well known but important enough to justify an increasing importance and presence in territorial and urban planning and management (Abello & Bernaldez, 1986). For environmental, functional cultural and aesthetic reasons and as a way to profit natural spaces as special features to re-establish human balance in a stressed urban life. Green areas, parks, gardens, greenways, open spaces and fields are not urban and territorial forms to be used and to compose urban and natural scenerys but also psychological answers to human quality of life.

Aesthetic factors are important in the understanding of the urban landscape as part of the identification process. Cities are not only functional systems: memories, images, scenic and aesthetic values are part of its identity and for that the urban design process must also include them as a way to define uses and coherent functional systems, where the global image should reflect the complexity of this special human habitat.

Urban fringes are fragile spaces, suffering strong transformations and intensive changes of use, where people living there also suffer continuous rupture processes inside community links and in people's

linkage within the surrounding environment. Many times, in these situations affective links and emotional equilibrium are affected, increasing stress levels and reducing environmental quality levels.
What means that natural values are essential to understand that land use and urban planning processes are not technical ways or solving the problems of rational use of the soil but also balanced, aesthetic, cultural and social processes of human habitats where The studies on the landscape quality and on the subjective factors that determine the affective adaptation to the built environment are interesting contributions to the understanding of the way people lives his habitat and make close relationship with it.
By them it has been possible to identify common factors of pleasantness and attraction of spaces and situations giving us the possibility of composing new natural and urban structures and spaces of high environmental quality and scenic beauty. With which it is possible to design new landscapes, new urban spaces for a more qualified and comfortable human use. Through new expansion design schemes or through a regeneration process of upgrading and re-using degraded urban and industrial areas and the recycling of spaces for new uses and activities for natural conservancy purposes or green urban structures, parks, gardens and greenways.
The presence of natural elements in the urban structure, and in the urban landscape does not depends only on the application of rational criteria of nature conservation programs, but also on pragmatic decisions of urban regeneration planning as intentional decisions to link urban and rural areas and to keep cultural, and environemental links that make regeneration processes more than urban space production. The safeguard of rural, agricultural and forest areas in the urban fringes, for its economic or environmental interest, are a way to integrate natural fragments in urban structure and to give it quality and references for peoples use through the urban regeneration planning and design process.
To create new comfortable urban spaces and to redesign landscapes in order to reach human needs of beauty and pleasure are not only challenges in the planning profession and attitude but also a moral and social responsibility. To design and built urban spaces are not today a simple professional work of definition of uses, infrastructures, utilities and collective equipments and map them with a zoning methodology. More than that, planning, as a regeneration process to *build in the built*, is a process of design new organised balanced and contemporary adapted landscapes.
Or, to have organised and balanced landscapes it is necessary to respect the people's memories and culture, the collective and affective

images that give identity to the spaces and create the conditions of stability of change a landscape without traumas and social or cultural reactions against. Urban landscapes are described as what we see plus what we feel. If we change them, we change what we see. To keep them balanced and culturally integrated with those who live in and feel them as a part of his own heritage and environment, we only can change what people see; not what people feel. For that urban landscaape appears as "*a symphony of complex harmonies (...) of which all the inhabitants of a city are composers and interpreters*" (Spirn, 1989).

Urban regeneration is associated to the need of adaptation of cities to contemporary needs and to higher standards of life quality. As a concept of urban planning that integrates respect to the past and innovation for the future, its main field of application is the built territory. Urban regeneration as an urban planning process acts on the built space where affections, memories, identities, cultures, are present and acting as part of the mind landscape: The own landscape of each one and relevant stones and marks of the large unfinished building that makes up the city.

Urban regeneration is a process of making new cities in continuity with its past, respecting site and personal and communities memories, but facing the future.

In this case sustainability is essential as the cement that aggregates all the parts that compose a balanced urban landscape made of stones, bricks, iron, glass, light and shadows, memories and references. Urban regeneration planning process is also a process of reinforce social cohesion through the increase of urban functionality, environmental quality, life quality, and self respect to all who live in the areas under regeneration.

Cultural identity of local communities increases the pleasure to live in city and represents a part of the urban and architectural heritage that structures urban fabrics and landscapes.

Memory is a compromise with the past and with the future.

Urban regeneration as a process of building in the built is a compromise that gives sense to the perpetuation of the cultural and affective values that make cities as meeting places between generations and places of reinforcement of communities self identity. In this sense memory is not as record but a compromise with the past and with the future.

References

Abelló, R.P.; Bernaldez, F. G. (1986) Landscape preferences and personality. Landscape and Urban Plannig, 13, 19-28

Alkoven P. (1993) The changing image of the city: a study of the transformation of the townscape using computer-aided architectural design and visualization techniques : a case study: Heusden - Proefschrift Universiteit Utrecht. Utrecht

Bell, S. (1999) Landscape pattern, perception and process. E & FN Spon, London

Corraliza, J.A. (1989) El espacio libre urbano como ambiente restaurador: modalidades de usos y tipos de usuarios, In: Actas del Seminario hispano-portugués sobre jardines y espacios abiertos, Sevilla, 2-4 noviembre. Comité MAB/Unesco espanõl, Madrid

Corraliza, J.A. (2001) Vida urbana y experiencia social: variedad, cohesión y medio ambiente. In: Ponencias del seminario organizado por el Instituto Juan de Herrera y la Gerencia Municipal de Urbanismo del Ayuntamiento de Madrid. Madrid, 16 a 27 de octubre de 2000. Boletín CF+S 15.

Enrique L.C. (1996) Paisaje y fotografia : naturaleza y território. In Actas del II Curso El Paisaje. Arte y Naturaleza. Huesca 1996.

Fourneau, F. (1989) Quelques reflexions preliminaires sur la notion de paysage: ses "production et perceptions", son aménagement. In: Seminário sobre el paisage (Madrid 1987). Junta de Andalucia. Sevilla

Galindo, M.P.G; Corraliza, J. A. (2000) Environmental aesthetics and psychological wellbeing: relationships between preference judgements for urban landscapes and other relevant affective responses. In: Psychology in Spain, vol 4, nº 1, 13-37

Jackson, J.B. (1996) The necessity of ruins, and other topics. University of Massachusetts Press.Amherst

Kaplan, R.; Kaplan, S. (1982) Cogniyion and environment functioning in an uncertain world. Praeger. New York.

Kaplan, R.; Kaplan, S.; Ryan, R.; Ryan, R.L. (1998) With people in mind: design and management for everyday nature. Island Press. Washington, DC.

Kevin L. (1973) What time is this place?. MIT Press, Cambridge, Ma

Llamazares, J.(1990) El rio del olvido, Seix Barral, Barcelona

Schauman, S. (1988) Scenic values of countryside landscapes to local residents: a Whatcom County, Washington, case study. Landscape Journal, 7, 40-46

Spirn, A.W. (1989) The poetics of city and nature: toward a new aesthetic for urban design. Places, 6 (1), 82-93

Spirn, A.W. (2000) The language of landscape. Yale University Press. New Haven

Tuan, Y. (1990) Topophilia: a study of environmental perception, attitudes and values. Columbia University Press. New York

Tuan, Y. (2001) Space and place: the perspective of experience. University of Minnesota Press

Wall, A. (1999) In: Corner, J. (ed) "Recovering Landscape: essays in contemporary landscape architecture". Princeton Architectural Press. New York

Urban Regeneration Policies in a Medium-sized City of Southern Italy: Salerno, a Town in Transformation and the Strength of Images

Ivonne de Notaris and Elisa Pozzoli

The study case which is going to be presented will describe the urban policies realised in the last ten years for the regeneration of a medium-sized city in Southern Italy: Salerno. The second biggest town of the Campania region after the chief town Napoli, which is 60 kilometres far, Salerno has a territorial extension of approximately 0.52 square kilometres and a population of 150,000 inhabitants. This particular context allows dealing with some matters strictly connected with the regeneration of the average towns in the Italian context, using as an observation point the South of our Country, i.e. a territorial area which has been historically burdened with serious problems of socio-economic underdevelopment.

The Italian context of the '90s

The complex social and economic changeovers which involved the town and the territory in the last decades produced deep transformations in the meaning and the function of whole areas, increasing the decline and the marginalisation of some of them and the quick development of some others. In particular, the dynamics of transformation in the economic and social fields inevitably affected the evolution of the urban space and the extensive development of the population has been followed by a new 'reticular' organisation of the territory itself, structured *'more on the principles of complementarity and inter-dependence than of the principles of hierarchical- functional dependence'* (Dematteis, 1986).
As an effect of the economic globalisation, single 'local systems' gained greater importance inside a complex net of relationships among different subjects and territorial systems: this caused the overcoming of hierarchical relationships in favour of co-operative and concerted interactions. This situation, however, also caused the birth of a strong competition among towns with the consequent exploitation of local resources (Dematteis 1998/99) in order to attract new investments and/or tourist flows. The transformations which have been involving the urban contexts since the '70s thus determined a new geography of centralities, on whose basis even a medium-small centre such as Salerno can gain importance and propose itself as a quality and excellence knot inside a particular net and meaning system (i.e. the net of tourist valorisation of the Campania coast area).

Since the '80s also in Italy they showed the evolution (or involution) trends, the opportunities and the problems of the urban and metropolitan systems, which had affected the other countries of Western Europe. It is however necessary to take into consideration some features of the Italian situation differentiating the urban areas of Central–Northern Italy form the ones of Southern Italy.
The analysis of the two main indicators of social welfare – income and employment – evidently issues that in the Central – Northern areas the phenomena of urban degradation and uneasiness can be circumscribed to well-defined areas and situations. They are often linked to processes of restructuring of the manufacturing sector, with a consequent abandon and/or refunctioning of the industrial areas. Thus the problems of the Central–Northern towns are partially similar to the ones of many other urban centres of Central–Northern Europe, with the advantage of assuming sometimes less critical forms. Moreover, a not irrelevant factor for the solution of such problems is represented by the financial, functional and administrative conditions of local governments which guarantee a certain operative skill of intervention and initiative to the Public Services.
The scene of towns and metropolitan areas in Southern Italy is quite different. The areas of social problem, risen from the big delay of local development, gather there. The data on the employment index, the personal income, the school evasion and the crime (and 'micro-crime'), together with the lacks of basic infrastructures and services for the population draw a picture that, for the seriousness of the phenomena and their extension, has few comparisons in Western Europe. In Southern Italy, besides, the dominant models of the public intervention, which has not been capable of giving an effective and sudden answer to the demands of the population, are in crisis. Against such already critical scenery, the difficult situation of the local governments, in terms of financial crisis and operational skills, makes even more difficult to intervene effectively on the territorial emergencies.
Trying to redress the problems shortly mentioned and in accordance with the European context, the Italian Government, during the '90s, introduced some new laws and financial means of notable relevance for the changes generated on the processes of territorial development. In particular, since 1990 a relevant administrative reform started which involves all the levels of territorial government with remarkable relapses on the Local Bodies (Municipalities and Provinces). The new norms (Law n.59/1997 and the following) want, as their main aim, to make real the principles of autonomy and responsibility of the public administrators, giving concreteness to the principle of subsidiarity introduced at the European level by the Treaty of Maastricht.

Strictly connected with the administrative reform it was the reform of the electoral system which started in 1993 with a law (Law n.81/1993) that introduced the direct election of the local governments' the political representatives, determining relevant changes in the political management at the local level.
The administrative reform and the electoral one, started at the beginning of the '90s in Italy, determined a clear separation between the political and the technical components of the local administrations, conferring the role of address and co-ordination to the first one and more decisional responsibilities and a greater autonomy to the second one. Therefore, on the one hand politicians have to answer directly the community they govern, about their own work, otherwise they have to suffer electoral defeat; on the other hand public administrations should work better, since their managers are more and more responsible for the reached levels of efficiency.
This frames a context of greater opportunities for the public administrations themselves, thanks to new projecting and financial tools, of both national and European source, that every single town can use for the development of its own territory. Again starting form the '90s, in fact, at a national level, new tools have been introduced to intervene in a more effective way on the transformation dynamics of the urban areas and on the delay of development of some parts of the Italian territory. This is the frame in which the experimentation of the so-called 'Complex Programs' is inserted: normative tools which aim at realising the integration among the subjects involved in the planning and management of the interventions, among various resources and among different use-destinations, in order to raise the quality of life through the endowment of services and the use of forms of socio-economic accompaniment. The most remarkable novelty introduced by these tools concerns the gradual overcoming of a sectorial vision of the planning intervention in order to affect the whole urban space re-considered in its physical, functional, economic and socio-cultural complexity. In Italy the '90s are also the years of the 'Negotiated planning' (*Contratti d'area*, *Patti territoriali*, etc), and of other specific initiatives aimed at the socio-economic development of the depressed areas of the national territory.
A decisive push for shaping new operational means for the local administrations were finally provided by the Italian reply to the opportunities introduced by the tools of the European Union's structural politics: the success locally obtained by Community Initiatives aimed at the resolution of remarkable problems at the European level is revealing (this is, for instance, the case of the Urban Programme's success).

The case study: Salerno, a town in transformation

Salerno is a town in fervent transformation, which has been laboratory of projecting and incubator of new energies in this last decade. The '90s in Salerno were, in fact, years of growth, of 'sense making' of an uncertain identity and affirmation of a new model of urban development that considers the town system as a primary resource for the territory development. But the '90s were also years of great expectations, of new needs emerging from a more and more demanding population requiring a high quality of the urban life.

If we look back, at the beginning of this last decade, we find a town with problems which are not very different from those of the other southern realities of our Country. Salerno is, in fact, a town grown frantically during the '50s, on the wave of a phantom economic boom that has been feeding, for about twenty years, a substantial migratory flow and, as a direct consequence, an uncontrolled expansion of the town towards the grounds which were still free to the East of the historical town. The town Administration did not prove capable of governing the occurring transformations and the town widened in the total absence of a project for the territory that could guarantee the safeguard of the environmental values and the realisation of quality interventions.

Salerno has therefore grown because of the addition of suburbs, monofunctional districts that for years have been suffering for the lack of integration with the rest of the city.

But which concrete opportunities does Salerno offer in order to activate development processes that can exploit the current (real and latent) resources and contribute to the growth of the local community?

It has been tried to give an answer to this question during the '90s, when the city began to affirm itself as a strategic pole of an urban system with great potentialities of growth, as knot of the relationships at local staircase system and, above all, as potential knot of a system of relationships at over local scale. Salerno lies, in fact, in the middle of one of the most appreciated tourist districts in Italy for its historical, cultural and environmental heritage. The economical dynamics of the last years give us in return the image of a city with high potentialities of development, a junction of commercial traffics with the areas of Cilento and Lucania. In detail, the presence of the harbour with a great volume of traffic in rapid growth and the foreseen realizations of an airport and an interport, witness the wish of making Salerno a point of reference for the intermodal transport, being supported by the whole southern territory and confirming the hypothesis of a city for *commerce and services.*

In this context, starting from 1993, an important inversion of tendency in the planning policies took place: the Electoral Reform for the local Governments meant, first of all, the affirmation in Salerno of a new and

strong self-promotion and contractual power of the proclaimed Mayor and his Administration, not only at the local level but, above all, at an over local one.
The main protagonist of this change is the new Government Team, chosen in 1993 by Mayor Vincenzo De Luca and confirmed in 1997. It proposed the development of the latent potentialities of the territory of Salerno through the definition of 'territorial strategies necessary for the conjugation, in the respect of the possibilities of the environmental load and a sustainable development, of those functions which are coherent with the idea of Salerno as city for tourism, for commerce and for all the services' (De Luca, 1999). The criteria which led to the identification of the parts of the territory where to operate with priority, followed the logic of giving direct realisation to the projectual proposals to be realized in short times, in order to make the process of urban renewal visible at first sight.
Some strategic lines of priority intervention have been defined to reach such an aim:

- the retraining of the whole coastline of the town territory, in order to promote the affirmation of a qualified tourist offer;
- the exploitation of the agricultural territory on the hills and the retraining of the area of the Irno river;
- the reorganization of the infrastructural system (road and railways), as an important transversal strategy for the urban rebalancing;
- and finally, the intervention on the 'existing' to be realized through a widespread bettering of the urban quality and, above all, through the recovery of the Historical Centre and the other urban suburbs.

These strategic lines represent as well the unbreakable priorities for the planning rearrangement of the town territory and they are the basis for the Programmatic Planning Document, as guidelines for the drawing of the new Master Plan. Since 1991 the MBM studio of Barcelona (architect Oriol Bohigas) was involved by the Municipality for some analysis: in 1993, after the elections of the new town Council, it was charged with the editing of the new Master Plan.
Starting from 1993, the Administration has been operating contemporarily at different levels. The drawing of new tools for the territorial Government (Master Plan, Plan of Commerce, General Plan of the Urban Traffic, Urban Parking Plan, etc), was accompanied by the realisation of a wide scheduling of public works and the activation of new actions both in the social and the cultural field. In this way the synergy and the comparison between two 'projects' for the city took its body, two operative methodologies guiding the planning and social politics respectively: 'working for a new Salerno' and 'working for a normal city'.

'*Working for a new Salerno*' has been the project, the suggestion that Mayor De Luca has brought ahead with continuity by consolidating with effective actions the image of a city in fervent transformation. This meant a concrete engagement to retrain the territory through an ambitious program of public works, with the aim to mark a sharp inversion in comparison with the politics of the past, giving breath to the entrepreneurial activity and creating the premises for the local development.
Paraphrasing the *motto* of the compiling Master Plan - *Salerno new conscience of identity, new demand of urbanity* – it is possible to say that the Administration tried to answer the necessity of rebuilding the identity of Salerno ('*giving Salerno a soul*') through a spread recovery of the urban livability. Speaking of identity is however often dangerous, so much more when the binomial identity/development can be reduced to a commercialisation of some urban areas to the detriment of others.
In the same years, the Administration also made the effort to construct a *normal city* with remarkable relapses on the social inner of the city itself. This proved a certainly less visible action than the many other realised public works, but it was at the same time very relevant, because of its contribution to the growth of the sense of belonging, of being citizens and part of a community.
Following these two operational methodologies, the greatest engagement of the town Administration, during the last ten years, has affected the urban suburbs in their whole: both the *suburbs of the Post-war period*, located along the coastline in the eastern zone of the city, and the *Historical Centre*, settled down between the hills and the sea, in a diametrically opposite position to the first one.
The suburbs of the urban expansion of the *Post-War period* presented all the problems of a growth originated by a building speculation, without putting attention on the real demands of the territory and the inhabitants that moved to live there: so many residential buildings and infrastructures exalting the sense of a territory to be crossed, compressed between the slowly attacked hills and the sea. An urban environment strongly degraded an evident social decay under the shapes of marginalization and isolation, the absence of crucial service structures.
The *Historical Centre*, was instead the territory of the abandonment, of the physical decay, memory of the medieval city progressively becoming the suburb of the new city, symbol of the underdevelopment, rather than place of historical identity.
Intervening for the recovery and the retraining of the urban suburbs meant, necessarily, to integrate the above mentioned two approaches: a careful work of urban retraining and remeaning of the places and, at the

same time, the creation of a better livability for the inhabitants by offering them new services. On the one hand, therefore, the building of a more beautiful, safer and more livable city, and on the other hand the attempt to overcome the logics of welfarism in order to offer effective services to the territory. The former strategy produced the creation of public parks, the recovery of the coast line, the repaving of the streets, interventions of renewal of public lightening and of public and private mobility. The latter caused the decentralization of the social services, the re-use of discarded school buildings for service activities addressing the districts, the creation of health structures nearer and nearer to the citizens and, in general, the consolidation of an operating methodology that, even if slowly, could support a strategy for the development of the social enterprises.

Starting from 1997, a strenuous examination activity at the international level was activated, in order to attract the attention of the operators upon the rebirth of Salerno, and to raise the level of the architectural interventions in the city. This is the case of the contest of ideas for the recovery of part of the Historical Centre and the contests of planning for the realisation of the Judicial Citadel -won by David Chipperfield-, the Maritime Station -won by Zaha Hadid- and the Sport Building.

These years of ferment and transformations corresponded to the planning and realisation of the 'Urban' Community Initiative Programme (1994-2001). For the Administration of Salerno Urban represented, first of all, the opportunity to experiment a strategy for the local development, beginning from the Historical Centre as a *laboratory* for the city in its whole. Urban offered, in fact, the unrepeatable chance to coordinate a series of interventions with the aim to exploit the cultural and landscape resources of the Historical Centre, so to give concrete form to the project of integration of the district to the rest of the city. The intervention in the Historical Centre offered the opportunity to give concrete form to the project of building/rediscovering the cultural-historical identity of the city, essential premise for the start of a real process of change.

It is therefore interesting to deepen the study of the carrying out of the Urban Programme, by estimating the (expected and unexpected) effects of its projects on the whole town territory and the transferability of the well experimented practices to future initiatives.

Starting from the historical centre to retrain the town: the success of the Urban Programme in Salerno

As already said, starting since 1993, the Administration of Salerno has been promoter of a wide program of single interventions that, through the different scales of the architectural projects, qualified the town in its whole and helped the rise of the local economy.

The intervention on the historical centre joined together several resources: a heritage of ideas and projects accumulated during the years, which converged in the Urban Programme, in the proposals of the Master Plan, in the suggestions of the international architecture contest 'Edifici Mondo', in the interventions to improve accessibility to the district and, in general, in the projects of big and small works to recover the historical buildings and open areas.
At the same time they were programmed and implemented specific actions for the rise of the economic activities, for the starting up of new socio-sanitary structures and specific services for the inhabitants of the district managed by voluntary associations (play-room, recreational circle for elderly, etc).
Besides, during the last ten years several initiatives and cultural demonstrations (musical itineraries in the churches, theatrical and cinema reviews, etc) were realised and proved fundamental for the rediscovery of local identity, the promotion of the image of the town and the rise of the 'leisure time economy'. The results of this work determined a real 'rebirth' of the historical centre, allowing the inversion in the trend to the abandonment of the district that was progressively repopulated by inhabitants and by new economic activities.
So, the historical centre of Salerno regained its urban centrality and, through the rediscovery and the exploitation of the historical roots of the town, it offered the possibility to re-launch an image of the territory capable to support better and better the realisation of the ambitious project of making Salerno the crossroad of a tourist system of international relevance.
But how did the Urban Programme allow all this?
The main objective of the Urban Programme in Salerno was the improvement of the general quality of life in the historical centre through the planning of integrated interventions aimed at the planning and productive recovery of the area. In order to gain this target, acting contemporarily on the physical and on the socio-economic structure of the district, the Programme aimed at the improvement of the accessibility to the historical centre and at the starting up of modern functions for the social and cultural development, to be placed inside public buildings to be retrained.
The Programme started operationally in 1996 and in the time of five years it helped the gaining of important results on the physical and socio-economic status of the district. As already said, the area of intervention was the Historical Centre, with a surface of 4,000 square meters and a number of inhabitants (6,472 up to 1991): corresponding to 5% of the whole population of Salerno. The total cost of the Programme was around 18 million Euros.

In detail, with regard to the physical retraining of the historical centre, they were realised the recovery of important buildings for remarkable social functions (centre for children, centre for the entrepreneurs, centre of aggregation of district, receptive structures, exhibitions, etc), the retraining of open spaces (roads and squares), the environmental recovery of the historical gardens (the public gardens and the botanical garden) and interventions of public lighting which actually improved the safety of the area.
For the socio-economic rebirth of the district, actions of promotion of the local companies and the typical handicraft products were activated. This was supported by accompaniment measures aimed at the professional training of young managers and of the potential managers of functions started through the retraining of public buildings: in particular, social operators for the 'centre for young people' and for the 'centre of aggregation and specialised workers' for caring the botanical garden.
Today it is possible to say that, because of the realised interventions, the awareness of the important role of the historic centre for the general development of the whole town and its tourist vocation has grown. The evident and deep improvement of the physical quality of the territory determined, in fact, the rebirth of the district and helped the creation of new managerial activities. The historical centre of Salerno has come back to be an area of privilege and has been progressively repopulated by a middle-upper class.
As already said, the contribution of the Urban Programme proved important in order to get these results, because it offered the possibility to implement on the whole historical territory a policy of widespread urban recovery, supporting the bigger program of interventions planned by the town Administration. In this sense, the positive consequences of the Programme cannot be simply interpreted as intentional and direct results of the undertaken actions, considering that the unexpected effects are much more remarkable. With regard to this, a meaningful example is the start up of new economic activities: it is not possible, in fact, to measure the impact of Urban in creating new jobs considering exclusively the number of new companies directly started up through the Programme, since the general improvement of the district, in terms of physical retraining and recovery of the life quality, has made this area of the town more attractive than others, with the consequent birth of new economic activities linked to the leisure time.
What said above gives us a synthetic picture of the actions addressed at the district. The Urban Programme, however, allowed to prime important changes in the ordinary work of the Public Administration as well. For the drawing, the realisation and the management of the community initiative, the Administration of Salerno decided to use since the

beginning projecting and managerial resources almost exclusively internal to the Public Body. In this way, it succeeded in organising an innovative structure inside the Administration Body itself, capable of setting efficient instruments to support the flexibility and feasibility of the Programme. This determined an innovation inside the Administrative Body through the acquisition of new competences, procedural and managerial skills, in accordance with the more general process of improvement of the local Administration's efficiency. In conclusion, it is possible to say that the organisational model experimented in Salerno represents one of the success factors of the Urban Programme.
At the core of this success there is a simple principle which guided, more generally speaking, the whole process of re-organisation of the 'town system', started by the Administration since 1993. This principle was to empower the existing 'human capital', too often mortified by bureaucracy, and to identify the subjects capable of acting with managerial spirit, with the main aim of growing professionally. This was pursued by stimulating experiences, supporting the active spirit of the individuals and the better co-operation for the success of specific initiatives. From this point of view the experience built in the last ten years represents a 'success story', not only for the efficiency of the applied organisational model, but also for the individual growth of the professionalism and, in general, of a new way to conceive the projecting activity within the Public Body. Urban had, in fact, the merit of spreading inside the Administration a new projecting culture aiming at integrating different actions, helping synergies among projects, resources and mobilised and mobilisable subjects.
Beyond the real success reached in this sense by the Initiative, it is true without any doubt that the logic of isolated interventions on the territory has been put into crisis by the necessity of programming and evaluating *ex ante* the interventions to be realised as part of a more complex global strategy.
Moreover, the realisation of the Programme offered the Town Administration the possibility to activate innovative actions gathering a rich projects heritage for the planning of future actions. From this point of view the exchange of experiences among Urban towns inside and outside the Committees of Overseeing proved particularly fertile: solid informal nets have been built among those who worked at the Programme and, between the co-operation and the competition among towns, a common appointment was progressively affirmed for the resolution of problems emerged during the work.
The part-taking in the Urban Programme finally consolidated the relationships of the Administration of Salerno with the European Union, also owing to its new negotiating ability shown in the relationships with

other institutional local and over-local subjects. Hence the activation of the first European Info Point in Italy, the constitution of the Study Planning Resources and European Community Policies Service and the new ferment in the activity of the Corporate Body, which seems to find a greater support to the local development projects at the EU level, rather than at the regional or national ones.
In conclusion, it is possible to observe that, within the frame of a wider strategy, Urban helped the Administration of Salerno in the recovery work of the life quality of the central district, activating a multiplying effect to support the public and private interventions and concretely contributing to the rediscovery of the historical-cultural identity of the town. The realisation of the Programme contributed, besides, in modifying the intervention on the existing town, introducing a new way of planning actions on the territory and a new necessity to integrate different instruments and resources.
This reading key becomes much more interesting if correlated to the transformations/innovations that during the '90s characterized the Italian context of norms, by modifying the relationships between 'public' and 'private' actors and by proposing new tools of intervention on the urban areas.
From this point of view, it is impossible not to recognize the merit of the fruitful experimentation offered by the Urban Programme, neither it can be underestimated that such experimentation, particularly in Southern Italy, focused predominantly on the Historical Centres: this allowed many Italian cities of different size to compare themselves thanks to a different and integrated approach to the resolution of the problems of their own territory.

Conclusions

From what said above it is possible to say that during the '90s some of the main European and Italian innovations seemed to find in Salerno a fertile ground for their experimentation. This can be pointed out in particular in the new methodology of intervention on the territory that affirmed itself by having a preference on the practicability and the visibility of concrete actions of retraining and recovering. The guiding principle seems to be '*from the plan to the project*', on the basis of a generic definition of strategies for the development of the city, gauged on the ambitious target of making Salerno a '*city for tourism and services*'.
In this direction the Administration leads the drawing up of the new Master Plan, entrusting the professional mansion to architect Oriol Bohigas, one of the fathers of the rebuilding of Barcelona. So, the beginning of the experience of Salerno sinks its theoretic and practical

roots into another big urban adventure (the Barcelona of the '80s) and it is based more and more firmly on the opportunities offered by the new Electoral Law (Law n.81/93), that actually determined innovative changes in the behaviour of the Administration.

During the '90s the town Administration showed bigger abilities in treasuring what previously programmed (but not realised) and, in the meantime, succeeded in gathering new funding opportunities introduced at different territorial and institutional levels. Its engagement focused, first of all, on a never ending work of urban retraining, by intervening on the whole city, so to recover years of stillness and to solicit among the inhabitants the rebirth of the sense of belonging to a community ('*rebuilding Salerno to rebuild Salernitans*'). The perception of the occurring change was immediate and the target of making Salerno '*a city for tourism and services*' draws more and more its concreteness from the image of a retrained 'beautiful city', or better, from the image of a favourable context for the development of tourism, commerce and services.

In this sense, from the analysis of the study case it is possible to draw up some considerations around the role that the image of 'beautiful city' has played in the policies of urban regeneration, realised in Salerno in the '90s.

First of all, it is necessary to say that this image is offered as the 'manifesto' for the development of the city, a guiding strategy that sums up in itself the many dimensions of the development: it does not aim only at the physical regeneration of the urban territory, but also at the cultural and identity promotion, for the economic and social raising of Salerno into a net of relationships at the over local level. The target of the Mayor and his Administration is the general raising of the city, starting from the retraining of the Historical Centre considered as a *laboratory* of experimentation: here the most meaningful initiatives have been carried out, thanks to the implementation of the Urban Programme.

It is noteworthy to underline that this rebirth of the territory was achieved starting from small interventions that effectively dynamized the territory, thus contributing to the building of the image of an active context for local development. The experience of Salerno is a further demonstration of the fact that big changes are not necessarily caused by the realisation of big works, but through the ability of identifying and connecting the different resources of the territory, conferring new meanings to the resources themselves and to their mutual interaction.

The element of connection and re-meaning of the local potentialities was, in this case, an image: the '*tourist, commercial and services-like Salerno*' constantly and strongly proposed by the 'official' rhetorics of the

local Administration and supported by the economic operators that drew up big progressive advantages from this rhetoric.
However, a process of economic development affecting the physical retraining of the city can sometimes risk to underestimate the social implications and consequences of the intervention, producing conflicts within the local community. This occurred also in the case of Salerno and it can be clearly seen looking back at the process from a point of view different from the 'official' one: to the rebirth of the historical centre it corresponded also the uneasiness of part of the inhabitants, seeing their own district invaded by 'a population of consumers'. This determined the birth of strong remonstrances and demands for a safer district, which were answered simply by strengthening the presence of policemen in the streets. On the contrary, it would have been more interesting and useful to activate a real confrontation among the different demands -of the inhabitants, of the local contractors and of the consumers- in order to arrive at the definition of a shared strategy for the tourist and cultural development of the Historical City.
In extreme conclusion it is necessary to say that processes of urban transformation like the ones activated in Salerno need to be looked back and evaluated in a wide temporal frame.
Currently, ten years after the elections of the new Administration in 1993, the analysis of the study case seems to give to the observers the elements to affirm that Salerno has at its disposal the necessary conditions to orient and to govern the still in progress and frenzied process of transformation of the 'city container', avoiding the possible drift of its 'contents': inhabitants and meanings.

References:

Avallone, G. Basile, R.F. Ventura, E. (1999) 'Le botteghe artigiane del centro storico di Salerno, una ricerca sugli artigiani e sull'artigianato artistico-tradizionale in una città media del Mezzogiorno d'Italia', Salerno.

Ceccarelli, P. (1997) 'Salerno: progetti per un Prg'. In: Fabietti, W. La sfida delle città europee, I° rassegna di planning europea, Roma, p.192.

Censis (1997) Le condizioni per un rilancio delle politiche di recupero e di riqualificazione urbana. In: Atti del XII Convegno-Congresso Nazionale A.N.C.S.A. 'Patrimonio 2000 - Un progetto per il territorio storico nei prossimi decenni', Modena.

-, (1998) Salerno città europea: analisi e previsioni per il nuovo piano della città, Roma.

Centola, L. (2001) Salerno guida alla città del futuro, Casino sociale di Salerno, Salerno.

CER Programació S.L. (1997) Piano Strategico per lo Sviluppo Turistico della città di Salerno, Barcellona.

Commissione delle Comunità europee (1994) Comunicazione agli Stati membri per un'iniziativa comunitaria concernente le zone urbane (Urban), GUCE C 180/6.
-, (1996) Decisione della Commissione relativa alla concessione di un contributo del FESR e del FSE per un programma operativo relativo all'iniziativa comunitaria URBAN Italia, GUCE C 290/96.
Commissione Europea (1994) Europa 2000+: cooperazione per l'assetto del territorio europeo, Bruxelles.
-, Guida alle iniziative comunitarie 1994-1999, Bruxelles.
-, DG XVI. (1995) Azioni innovatrici nel quadro dei fondi a finalità strutturale 1995/1999, Bruxelles.
-, Ministero LL.PP. (1999) Il programma Urban in Italia. Un grande laboratorio per la rigenerazione dei quartieri urbani degradati, Roma.
Cremaschi, M. (2000) 'Il Pic Urban – sei casi di studio'. In: EuroPass – dossier, 22.
Comune di Salerno (1994) Documento Urbanistico Programmatico, delibera GM 20/04/1994.
-, (1994) Programma di Sviluppo Integrato per il recupero funzionale e produttivo dell'area del Centro antico cittadino, delibera GM 26/09/94.
-, (1994) Salerno nuova coscienza di identità, nuova esigenza di urbanità - Preliminare del Piano Regolatore Generale, Studio MBM – Barcellona, Salerno.
-, (1996) Un anno per Salerno – rendiconto delle attività dell'Amministrazione Comunale, Salerno.
-, (1997) Edifici mondo: Concorso per il recupero del Centro Antico di Salerno, Salerno.
-, (1998) Quattro anni per Salerno – 1994/1997 rendiconto delle attività dell'Amministrazione Comunale, Salerno.
-, (2001) Linee strategiche di sviluppo urbano della città di Salerno, Salerno.
-, (2001) Progetto Integrato Territoriale – Salerno città dell'eccellenza, sviluppo sostenibile e nuova qualità della vita, Salerno.
De Luca, V. (1999) Un'altra Italia – tra vecchie burocrazie e nuove città, Bari.
Dematteis, G. (1986) 'L'ambiente come contingenza e il mondo come rete'. In: Planning 82, p.112.
-, (1998/99) 'Non basta una forte identità la città vive solo se è un 'nodo''. In: Telèma, 15, Roma, pp.67-68.
Donarono, E. (1997) 'A Salerno parte il concorso per rifare il centro storico'. In: Edilizia e Territorio – Il Sole 24 ore, 37, p.28.
Formez (1994) Europa e Mezzogiorno – dossier di documentazione comunitaria, Roma.
-, (1994) I fondi strutturali comunitari 1994-1999, Roma.
Laino, G. (1997) 'Note sul programma Urban in Italia'. In: Urbanistica Informazioni n.155, p.31.
-, (1998) 'Specificità e problemi dell'attuazione di Urban in Italia'. In: Urbanistica Informazioni, 157, p.6.
-, (1998) 'L'esperienza dei programmi Urban. Una partita un po' particolare'. In: Come fare cose (buone) con parole - vademecum per il piano regolatore di Napoli, Laboratorio Bagnoli DUN, Napoli.
-, (1999) 'Il Programma Urban in Italia'. In: Archivio di Studi Urbani e Regionali, 66.
Lucinese, A. (1996) 'Avanti con Urban'. In: Costruire, 174, p.18.

Martino, F. (2001) 'Un sistema di progetti urbani per riqualificare Salerno'. In: Urbanistica Informazioni, 178, p.7.
Martinetti, G. (1993) 'Metropoli. La nuova morfologia sociale della citta ', Bologna.
Ministero LL.PP. (1997) PIC Urban Italia. Primo rapporto annuale di esecuzione, Roma.
-, (1998) PIC Urban Italia. Rapporto annuale di esecuzione, Roma.
-, (2001) 'Urban', 1, 2001.
Persico, P. (1997) Identità e sviluppo – cronaca e metodologia di un cambiamento, Salerno.
-, (1998) 'Tutti contenti di Urban tranne Urban'. In: Il danaro, 4.
Progressisti per Salerno (1993) La concretezza del cambiamento - Programma elettorale per le elezioni comunali, Salerno.
-, (1997) Solo per Salerno - Programma elettorale per le elezioni comunali, Salerno.
Sichelgaita (1998) Salerno città europea, Salerno.
Sundry Authors (1998) 'Salerno in a European dimension'. In: Speak Europe, 4.
-, (1998) 'Salerno - I nuovi interventi urbani - progetti e strategie per la città'. In: d'Architettura,19.
-, (1998) 'Progetti per il centro antico di Salerno: Chipperfield, de las Casas, Monestiroli, Sejima, Venezia'. In: Casabella, 667, pp.22/51.
-, (1999) 'Salerno: un'altra Italia'. In: Giornale dell'Architettura, 22.
Wwf - Italia Nostra (1997) Dossier Salerno. Riflessioni sul futuro planning della città, Salerno.

Big Projects, Festivalisation and Visions as Strategies of Urban Planning in Global Times

Case Study Metropolis Hamburg

Jörg Knieling

This paper intends to illustrate present processes and strategies of urban planning and discusses these in the context of the general setup of globalisation. The metropolis of Hamburg will serve as the empirical case study. With about 1.7 mill. inhabitants in the Free and Hanseatic City of Hamburg and a total of about 4 mill. in the metropolitan region of Hamburg, this metropolis is one of the main agglomerations in Germany and as a location it competes with comparable metropolises on the global level.

Globalisation is the process of growing international flows and linkings of finances, economics and communication. The globalisation process is leading to a change of standards in competition for location between metropolises and between metropolitan regions. Demands like the internationalization of education and research, the capacity to integrate foreigners and the modernisation of the economic sector and the public administration are gaining in importance.

These changes in the general setup also have an impact on urban planning. Issues which must be considered are how to deal with the new location demands and what the effects on urban development are and will be with respect to economical, social and environmental aspects (see Häußermann/Roost 2000). In the first part of this paper, three strategies of present urban planning are described and illustrated by means of a case study of the metropolis of Hamburg. All of them have in common that they are characterized by "focusing" - in terms of space, time or theme:

- Urban planning by Big Projects: The HafenCity Hamburg is currently the dominant project of urban development in Hamburg. The Masterplan calls for implementation to take about 25 years. The HafenCity is an example of spatial focusing of urban planning.
- Urban planning by Festivalisation: Hamburg's candidature for the Olympic Summer Games 2012 is an example of both a temporal and a thematic focus of urban planning. Topics that are connected with this extraordinary sports event receive intense political attention, a short period of time in 2012 moves into the centre of public interest. Besides this the candidature is organized as a public-private partnership which comprises the Senate, local businesses, and sports associations.
- Urban planning by Visions: The *Leitbild* "Metropolis Hamburg – Growing City" bundles all efforts of urban planning and strives for a new

push of activity and innovation. The "Growing City" includes and promotes a certain array of topics, but at the same time it excludes other themes, interests and population groups. As a result of focusing, visions obviously are highly selective.
In the second part, these strategies are discussed in the context of urban planning in global times. As a result there are questions and recommendations which effects focusing have on urban planning and which requirements there are from a point of view of good urban governance.
The selection of the three examples for urban planning in Hamburg presents only a part of the activities in the city and the region, and they were not necessarily chosen because they are the most important. Indeed, besides HafenCity, the 2012-candidature and "Metropolis Hamburg – Growing City", there are further important projects, e.g. the development of the industrial site for the Super-Airbus A 380 or the candidature for the International Horticultural Exposition 2013. My choice of projects was rather motivated by the phenomenon of focusing and the intent to consider this in the context of planning theory.

Urban planning by Big Projects: HafenCity Hamburg

Initial situation

The HafenCity is the biggest project of current urban development in the Free and Hanseatic City of Hamburg. In 1989 the Senate and the Parliament decided to develop one section of the northern harbour as a housing and business site located next to the city centre: Their intent was to create 5,500 homes housing 10-12,000 inhabitants as well as 20,000 jobs. A development agency was founded. Property and infrastructure provisions are being financed by potential investors. The Masterplan calculates that the project will be realised step by step within 25 years. During this time period the project will be able to be adapted to changing fashions and demands (see GHS 2000).
The development of a district in such a central position presents a huge opportunity for urban planning and urban development. For Hamburg the HafenCity offers a unique possibility to confront the trend that the city is spilling out into the surrounding countryside -- and losing population because of it -- by providing an attractive offer in a central location. The HafenCity will increase the area of the inner city of Hamburg by about 40% and is meant to provide metropolitan services, culture and housing (GHS 2001).
Today, about 80% of the area of the HafenCity is owned by the Free and Hanseatic City of Hamburg. This real estate was established as a

special property package called "Harbour and City" and transferred to the publicly owned GHS Hamburg Port Area Development Cooperation. Further owners in the HafenCity are the Deutsche Bahn AG and private investors.

The territory

The HafenCity is situated in the northern part of the harbour next to the historical *Speicherstadt*, which is close to the city center. The close proximity to the inner city is shown by the short distances to the town hall (800 m) and the central railway station (1,100 m).

The territory of the HafenCity contains 155 ha. Leaving aside the water areas, traffic infrastructure and open space, the HafenCity has about 60 ha of net development area. Scale and density of the new area are comparable to that in the city centre and the *Speicherstadt*.The former harbour area was not included in the zoning plan, but was regulated by a special harbour law. Meanwhile, some areas have been released from this status. Because of this special situation this part of the city had long been almost inaccessible to the public, so the degree of identification with it is low. The new status is meant to change this.

The traditional economic basis, namely the trade of piece goods, has been decreasing dramatically since the beginning of the 1990's. Instead of small-scale warehouses, large ones are in favor today. In the *Speicherstadt* there are still about 5,500 employees in 600 businesses. To modernise this historical site, about 120 enterprises with 2,500 employees will have to move and be offered new sites in the harbour.

Urban development

After the decision was made by the Senate and the Parliament in 1989 for the renewal of this harbour area, initial planning propositions were presented. Two years later the Senate commissioned the publicly owned Hamburg Harbour and Warehouse Company (HHLA) to develop the area. The GHS was founded. The GHS' main task is to manage the development and the marketing of the HafenCity.

In 1999 the German-Dutch team „Hamburgplan"with Kees Christiaanse / ASTOC won an international urban development contest. Their concept was based on three aims:

- The new site is supposed to become part of an ensemble together with the old Speicherstadt and the historic city of Hamburg,
- There has to be a big variety of contemporary and modern types of urban design,
- The site is divided into eight parts, each of them with a wide range of uses, and each part will be completed one after the other rather than simultaneously.

On the basis of the contest the Senate agreed on a Masterplan which forms the framework for the urban development of the HafenCity. The Masterplan divides the area of the HafenCity into different parts, each of which has a unique colour scheme and its own specific characteristics, intended use and urban typology. The development will be realised in stages of five years each. In summer 2002 the implementation started with the first complexes of business buildings and housing.

Principles and goals of urban development

The principles and goals of urban planning are based on the main idea that each area is arranged very flexibly with regard to the design and use of the buildings. Because of the long time that is needed to implement the whole project, it is necessary to maintain a dynamic adaption policy in order to accommodate changes in customers' interests or external conditions. But nevertheless, the planning process needs detailed definitions that guarantee that the new district gets a specific profile.

From this perspective, the following principles are of main importance for the development of the HafenCity:

- The structure is to be small-scale with an urban character (compact structure / urban mixture),
- Typical structures of the harbour are to be characteristic for the HafenCity,
- Particular attention is to be given to the design of the open spaces, especially of quay reinforcements,
- The close connection of the HafenCity with the inner city has a high priority, but the link to the neighbouring districts is also very important because they are to be supported by the new development,
- The HafenCity is seen as a project of sustainable urban development aiming at a "city of short distances",
- By developing the HafenCity from west to east, the intent is to create a small-scale urban structure that will guarantee a lively district.

For Hamburg the HafenCity contains the extraordinary chance to strengthen the city by building attractive housing on this nearby site, to make urban living more attractive, to reduce sprawl and to create space for new activities in services and retail trade. In addition, the HafenCity offers the opportunity to vary Hamburg's profile as a destination in international city tourism.

Besides the development of the HafenCity itself, this project will include refinancing for harbour growth in a new area, where modern harbour infrastructure has been built to compensate for the loss of places where harbour activities can be carried out.

Urban planning by Festivalisation: Hamburg's candidature for the Olympic Summer Games in 2012

Organisational setup for the candidature

The Senate of the Free und Hanseatic City of Hamburg decided in July 2001 to carry out a feasability study on a candidature for the Olympic Summer Games 2012. The study was presented in Parliament in October 2001, with the conclusion that it would be possible to host Olympic Games in Hamburg (see FHH 2001).

In November 2001 the National Olympic Committee (NOC) decided that Germany could compete to hold the Olympic Summer Games in 2012, and it asked all interested cities to send their concepts for candidature. Besides Hamburg, the city-regions of Düsseldorf / Rhein-Ruhr, Frankfurt / Rhein-Main, Leipzig und Stuttgart are also competitors.

After Hamburg founded the „Hamburg for Games 2012 GmbH" in a public/private partnership of Senate, business and sports associations, the city presented its concept for the Olympic Summer Games in 2012 in May 2002. The NOC will nominate the German candidate in April 2003. The final decision of the International Olympic Committee (IOC) as to where the games will take place in 2012 will be made in summer 2005.

Goals of Hamburg's candidature

Besides the positive effects for the sports infrastructure, the Olympic Games promise that projects of urban-regional development like traffic infrastructure that have been planned anyway, could be completed earlier. Beyond that, the popularity of Hamburg could be increased nationally and internationally. From the point of view of sports, the Olympic Games would improve Hamburg's image as a top sports location (FHH 2002a).

Keeping these arguments in mind, Hamburg's candidature is seen as an important means of implementing the Senate's vision to transform Hamburg into a "growing and vibrant metropolis with international popularity“ (see chapter 4).

The concept of the candidature

Locations and organisation

The concept for locations and organization aims at concentrating most of the sports locations inside Hamburg and at holding nearly all the final rounds of the various events within a radius of 10 km around the Olympic centre. Primarily, already existing and established sites with an international reputation have been chosen as locations. The main infrastructure, the Olympic stadium, the Olympic village, the swim stadium, the Olympic dome and the media centre would be built in or next to the HafenCity, forming the Olympic centre.

By choosing this central site, Hamburg would have the extraordinary chance to hold the Olympic Games in the centre of the city. The concept would allow easy access to most of the Olympic locations – "Olympic Games of short distances". The close proximity to the inner city also would offer the opportunity for an intensive cultural and personal exchange in the Olympic centre.

The use of existing locations would have the advantage that an economic reuse of these sites would be guaranteed after the Games. Only some of the new buildings would have to be pulled down after the Olympic Games because of a lack of demand. That would be particularly the case for the Olympic stadium.

The concept proposes different options for the reuse of the locations that will have to be more detailed (see figure 1; FHH 2002b). For the Olympic park there is the option to be transformed into an "Urban Resort", a development project that would combine overnight accommodation, leisure supplies, sports and education in an urban atmosphere. Good chances are seen for an integration of maritime tourism with sports and education. Beyond this the Olympia park would offer interesting connections to the cultural world of the inner city, to the natural world of the International Horticultural Exposition 2013 (which Hamburg is also competing for and that would be situated south of the harbour), and to a site presenting the history of emigration.

Option	„Maritime“	„Sports and Education“
Target group(s)	- mainly tourists - local demand as important target group	- tourists and locals - top athletes (Olympic centre) - students
Content	- fun and entertainment	- performance and entertainment
Necessary facilities	- overnight accommodations to increase the number of visitors and profit - wide range of leisure activities (in addition to the HafenCity) - musicals, conferences, casino	- indoor und outdoor sports facilities - educational institutions, housing facilities - optional: science centre (sports, life, health)

Figure: Reuse concept of the Olympic park (see FHH 2002b, p.12)

Mobility concept

In addition to locations and organization, the candidature proposal includes a mobility concept which comprises the following principles:

- Priority to be given to public transport,
- Accessibility on foot to the sports and event locations that are situated in the city to receive special attention,
- Waterways to be used for transport,
- The short distances of the "City Olympics" to reduce transport demand.

The mobility concept is meant to fulfill the high environmental standards the IOC has set. The capacity of Hamburg's transport system would be optimized by holding the Olympic games during the summer holidays, so that the traffic load would be freed of pupils and students. In addition, businesses would be requested to schedule their holidays during this time period to further ease traffic levels.

Accommodation concept

Accommodation has top priority in Hamburg's candidature because the IOC demands for high standards in terms of quantity and quality. Because Hamburg would integrate the harbour into the Olympic area, it would be possible to reach the required number of 42,000 rooms by using luxury ships for accommodation. This would calm hotel owners' fears that building hotels for the Olympic Games could lead to overcapacities after the Games, thus resulting ineconomic damage to the hotel sector.

Communication concept
As part of developing the concept for Hamburg's candidature, a contest for the best communication concept was launched. Agencies with international reputations cooperated in teams. The winner was a collaborative effort between Springer & Jacobi, Jung v. Matt, fischerApelt, Brand stage und upsolut Event. The main components of the communication campaign are a coloured logo showing the Olympic flame connected to a blue wave, and the slogan "fire and flame for Hamburg 2012". Business and media enterprises have formed a "Premium Club" and support the candidature by sponsoring events and the communication campaign.

Urban planning by Visions: *Leitbild* "Metropolis Hamburg – Growing City"

Initial situation
In the 1990's the general setup for the development of the metropolis Hamburg changed. The expansion of the European Union moved Hamburg into the centre of an important European economic region, and at the same time globalisation, new economic markets and modern information and communication technologies increased the speed of structural change dramatically.
From the point of view of the Free and Hanseatic City of Hamburg, the growing international competition for location is seen both as an opportunity and as a challenge. On the one hand, in recent years Hamburg has been able to hold its top position in comparison with the other German states. On the other hand, Hamburg has lost ground in competition with national and international metropolises. Economic growth and the development of the population are indicators for this.

Leitbild „Metropolis Hamburg – Growing City"
With the *Leitbild* „Metropolis Hamburg – Growing City" the Senate is trying to stimulate the city's economic development so that Hamburg transforms itself into a "growing and vibrant metropolis with international popularity". Metropolises such as Copenhagen, Barcelona, Vienna, Seattle or Toronto are the benchmarks Hamburg is comparing itself with; these metropolises have enhanced their reputation as locations for

housing, working and living as well as their international popularity by means of calculated strategies (see FHH 2002a; Heeg/Klagge/Oßenbrügge 2002).

The *Leitbild* "Metropolis Hamburg – Growing City" concentrates on "smart growth" as an intelligent form of growth. The conceptual background is sustainable development that meets the expectations of the present population, but does not endanger the options of future generations. One advantage is Hamburg's low population density, which means that some reserves for development still remain and could be mobilized without threatening Hamburg's character as a "green metropolis".

The Senate intends to use the "*Leitbild*" as an orientation for its politics consistently. The main goals are:

- An increase in the number of inhabitants
- More available sites for housing and business
- Economic and employment growth
- Support of families
- A better traffic infrastructure
- An increase in Hamburg's international attractiveness and popularity

Implementation of the *Leitbild*: Fields of activity and the development process

Key projects for the implementation of the *Leitbild* are the HafenCity, a new urban connection between the city centre and the southern part of Hamburg across the harbour, and Hamburg's candidatures for the Olympic Summer Games in 2012 and the International Horticultural Exposition in 2013. There will be a broad communication process which will promulgate a positive public opinion throughout the city and will integrate the population and interest groups of the urban society into the process. For the realization of these goals the Leitbild includes several strategies and compilations of measures:

Increase in the number of inhabitants

One step will be to reduce suburbanisation by offering attractive and cheap housing sites mainly to young families. Further steps include increasing migration of qualified employees to Hamburg from the rest of Germany and from foreign countries and improving the living conditions of families.

More available sites for housing and businesses

The availability of sites for housing and business development is one of the conditions for implementing the *Leitbild* „Metropolis Hamburg –

Growing City ". Those sites are to be reserved and newly developed for industry, business and different forms of housing. Modern site management will ensure that existing and interested businesses are supplied with new sites in the case of growth, change of location or new development.

Economic and employment growth
To achieve growth in employment and economics, Hamburg will concentrate on six "clusters of competence": the life sciences, nano- und optical technologies, information technologies und new media, the aviation industry, harbour and logistics, and china. In addition, the Senate suggests implementing new measures in fields of activity such as Eastern Europe, SME politics, education and science, employment policies and tax policies.

Support of families
Measures in areas such as day nurseries, schools, housing and the combination of family and career are intended to improve living perspectives for families.

Better traffic infrastructure
Measures for mobility management integrate telematics and selected infrastructure.

Increase of Hamburg's international attractiveness and popularity
To increase Hamburg's international attractiveness and popularity, representive events in the fields of politics, sports, culture and the sciences are of importance. The fields of activity will be selected according to an internationalization strategy.
There already is a range of attractive events such as the Hansaplast-Marathon, the HEW Cyclassics, the Soccer World Championship in 2006 with games in Hamburg, and the candidatures for the Olympic Summer Games in 2012 and the International Horticultural Exposition in 2013. The Hamburg marketing strategy is to demonstrate that the city has a high potential for culture, sports and the sciences that is attractive for tourists and also for foreigners who might be interested in working and living in Hamburg.

Organisation and the process of the implementation
Besides these strategies and measures that aim at realising individual goals of the *Leitbild*, there are further aspects that deal with the organisation and the process of the implementation:

-Metropolitan region of Hamburg and metropolitan cooperation

As a „Growing City“ Hamburg needs to strengthen its connections to neighbouring communities and - on another level - its cooperation with the northern German states. This will entail examining the already existing metropolitan region of Hamburg and optimising íts organisational structure.

Since the cooperation between Hamburg and Berlin has been so successful for some time now, this sort of metropolis cooperation will be expanded to include Copenhagen and Malmö.

-Public participation

The *Leitbild* process aims to integrate urban-regional society at different levels of communication. In a first step, an internet-based dialogue that took place in autumn 2002 concentrated on the inhabitants. In the future, representatives of economics, social life, politics, and other interested persons will have the opportunity to participate in a differentiated dialogue.

-Fund for innovative actions for the „Metropolis Hamburg – Growing City“

A special fund has been set up by the Senate as an incentive for implementing the *Leitbild* „Metropolis Hamburg – Growing City“ by means of innovative actions. From 2003 to 2005 the fund will contain 5 mill. EUR each year.

Conclusion: Urban planning in global times – opportunities and restrictions

Globalisation aggravates the competition for location on the international level. Metropolises like Hamburg come under pressure to change routines and thought patterns and to look for adapted strategies of urban development. Enterprises loosen their connections to their traditional locations. Because transport costs are low and international communication is becoming increasingly easier and the quality of products is becoming comparable at the global level, companies situate their headquarters, research or production locations wherever markets are close and where skilled or cheap labour or soft factors like quality of life are available.

As a consequence of globalisation, urban politics is faced with the challenge to change some of its logics of action:

- Aside from the already existing regional or national competition for location, international aspects are gaining more importance. The metropolises need to raise their location quality to meet the demands of the international financial and economic markets who are the crucial customers. This also means offering foreign professionals an attractive place to live and work and to demonstrate open-mindedness when dealing with questions like the integration of immigrants. Besides this, existing businesses have to be interested in the new global dimensions of economy. There are still a lot of restrictions that have to be cleared away, a basic one being, for example, the fact that not everyone can speak English, the global business language.

- At the global level, it is more difficult to gain a good reputation and popularity as an ecnomic location or a tourist destination than it is at the national level. So urban marketing has to concentrate even more intensively on specific target groups and has to communicate the strengths and perspectives of the metropolis as a unique profile. That means that there is high pressure on urban politics to organise extraordinary projects and events that can be used for global marketing. Big projects, festivalisation and visions correspond with this profiling strategy of global marketing.

Big projects, festivalisation and visions can be interpreted as instruments of urban planning to adapt to these conditions of a globalized setup. On the one hand, they seem to promote innovations of urban development, and on the other hand they cope with marketing demands to focus on unique and big projects or events that attract international attention. The following passages concentrate on the opportunities and restrictions, chances and risks that have to be considered when dealing with these strategies in urban planning.

Urban politics in global times acts under restrictions such as a lack of resources and demands for sustainable urban development. If global marketing needs unique action and attention and if financial resources are restricted on the urban as well as on the national level, there has to be a selection of projects that really are able to attract international attraction.

Urban planning by Big Projects

Big projects like the HafenCity have enormous influence on urban structure because of their dimension. They can promote the definition of new districts or centers, their identity and their images, and they can be motors of urban development.[1] The HafenCity proves this: The inner city of Hamburg is being enlarged by a big areal so that more population, jobs and spending power come into the city. There will be an attractive site that combines living and working inside the city. This will prevent certain target groups from moving out into or beyond the suburbs.

For some years now, Hamburg has been eager to broaden its positive image as a "green city near the water" and as harbour city and to present the city as an international metropolis for services and high-tech industries. Efforts have been made in the sectors of ICT, new media, the life sciences and aviation industries. The HafenCity demonstrates this change in structure: While in former times harbour activities constituted the main use, in the future there will be open space, housing and "dry businesses".

This change is not easy from the point of view of politics. The HafenCity can be seen as an example of the "organization of innovation" (see Häußermann / Siebel 1995). The structural change in economics stimulates the demand for flexible and quick reactions. To win political majorities, a big project with a positive expectation can help, but it must not produce any major disturbances. The HafenCity obviously is a favoured case because the site had been closed to the public, so there is hardly any opposition to changes, and moving the existing businesses is mainly a question of compensation of land or money.

In addition, the big project HafenCity can become a catalyst and establish new qualities of urban development in Hamburg. These could include urban design, modern and efficient building techniques or socially integrated methods for the planning of open space. The politicians have to make sure that these qualities are realized during the period of implementation and that innovations and new qualities are integrated regularly.

Some other risks of big projects like the HafenCity are, for example, that they tend to have selective effects, in particular, that they tend to neglect social and ecological aspects. This can have a direct impact on the planning results and their implementation in the district, but also an indirect one when priorities and investments of urban politics are changed (opportunity costs). A big project like the HafenCity can affect the implementation of parallel projects that are important for other districts.[1]

Urban planning by Festivalisation

The context between big events and urban planning has recently been discussed in planning theory under the topic of "festivalisation".[1] The festivalisation debate is connected with aspects of steering and innovation theory. In the context of urban and regional development, public steering capacity is currently considered to be pessimistic; the instruments of a hierarchical way of public steering are not designed to be very efficient (see Voigt 1995). From this point of view, festivalisation is a way of modern steering because it coordinates the different urban actors and their activities into a joint direction without using pressure or regulative instruments.

Hamburg's Olympic candidature illustrates this. After the Senate had given the impulse, it was possible to integrate the main business and sports associations, important companies, the counties, cities and communities of the region and the neighbouring states into the joint vision of Olympic Games in Hamburg in 2012. The condition was that the Olympic Games promise benefits for all participants:

- Businesses expect impulses for marketing the location at the international level and for a quicker realization of infrastructure projects (e.g. motorways, harbour expansion);
- For sports associations, it is a unique opportunity to modernize the sports infrastructure and to implement measures of sports promotion (e.g. more sports lessons in schools, international sports events);
- Between politicians there has been a broad consensus because the choice of the harbour as the main location does not provoke major conflicts and the international reputation of the city is seen as an opportunity.

The candidature promotes a vision for developing this central area next to the inner city. The broad support can be seen in the way the candidature has been organised: The "Hamburg for Games 2012 GmbH", that worked out the concept and organised the process, is financed by a partnership of the Senate, business and sports associations; the Senate's representative for the Olympic candidature is a former mayor of Hamburg who is member of the opposition party in Parliament; several Olympic ambassadors integrate further interests of urban society, particularly sports.

Another aspect connected with festivalisation is the innovation capacity of urban and regional planning. With reference to the Ruhr District, Häußermann and Siebel (1994) asked „how to organize innovation in a non-innovative milieu". Although this might be a special topic for the Ruhr District with its dominant mining structure, there are analogies for Hamburg: The influencial position of the harbour businesses and the expanded networks of administration and politics tend to slow down innovation. The vision of Olympic Games supports innovative actors and creates new coalitions of change agents, who receive the necessary backing for implementing their ideas.

An example of this "self-doping", as it is called by Häußermann and Siebel (1995), is the new harbour bridge from the HafenCity to Wilhelmsburg, which makes it easier to reach Harburg, and which thus plays an important role for the integration of Hamburg and Harburg. The candidature provides the conceptual framework from which to communicate this project and to mobilise public support for it. Even if Hamburg does not win the competition to host the Olympic Games in

2012, it can be expected that the new harbour bridge will remain a main project of urban planning.
In addition, festivalisation is a strategy that motivates public administration. The "self-doping" includes "*den Zwang, ein anspruchsvolles Projekt in einem begrenzten Zeitraum zu einem definierten Termin zum Erfolg zu führen*" (the pressure to realize a demanding project in a limited time by a fixed date successfully)[1]. Thus, big events can lead to more efficiency and to economic management methods within the administration.
Besides these potential positive effects of the festivalisation strategy, there are risks such as a poorly balanced use of public finances, the question of reuse of additionally needed buildings or a closed planning situation because of a fixed deadline.
In comparison to other policy fields of urban development, the Olympic candidature gives priority to sports topics. This effect is reinforced because the application committee demands proof that the Olympic candidature really does have high priority in the city. So conflicts with other policy fields and their representatives are generated with regard to the distribution of limited public resources. These "oasis effects" may cause important policy fields to be neglected or discriminated against: "*Festivalisierung ist das organisierte Wegsehen von realen Problemen*" (Festivalisation is the organized ignoring of real problems) is Siebel's (1992) critical judgement.
The problem of how to reuse additional Olympic buildings can only be solved by determining, for example, whether the costs of a new Olympic stadium can be offset by hosting the Olympic Games. It is almost impossible for a city to operate stadiums of the required size and standard economically nowadays. But this is a fundamental problem of the Olympic Games which the IOC and all candidates alike are faced with.
The period of time that was available to work on the concept for the candidature was strictly limited to about half a year. This allowed hardly any opportunity to have a broader discussion with different interest groups and citizens or to integrate the concept into a new urban development masterplan. The limited deadline as a restriction could lead to a closed planning situation, which might obstruct innovations or the achievement of modern quality standards.

Urban planning by Visions

Visions, models or *Leitbilder* can have different functions for urban and regional development. They include coordination, reflection, innovation and marketing (see Knieling 2000, 92 ff).

The *Leitbild* "Metropolis Hamburg – Growing City" is meant to be a vision for Hamburg that coordinates the actions of the various actors. Again the theoretical basis is that public steering has to change from a hierarchical to a cooperative mode (see Scharpf 1991). Steering by visions or motivating models is gaining importance. The *Leitbild* "Metropolis Hamburg – Growing City" demonstrates this mechanism. It contains goals, measures and projects, most of which have been discussed in the city for years and some of which have already begun to be implemented. The *Leitbild* bundles these projects, so that the wide array of individual activities is put together into an abstract model that increases the legitimation of each.

But a *Leitbild* is not able to solve all conflicts between competing interests or to balance the differences of power the actors possess. It favors individual policy fields and actors, and neglects others at the same time. The *Leitbild* requires financial resources to implement its goals, and these resources might be lacking in other policy fields as long as financial problems limit public spending as it has in recent years. During the implementation of the *Leitbild*, conflicts are to be expected.

Citizen participation and a broad dialogue at an early stage are meant to support compromises between the different interests. This process must show whether government and administration are willing to cooperate with the urban society. At the same time, the dialogue can help to gain more participants for a common urban development process and to motivate them as the endogenous potential of the city. Conflicts in this process can then be seen as productive if they lead to better solutions or to higher standards of quality.

Innovations will have a key function for the "Metropolis Hamburg – Growing City", particularly once the *Leitbild* with its strategies and goals is implemented. Although the submitted proposal for the *Leitbild* contains a lot of aspects, it also leaves several questions unanswered. The competition for location certainly stimulates innovations. But obstacles can arise if politicians act with an eye to short–terms, e.g. in election periods, if interest groups representing fixed positions are dominant or if the consensus between all participants is of major importance.

With regard to marketing demands for urban development in global times, the *Leitbild* "Metropolis Hamburg – Growing City" gives Hamburg a nearly unique position in Germany because, in contrast to the population decline that is expected for most of Germany, Hamburg is planning to increase its population by urban development. For national and international marketing, it will be important to communicate the *Leitbild* and its goals. For example, the clusters of competence such as the life sciences, ICT and new media, and aviation industries offer attractive aspects for that. Some of these topics have already got

enough substance to serve as the foundation for a successful marketing campaign, while others still have to be developed.
Moreover, there is the particular demand to connect marketing efforts with the institutional level of the metropolitan region. Internationally, it is Hamburg that is well known as the brand, but the strengths and potentials of the location are characterized by the cooperation of both the city and the surrounding region. Solutions for suburbanisation, a better traffic infrastructure or industrial projects such as the enlargement of EADS Airbus cannot be completed without the surrounding region. In addition, "soft" standards of the location like the quality of housing and living or cultural and entertainment facilities decide the reputation of a region from the point of view of foreign companies or high potential employees. These qualities are primarily available in the region outside the city limits, i.e. at the regional level of the metropolis.

"Focusing" as a strategy of (good) urban governance in global times?

All three strategies – big projects, festivalisation and visions - have in common that they are characterized by a "focusing" of urban planning: in the case of HafenCity the focus is spatial, the urban planning of the Olympic candidature is temporal, i.e. the focus is on a short period of time, and the *Leitbild* focuses on a special theme, so the focus is thematic. This empirical evidence leads to the thesis that focusing could be interpreted as a political logic of urban planning in global times. It seems to be the consequence of the increased competition for location. It can open up opportunities for urban development such as cutting through the administrative red tape that results from complexity, network structures and financial problems, or defining new standards of quality of urban planning, e.g. in terms of local economics, labor market efforts, social qualities, sustainable housing or open space planning.
Risks of the strategy of focusing are that it could result in selection and neglect in three forms: thematic, social and spatial. In any case, focusing leads to shifts in priorities of urban politics. So which topics and whose interests will be the successful ones becomes a question of power and political strategy.
From this perspective, focusing proves to be an ambivalent strategy: It can be beneficial in making public assets and resources available for individual interests. But it can also help to position a metropolis in the global competition for location in such a way that modern businesses become disposed to choose this location, and soft factors like environment, good housing or leisure facilities are held in high esteem. Therefore, urban planners are required to use the strategy of focusing in a socially and environmentally responsible way.

Finally: If used as a development strategy, focusing could strengthen the steering capacity of urban planning. This indicates that focusing could become an element of modern (good) urban governance (see Banner 2002; Pröhl / Sinning 2002) that places more importance on informal instruments such as festivalisation and visions or on intelligent "place-making" (Healey 2002), which big projects can represent.

References

Banner, G. (2002) Zehn Jahre Neues Steuerungsmodell – ein kritischer Blick zurück und ein Blick voraus, in: Deutscher Städtetag (ed.), Verwaltungsmodernisierung – Baustelle ohne Ende?, DST-Beitrag zur Kommunalpolitik, Reihe A, vol. 30, Berlin/ Köln

Buchmüller, L.; Keller, D. A.; Koch, M.; Schumacher, F. Selle, K. (2000) Planen Projekte Stadt? Weitere Verständigungen über den Wandel in der Planung, DISP, no. 141, p. 55-59

Culemann, R.; Ernst, B.; Schön, B. (ed.) (2001) Von Leuchttürmen und Taschenlampen: HafenCity – ein Ort zum Leben, Stadtentwicklungsbehörde der Freien und Hansestadt Hamburg Hamburg

Ehrenberg, E.; Kruse, W. (2000): Soziale Stadtentwicklung durch große Projekte? EXPOs, Olympische Spiele, Metropolen-Projekte in Europa: Hannover, Sevilla, Barcelona, Berlin, Dortmunder Beiträge zur Sozial- und Gesellschaftspolitik, vol. 30, Münster: LIT

FHH Freie und Hansestadt Hamburg (2001) Bewerbung Hamburgs um die Ausrichtung der Olympischen Sommerspiele 2012 (Machbarkeitsstudie), Senatsdrucksache 2201/1141 vom 15.10.2001, Hamburg

FHH (2002a) Leitbild "Metropole Hamburg - Wachsende Stadt", Senatsdrucksache: http://www.hamburg.de/fhh/behoerden/senatskanzlei/dokumentation/drucksache_wachsende_stadt_bearbeitet.pdf, Hamburg

FHH (2002b Bewerbungskonzept für die Ausrichtung der Olympischen Sommerspiele 2012 in Hamburg, Senatsdrucksache 17/2012 vom 30.04.2002 (Auszüge: http://www.hamburg-fuer spiele2012.de/6_bewerbung/bewerbung.html), Hamburg

FHH / Umweltbehörde (2001) Hamburg im Fluss - IGA auf den Inseln, Internationale Gartenbauausstellung 2012 in Wilhelmsburg, Hamburg

GHS Gesellschaft für Hafen- und Standortentwicklung (ed.) (2000): HafenCity Hamburg: Der Masterplan, Hamburg

GHS (ed.) (2001) HafenCity: Mitten in Hamburg, Hamburg

Häußermann, H.; Roost, F. 2000: Globalisierung, Global City; in: Häußermann, Hartmut (ed.), Großstadt. Soziologische Stichworte, p. 79-91, Opladen: Leske + Budrich

Häußermann, H.; Siebel, W. (1994) Wie organisiert man Innovation in nichtinnovativen Milieus? in: Kreibich, R.; Schmid, A.S.; Siebel, W. ; Sieverts, T. ; Zlonicky, P. (Hg.): Bauplatz Zukunft. Dispute über die Entwicklung von Industrieregionen, p. 52-64, Essen.

Häußermann, H.; Siebel, W. (1995) Politik durch Projekte. Von der umfassenden Entwicklungsplanung zum Projektmanagement am Beispiel der internationalen Bauausstellung Emscher Park, in: Buchmüller, L. / Meyrat-Schlee, E. (ed.), Stadtbild – Sinnbild. Planungsmethoden - Wertewandel, ORL-Bericht 91, p. 206-219, Zürich

Healey, P. (2002) Place Making and Governance, in: Fürst, D.; Knieling, J. (ed.), Studies in Spatial Planning of the Academy for Spatial Research and Regional Planning (ARL), vol. 2, p. 1-12, Hannover

Heeg, S.; Klagge, B.; Oßenbrügge, J. 2002: Metropole Hamburg – Wachsende Stadt, sudy of the University of Hamburg, Hamburg.

Keller, Donald A.; Koch, Michael; Selle, K. (ed.) (1998) Planung + Projekte. Verständigungsversuche zum Wandel der Planung, Dortmund: Dortmunder Vertrieb für Bau- und Planungsliteratur

Knieling, J. (2000) Leitbildprozesse und Regionalmanagement. Ein Beitrag zur Weiterentwicklung des Instrumentariums der Raumordnungspolitik, Beiträge zur Politikwissenschaft, vol. 77, Frankfurt a.M./New York: Peter Lang-Verlag

Meyer-Künzel, M. (1999) Städtebau der Weltausstellungen und Olympischen Spiele: Stadtentwicklung der Veranstaltungsorte, Hamburg

Müller, H.and Selle, K. (ed.) (2002) EXPOs, Großprojekte und Festivalisierung als Mittel der stadt- und Regionalentwicklung: Lernen von Hannover, Werkberichte der AGB, vol. 48, Dortmund: Dortmunder Vertrieb für Bau- und Planungsliteratur

Preisler-Holl, L. (2002) Gartenschauen - ein bundesweiter Überblick mit Exkurs über einen Bundeswettbewerb und seine Stiftungsinitiative, in: Preisler-Holl, Luise (ed.), Gartenschauen - Motor für Landschaft, Städtebau und Wirtschaft, Materialien des Deutschen Instituts für Urbanistik, vol. 6/2002, p. 161-182, Berlin: difu

Pröhl, M. and Sinning, H. (2002) Good Governance und Bürgergesellschaft. Verwaltungsmodernisierung, Bürgerorientierung und Politikreform als zentrale Anforderungen an Kommunen, in: Pröhl, M.; Sinning, H.; Nährlich, S. (ed.): Bürgerorientierte Kommunen in Deutschland. Anforderungen und Qualitätsbausteine, p. 17-27, Gütersloh: Verlag Bertelsmann Stiftung

Scharpf, F.W. (1991) Die Handlungsfähigkeit des Staates am Ende des zwanzigsten Jahrhunderts, Politische Vierteljahresschrift, no. 4, p. 621-634

Schubert, D. (ed.) (2001) Hafen- und Uferzonen im Wandel. Analysen und Planungen zur Revitalisierung der Waterfront in Hafenstädten, edition stadt und region, vol. 3, Berlin: Leue Verlag

Selle, K. (2002) Stadtentwicklung zwischen Erlebniswelt und Alltagsort. Überlegungen zu großen Projekten, Quartiersentwicklung und bürgerorientierter Politik, Manuskript des Lehrstuhls für Planungstheorie, www.pt.rwth-aachen.de/publikationen/manuskripte/ Stadtentwicklung.html, Aachen

Siebel, W. (1992) Die Festivalisierung der Politik, in: DIE ZEIT, 30.10.02, p. 62, Hamburg

Voigt, R. (1995) Der kooperative Staat: Auf der Suche nach einem neuen Steuerungsmodus, in: ders. (ed.): Der kooperative Staat: Krisenbewältigung durch Verhandlung? p. 33-92, Baden-Baden: Nomos.

The Production of Urban Space
A Field Study on Visual Perception of Architectural Space

Angelika Psenner

The Image of a city is defined, amongst other things, by the city's public space, its streets, and its open places. They play an important role in the social life of men, as they are the freely accessible areas, where people meet in their everyday life.
The article describes an interdisciplinary approach and the findings of an empiric research project on the perception of laymen of a special urban open space in Vienna. The empiric study is dedicated to the investigation of the interdependence of perception and architecture: To what extend is architectural planning taking influence on the personal understanding of urban open spaces?
For the carrying out of the project an innovative research design has been developed. Therefore the theme of the methodological approach is strongly emphasised in this article.

Introduction

What do we know about the real effects of urban architectural space? How is it perceived by those who use and inhabit it? Can the perception of that space be explored scientifically? Can one talk about an interaction between built space and its users? Or do (artificial) spaces and their perception stay unchanged; do they have the same impact on every perceiver in every situation? What does space mean? What is perception?
The first basic studies that dealt with this flood of questions were done in the 1960s and 1970s – i.e. "The Image of the City" by Kevin Lynch (1960), "Streets for People" by Bernard Rudofsky (1964) and "The Production of Space" by Henri Lefebvre (1974). Unfortunately this research work was not continued and developed further. The reason for this can be seen in the divergence of the various disciplines (this assumption is confirmed by the fact that in conceptional – and therefore transdisciplinary – *art* a strong and intensive debate about urban-space-perception takes place). At least with regard to sociology and architecture there seems to have been no constant interdisciplinary co-operation. The representatives of either field rather accuse each other of being out of touch with reality and of producing outcomes that are not practicable – or, of being unscientific and superficial: 'Architects can't read and they invent their own language that nobody besides themselves can understand' (Edward W. Soja at the Technopolis Congress in November 2001 at the IFK Internationales

Forschungszentrum Kulturwissenschaften, Vienna). Or 'sociologist make no attempt of a proper investigation, they rather verbalise everything.' (Quotation by an architectural colleague).
The city, the urban space is one of 'the most complex of all human artefacts' (Rykwert 1990). It is this complexity that in my view accounts for the difficulty of a scientific analysis of urban space. A big omission can be seen in an interdisciplinary context. Therefore in my work an attempt is made to study a single aspect of the theme *urban space* in a general and trans-disciplinary manner, by combining research tools from the fields of architectur, sociology and visual research. Moreover, the study sought to achieve practical results, capable of being applied in urban design and architecture.
This article deals with the analysis of *space perception.* The theme will be discussed by means of an existent urban example; so that street users, who in general are architectural laymen, are focused primarily. The field study refers to the *public space* of a street, which differs clearly from private (garden, courtyard) or semi-private spaces (passages, shopping malls...). It differs in function, organisation and equipment.
Two facets of approach
The research is based on two different approaches, both of which are of great importance and should be discussed at the outset:
On the one hand the study deals with the examination of the selected field, that is to say that the project was developed in order to find useful answers to the research question: 'How is a special public space perceived by its users?' or 'How/ what do people perceive in the chosen street?' On the other hand the intention was to develop an applicable method. In keeping with my educational background (architecture, urban design, sociology) and my intention, such a method should include analytic methods from architectural research and sociology. Therefore it was necessary to study the current practice in photo/image analysis and the possibilities of scientifically recognised methods.
The precarious attitude of scientists towards images and visual data (in contrast to speech and text); the significance of visual and aesthetical knowledge in philosophy; the historic evolution of the use of photography in science, especially in social science, and finally the problem of a certain claim of evidence of photography – all these significant problems in approach were discussed thoroughly in an introductory section in the thesis itself. In this article we will have to do with a simple addressing of those basic issues.
The 'Lesemaschine' (reading machine), described below, has been developed especially for the purpose of this study. The method of interweaving image-, text- and plan-analysis is novel, therefore an extensive comment on the approach and a thorough explanation of the

elaborated method are included in this text, whereas the description of the findings is kept rather short.

(Visual) perception

We keep in touch with the real world through our senses. The act of perception enables us to get a valid impression of the world around us and to learn from it. It is well known that beside the five sens organs – listening, smelling, tasting, seeing and the sense of touch – other physical regulators do exist. They help us to comprehend our presence. Our eyesight for example is complemented by the perception through additional light-sensitive receptors in the skin. In this article however I will concentrate on the visual aspect of perception, as it comes close to the possibilities of urban design.

Perception research is done in very different fields, this results in a big variety of different potential approaches to the theme: philosophy, psychology, medicine, biology etc. It can be said that the theoretical models, which had been developed in the last five decades, have gained complexity over the time. Especially in the last years researchers tried to strive for a comprehensive, trans-disciplinary approach, whereas in the 1960s very simple, linear information processing models were used. They gave a rather flat view of the process, which was assumed to begin with the stimulation of a sensory surface, and to end with the formation of a "percept", which then was combined with stored information given in consciousness (Bruce/ Green/ Georgeson 1996, 376ff). In this the whole process of events is inflicted on an absolutely passive perceiver – or receiver, who is just reacting to external circumstances. This model leaves many questions unanswered: Why do different eye witnesses give different accounts of the same events? How are units formed, so that some portions of input are treated as belonging to one object? How are successive glances at the same scene combined with one another?

Another difficulty concerns the production of images. A mental image does not begin with a retinal stimulation, but it is treated as a train of processes that arises in the middle of the apparatus. In this way one could never be sure of actually seeing or just imagining things one thinks of. As long as the process of perception is seen as a passive action, the multi-sensorial aspect of information processing can hardly be coped with. The sequential model does not explain in which way the different inflows of our simultaneously working senses are co-ordinated.

A much more complex model of information processing is shown by the so called "perceptual cycle model" developed by the psychologist Ulrich Neisser (Neisser 1978, 89ff.). Here perception is treaded as a constructive process, as a continuous activity – in this regard, it represented a radical break with most perceptual theories of that time –

not restricted to a single sensory system. The internal *schema* interrelates with the actual perception, and vice versa. The term *schema* with this nexus originally was used by Piaget and Bartlett (Neisser 1976, 97). It is that portion of the perceptual cycle that is *inside* the observer, modifiable by experience, and somehow specific to what is being observed. It is that part of the theoretical model that takes into consideration the psychological structure of the perceiver; it allows him/her to pick up information and to use it in an active way. So with the time we develop individual sophisticated schemata, that accept information from many sources simultaneously and direct explorations of many kinds. In this perception is inherently selective – we can select and even ignore information, we do not just "stare" at things neither are we "exposed" to them.

Visual perception is directly connected with our anticipation of information, with our curiosity, with our reflexes (eye movements and fine body movements, i.e. the turning of the head) or with real explorations and actions under the use of all senses. Therefore perception can be learned and trained. Neisser calls it 'a multimodal enterprise based on multimodal anticipations' (Neisser 1978, 92f). In other words: visual perception is not simply based on sight, but it also takes in the information flow that evolves from the other senses, and what is seen is also determined by what we *expect* to see. If this model of perception is improved by the spatial factor, the mental anticipation schemata can be complemented with a wider spatial schema, in which the perceived object or scene is set in. In relation to this Neisser speaks of a 'cognitive map'. The internal schema directs looking, whereas the cognitive map directs travelling, body movements of a larger kind. 'Cognitive mapping is an abstract term, that covers cognitive or mental abilities, that allow us to pick up information about our spatial surrounding, to arrange, to store, recall and to process it. These abilities can be developed and improved. Cognitive mapping is especially referring to a process of *action* that we take out when we examine the environment. The cognitive map is the outcome of this active process; it is the structuralised picture/illustration of a part of the spatial surrounding.' (Downs/ Stea 1982, 23f).

According to this model what people see depends on:

- the mental anticipation they develop (related to the schema and to the cognitive map)
- the perceptual exploration they carry out (peripheral vision, eye movement, haptic exploration, the use of other senses,...)
- the information they find available (by the use of *all* senses)

Gestalt theory also takes up the theme of mental anticipations, the schemata, and refers to them as 'good' Gestalt (e.g. Koffka 1990). Perception happens on certain levels of pithiness: not any geometrical form can be realised and seen. In this regard the Gestalt theory and Neisser's perceptual cycle model overlap, they both confirm that the percept is not just influenced by the available information but that our dispositions, our expectations, our past experience, that is to say our internal schema have a great impact on it.
There is a wide range of empirical studies concerning this matter: i.e. the space-psychological investigation by Janesch, the colour study by Katz and Rubins and also Hartmanns research work regarding the phenomenological figure-ground problem (all cited and discussed in Koffka 1990, 246ff). They all confirm that:

- perception is constantly evolved by experience
- perception is an active process, that combines and interweaves the picking up of external information, thinking and acting, so that they correlate with each other.

When we start from the idea that active perception can be learned and that the skill of seeing is improvable, we can directly draw the conclusion that the way we perceive is highly influenced by our social life. This is my starting point. The society in which we live teaches us to *read* the world in a special way. The perception of urban space is – besides other things – also depending on the social conditions of the perceiver himself.

Space perception

As mentioned before, 'space' in this context does not mean the euclidic geometrical space nor the material three-dimensional extension. Space and the experience of space exceed the simple qualities of territory, cubic meters or the texture of the defining/limiting surfaces. The term 'space' in its singularity might be seen as misconceptional, as it suggests the existence of an all-embracing, all-covering, for ever (all the time) present space. In philosophy this concept is called *Behälterraum* 'container space'. It relates back to the ancient world, to the historic idea of the geocentric *Weltbild*: a finite space, that is defined by the fixed stars and the centre of which is formed by the immovable spherical earth. But modern physics gives evidence, that space – just like time – is a relative and dynamic unit.
Even in everyday life *the* space does not exist, we rather have *spaces*. The emerging of spaces, the perception and the experience of them are parts of a process which itself is a social construction. Corresponding to our own biographical experience we form a unique and individual spatial structure, by combining all the different spaces that we meet and that we construct day by day.

Social *Verinselung* – here, with reference to Martina Löw's work (Löw 2001), a particular spatial socialisation in our time is meant: as they grow up, children do not experience a continuous enlargement of their living space, but they are introduced to single spaces, that are spread like 'islands' (Inseln) all over the city – technological evolution and globalization lead to a certain weakening of the container space conception. We move towards the idea of relational spatial units, that are renewed and developed constantly and that in consequence are connected with each other in an individual and personal space system. This aspect proves that space can not be seen in a static way, but that it is formed individually according to our way of being and living. Therefore it can be said, that

- the construction of space is a social and procedural phenomenon;

In addition to this thesis Löw in 'Raumsoziologie' proposes, discusses and proves the following additional assumptions:

- space is a relational arrangement of living beings and social goods;
- space is produced in interaction between acting and structures, it is conceived under pre-structured conditions;
- spaces are normally produced in repetitive actions, in routinely behaviour (Löw 2001, 271f).

We develop a socialised and symbolised way of perception (c.f. Picture 1), that enables us to handle the oversupply of visual information. According to Neisser, anticipation and schemata (or cognitive maps) are learned socially. This implies the assumption of certain interdependence between perception and society, it also leads to the conclusion that people from different social backgrounds perceive differently. Which means that they also perceive – and with that conceive – space differently.

Figure 1: Visualisation of a perceptional performance by the test person 03WM: the picture of the "Galaxy" tower block is compared with the matching interview text and the indicated symbolisation (plain-clothes soap Columbo).

The discussed street project clearly shows that people tend to compare places – even if they are well known – with images, and that those images are influenced or created by mass media, like TV and cinema. This connection is still intensified when it concerns unknown places, that had not yet been experienced and where the internal *schema* cannot establish direct, personal references.

The research field – the Praterstrasse

The data survey – documental research and on the other hand an elaborated time-consuming field study – needed a clear definition of the research field: the Praterstrasse, which is situated in the second district in Vienna, the so-called Leopoldstadt.

Several circumstances had lead to this choice:

- the urban relevance of the street is very notable
- the history of the street and its district is rather diversified with a high impact on its architecture

- this history and the different positions within the urban system are very well documented in historic accounts and in literature (as in many biographies of Viennese Jewish writers detailed records can be found concerning their home district, the Leopoldstadt and very often they also refer to the Praterstrasse.

The most prosperous period in the street's history was the beginning of the 19th century, when the northern railway station was build and the coal trade started to boom. As a result, the street became part of the economic and organizational centre of the city. Coffee shops, restaurants (the traditional place for trading), theatres, stages and several rather elegant city houses were erected and lined the fashionable street. 'It was a rather exclusive quarter, high on reputation', wrote Arthur Schnitzler in his autobiography "Jugend in Wien" (Youth in Vienna).

With the Holocaust and the extinction of the Jewish Culture the district, and with it the Praterstrasse, lost its importance and did not recover it after the war. Only in the past fiew years the first signs of gentrification could be observed.

The current condition of the Praterstrasse could be described as follows: The street has been laid out with spacious standards that are rather untypical for Viennese suburbia: there are magnificent multi-storied townhouses with generous street level zones and spacious pedestrian areas and pavements. Its wide and open character and the special position within the traffic system predestined the Praterstrasse to take over the function of a key connection route between city centre and periphery. In addition the interweaving of different functions leads to a certain urban boulevard-like appearance. Beside the intensity of its traffic, the Praterstrasse also functions as a supply- and shopping street; and the residents and day trippers (to the nearby recreational area of the Prater) use it for walking and promenading. This multi-functional and highly faceted appearance ensures highly valuable findings within the research field.

The fieldwork study: structure and order

'How is urban open space perceived?' in order to deal with this question within the qualitative fieldwork study a special testing order was developed. The single tests are called *walks* as they can be seen as little city-walking-tours, in which a range of people, such as architectural laymen, residents, street users, tourists, etc. participated. They were personally confronted with the street and its architecture, and were asked to experience it along a special standardised, two kilometre long route. They were also asked to produce a series of photographs of the

visual material – no restrictions were made on the potential motives or the amount of pictures. A standardised camera was used. Its technical standard allowed the production of good data (with the possibility for zooming) and it was at the same time rather easy to use. The professional photographer was the only exception to this role - she worked with her own equipment. In this way a common prejudice was proven wrong, according to which 'the average man/woman is not able to use the camera properly; pictures are photographed by chance; every connection to the original intention is accidental.' Considerations like this were expressed when I first presented the preliminary study at the Jo Reicherts seminary at the University of Vienna in spring 1999. In the end the 'professional' photos could not be told apart from the laymen-pictures.
Accompanying open interviews and participant observation complemented the research. The fieldwork covered an entire climatic year, so that it would enclose all four seasons.
In order to enable an interpretation that goes beyond a text-orientated, matter-of-fact reproduction, language and dialect of the interviews were not edited.

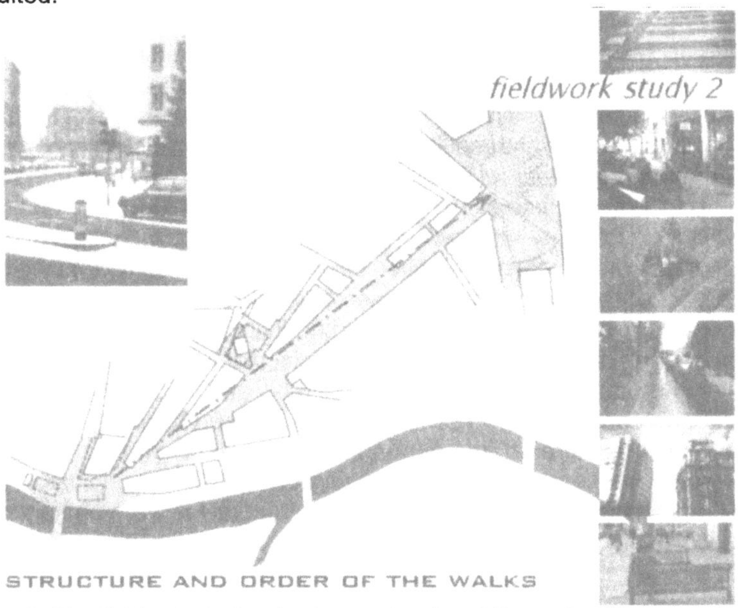

Figure 2: The fieldwork study: structure and order of the walks. The arrow in the ground plan of the street shows length and direction of the standardised route. The pictures are a small selection of the different images and themes that were chosen by the test persons: the roadway, the lane, the pavement, stairs and floor coverings, architecture, street furnishings etc.

Analysis and method

The output of the *walks* in terms of verbal and visual material was enormous. In order to be able to handle it, an appropriate technique had to be developed. For the evaluation of the photographs scientific methods from sociology and visual research were used, which were complemented by architectural analytic methodologies (i.e. cartography following differing criteria). This was done in order to guard against certain professional prejudice and a possible expectational attitude (regarding my architectural training), so that a new approach to the matter was allowed. The following qualitative sampling procedure was then related back to the initial classificatory analysis of the relevant visual material.

In this work photographs are not equated with perception. Looking through a lens makes you behave differently; it is not like exploring the space incidentally while moving through it, or like 'scanning' it with the eyes and with all senses. But photos can give reference to the percept, as long as they are used in combination with the textual information of the interviews.

"Lesemaschine" the reading machine

All in all 373 photos had to be arranged in a clear and readable form. For this reason the "Lesemaschine" LM (reading machine) was developed, which is actually a system of different cardboard stripes that can be moved. In that way the resulting interpretative work is slightly conducted, ordered and simplified. LM allows a good overview over all the material and on the same time single pictures (either within the same test series, or within all series - concerning one single place or building) can be compared with each other rather efficiently. The machine consists in a line up of the different photo series of all the test persons TPs. Every vertical stripe corresponds to the shooting carried out by one test person. The horizontal line marks a special place in the street.

With this analytic method overlappings and discrepancies in the perception are shown. At one point of the street 13 out of 15 TPs took very similar pictures of the same motive: the 'yellow house' (c.f. picture 4); some are even congruent. Whereas in the place in front of the Nepomuk church a great variety of different motives were photographed. This diversity in perception is also shown below in picture 4 'church place'

Figure 3: The "Lesemaschine" in two different positions. Every single vertical stripe corresponds to a photo series (shooting) of one TP. The horizontal line marks a special place in the street.

Cartographic mapping

Cartographic mapping is used to carry on and to deepen the visual analysis. The photographs and the motives together with the spatial motion of the TPs (during the walk) are thus recorded and subsequently mapped in the street plan. Trough the use of ordinary graphic systems and plan features, like legends and symbols, the testing process and the perceptual results are visualised in a precise and comprehensible way. The different plans show (c.f. legend in Picture 4) whether photos were taken with normal lens, with zooming, detail-zooming or panoramic views. This distinction reveals potential connections between the spatial possibilities and the actual perceptional performance. Plan 08AH illustrates a special detail perception (it mostly shows small objects in occasional shots) whereas 05KS indicates a more spatial perceptive gesture with spacious flights (it fairly reproduces the ground floor plan as a whole).

The superposition of the 14 usable and evaluable plans (Test 01RM was done with a four years old girl. In this case a shorter, easily manageable route was chosen and the child refused to take pictures. In spite of these irregularities the test run gave a good insight into the perceptional behaviour of a child. Nevertheless the data could not be compared and analysed with the other photos in an equal manner) results in the cartographic plan *"all"*. This plan consents to a great potential for interesting and informative interpretation, such as the theme of density/ emptiness (places that were documented by many people respectively by none).

CARTOGRAPHIC PLAN "ALL"

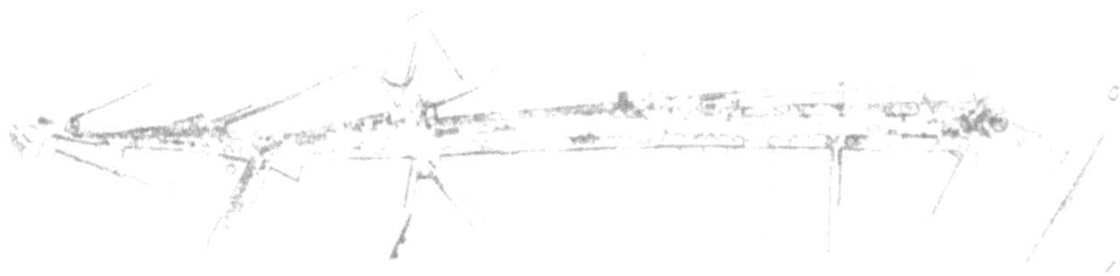

Figure 4: The superposition of all the single plans

above

below

other side of the street

Figure 5: Beside the cartographic plan "all" three additional superposition-plans were provided: above, below and other side of the street. They are drawn up after special criteria and therefore reflect a selected number of photographs.

Beside the cartographic plan *"all"* three additional superposition-plans are provided: *above, below* and *other-side-of-street*. They are drawn up after special criteria and thus they reflect an exclusively selected number of photographs. The criteria *above (a)* and *below (b),* which actually means *above eyelevel* und *below eyelevel* is based on the following thought:

a describes the viewing angle when the head is in upright position. It includes objects that are situated in the upper field of the horizon. The required physical and psychical attitude for this can be described with general attention and awareness: the preservation of the surrounding, the search of a special object or person, or the investigation and verification of a certain sensual stimulus (i.e. a special and unusual sound). The raising of the head the viewing angle *a* not only brings an enlargement of the range of vision, but it also disconnects the visual perception from the act of locomotion. If it was necessary to watch the steps – due to irregularities of the soil – or to walk in a special non-rhythmical way, it would be dangerous to raise the head. Under those circumstances a constant upright head position is definitely out of place. The head can be raised now and then to check the surrounding world quickly.
The *b* plan contains 95 of 347 (usable) photos that is less than a third (a-plan: 252 photos). In the evaluation of *a* and *b* the following can be observed: altogether most TPs have shot more *as* than *bs*, only single TBs showed an intensified *below eyelevel* perception. Some have alternated rhythmically the *a* and *b* views, they checked vicinity and distance by turns. In contrast to the *a*-plan the *b*-plan fairly reproduces the ground floor plan as a whole. That way the other side of the street normally is not included in the *below eyelevel* view, but it contains street furniture like trees, benches, lamps, dustbins, street signs, etc. Some parts of the street are completely excepted from the *b*-perception. The fourth plan that is named *other-side-of-street* (v. picture 6) equally shows several blanks.

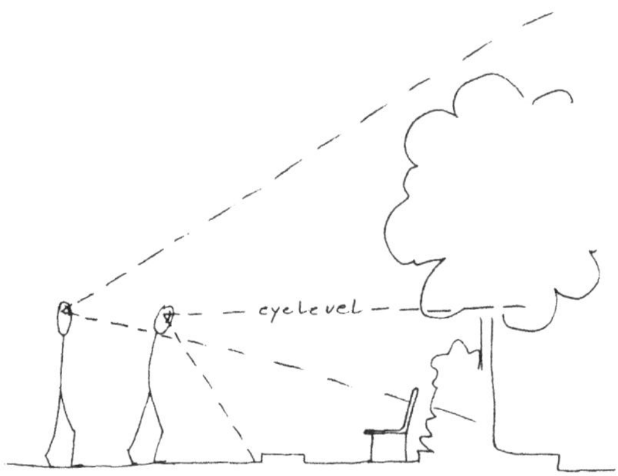

Figure 6: sketch; visualisation of the distinction of above eyelevel und below eyelevel

The planimetric analysis of the different maps enables the elaboration of single aspects and the concentration on certain sections of the walk. Therefore the whole walk was divided into seven portions (TB0 – TB6), five of which are examined closely. Due to irregularities the beginning and the end of the walk were left out: In TB0 the TPs had to get used to the unusual situation of the set, at the end of the walk the TPs were affected and exhausted by the length of the walk (2 km) and the fatigue of an atypical activity. The *cartographic plan "all" Section TB2* shows the last analytic step: the different plans or sectional plans (which are based on the above mentioned portions, TB and which allow a more detailed processing) are related back to the corresponding interviews.

CARTOGRAPHIC PLAN "ALL" SECTION TB2

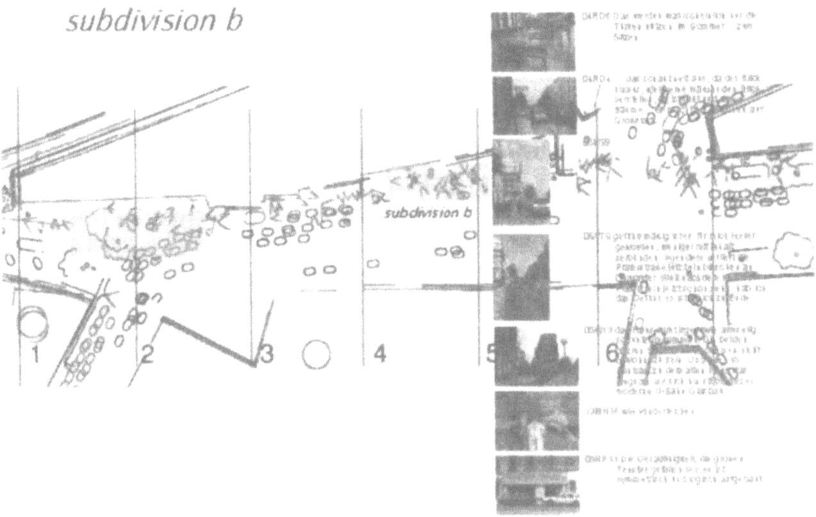

Figure 7: Sectional plan: superimposition of text and visual material. The chart shows the longest of all sections TB2, it measures approx. 500 metres. In this sector the street is not lined with trees and it is augmenting constantly in width. With a view to the clarity of the survey results, this large-seized sector was split into six regular geometrical divisions. In the plan they are marked with vertical lines and with numbers. The light blue field shows the third and last subdivision, it is named with "subdivision b". Only at this level a sensible superimposition of text and visual material is functional: the pictures shown on the plan had all been shot in that "micro space". The matching interviews are indicated by a few words. At this point words and images are related to each other and analysed mutually.

Findings

The construction of space is a social phenomenon; as such it is highly dependent on social developments. Consequently the perception of space has to be seen as a procedural event.

> 'Space is constituted in a synthesis of social goods, people and places. It is constructed through anticipation, through perception and through memories. Moreover in special places space is psychologically constructed by *spacing* and physically by *placing* goods (building, erecting) and people (survey) in relation to other goods and people.
> In every day life spaces are produced in routinely behaviour. Spatial structures are reproduced in repetitive actions. Spatial structures are a variant of social structures, like those they are embedded in institutions. With the reproduction of spatial structures these institutions are replicated and thus repeated persistently' (Löw 2001, 263. Translation by the author).

The idea of an 'absolutistic' space is outdated (Hawking 2001, 51); this concerns the concept of the *container* space and the scheme of the existence of space as an independent reality – instead of space as consequence of human acting. This idea can no longer be applied to our life and society. If space is no longer seen as a invariable background to our action, but if it is understood as part of the context of all action, we are getting nearer to the procedural concept of space, as outlined above. This understanding of the term directed the analysis of the fieldwork study "Praterstrasse". What can be said about the perception of the chosen space generally? And what lesson does this hold for the planners? How shall future urban developments be dealt with? These issues shall be discussed by means of the following realms of investigation.

Seasons

The perception of urban public space is directly corresponding to temperature, climate and other natural phenomenon. The final percept is therefore considerably influenced by seasonal changes. In winter time the TBs showed a certain sensitivity for the perception of single objects; whereas in the warmer period the reading of spatial impressions – of spaces – predominated. The detailed "shots" of single objects like street furniture or pieces of façades, in warmer seasons fused to a spatial unit. Then the TPs would mention phrases like *place, nook, spot* and *characteristic corner.*

Therefore provincial place design and units with small town character are duplicated by the perceiver just when the conditions for spatial perception are adequate and convenient. If pre-arranged spaces are not realized according to their design and the intentional connotation they are left out of consideration, or they are even criticised and detracted.

Planned and conceived space

Perceiving is a socialised behaviour, therefore spatial concepts are realized when the perceiver is able to understand and to "read" those constructs, when the used symbols and codes correspond to personal experience and to his/ her way of life. Consequently TPs that live (or grew up) in the country or in a small town are more likely to respond to place-clichés, like a cobble stone pavement, a rustic wooden bench, a tree or a little well. While so-called "town children" will not be able to filter out these codes, they will rather be lost in the jumble (medley) of other impressions. Architectural performance in public space in not seen/ perceived/ understood by everybody in the same way.

Axes

The distant view is nearly always taken in, provided that the layout of the street gives the possibility to do so. In the actual situation of the "Praterstrasse" this distant view does not focus the monument – which would be the planimetric focal point of the street – but it is oriented on various chief attractions that change with the differing position in the street: the beginning of the avenue of trees at the "Nestroyplatz" or special boarder marks, like the typical 'front houses'. This front houses mark the beginning of a new block, they take especially prominent positions as nearly every incoming street does meet the Praterstrasse at sharp angle.

The planning authorities and the planners are supposed to take this fact more seriously into consideration. The street users' potential field of vision is still overrated. This by no means does deny the merit of large-scale urban axes; but I believe that for a high-quality experience of space and for a secure orientation also small-scale processing of space should bee worked out. The quality of streets and of urban space in general should be proved and confirmed for single segments by adjusting it to the human potentials concerning the perceptional capability.

Perceptional blanking

In the act of perception people tend to blank out, to 'overlook' unpleasant factors. In moments of insecurety we rather search for more attractive eye catchers. When I am confronted with a boring or upsetting environment, my eyes automatically start to wander, at that point the other side of the street suddenly becomes more fascinating. Provided that nothing (trees, cars and other barricades) prevents me from looking at it.

This statement was proved by the individual reactions of the testing persons - especially at the Nestroyplatz and before that in section TB2: they tried to overcome the confusion of the traffic-loaded space and the unclearness of the euclidic geometry by the search for beauty, firmness or for special details in the facades.

Narrowness – vastness

When the geometrical moving space is narrowed down, this obviously has an impact on the perception and on the way of behaving. In the study the street users started to walk quickly, they preferred to look ahead, because they did not see things that are worth talking about. In such situations less photos were shot. It seems that the TPs tried to quickly escape that narrow and uncomfortable space.

But one and the same narrow stretch (i.e. in the first half of TB3) is not always perceived as being too constricted. In midsummer this shadowed zone between building and trees is felt to be a pleasant pergola, as it offers a certain protection against heat, dust and supposedly also against noise. However the flowerbeds with high-growing bushes and shrubs are still seen as an unusable zone with a strongly limiting character: *'One cannot pass there. Just on a few points you are actually allowed to cross the street. That's bad, but that's probably due to the traffic. Road safety. You actually have two sides of the road that are not connected with each other. Just by a few zebra crossings. (...) Those slanting concrete slabs too are really odd and ugly.'* (quotation: 04RD) *'What I really don't like are those things, actually they are dog toilets. Disgusting.'* (quotation: 14FM)

The enlargement of the pedestrian area after that narrow situation is a special moment: In winter nearly always a certain relieving all-around view followed immediately after the cramped spatial conditions were left behind. As if the TPs were grasping for new orientation. The perception is directed to the other side of the street. In summer – due to a intensified spatial reading – the place in front of the church was inspected carefully. What is offered here? What's new? What have I missed?

Large spaces are likely to be framed. The TPs normally would search for boundaries (head buildings, which are corner buildings with a particularly elaborated design) or they would centre the space by an object that radiates a certain (historical) atmosphere. If spaciousness predominates for a long time and if it is superposed by over-excitement and strain (noise, strong traffic...) the TPs react by the "retreat" to small, protected and clear units.

Figure 8: Liebes Gässlein (nice tiny little alley). If spaciousness predominates for a long time and if it is superposed by over-excitement and strain (noise, strong traffic...) the TPs react by the "retreat" to small, protected and clear units.

Conclusion

The evaluation of the field-study data might be continued; further aspects might be taken into consideration. The potential of the discussed textual and visual data, as well as of the applied method is not yet exhausted. Gender could of course be a possible point of view for further investigation: does the perception of men and women differ? Or in which way does age influence our way of perceiving? These aspects could not be covered in the present study, as the analysis itself was held short in favour of a accurate elaboration of the combined visual method.
However the initial target was reached: by the use of a (new) scientific instrument the chosen street block was analysed and findings were made that are usable for future urban planning. The research question: 'How is a certain open urban space perceived?' is answered according

to a special aspect and – concerning a concrete and practical use – the statements are phrased for a determined group of readers, above all for planners and architects.
I did not aim for general findings and rules, as they lie out of context and out of the above defined concept of "space perception". Nevertheless a general regulative that can be stated here would be the perceptual scheme status of "town" and "country children": they obviously react differently to architectural place concepts. For planning a current assumption could be proved: the behaviour of street users – and with it also the perception, as this is acting! - is strongly influenced by the "spaciousness" of a street space; by its narrowness and vastness, both seen as relational terms.

Special thanks to Wolfgang Sützl for his help in editing this article.

References:

Achleitner, F. (1996) „Ein Stadtbild gibt es nicht", in: Ehalt, H. C. and Konrad, H. (ed.) *Wiener Architektur,* Böhlau Verlag, pp. 211-222.

Atzwanger, K. and Schäfer, K. (1999) "Evolutionary Approaches to the Perception of Urban Spaces". *Evolution and Cognition*, Vol.5, Nr.1, pp. 87-92.

Becker, H. S. (1981) "Introduction", in: Becker, H. S. (ed.) *Exploring Society Photographically*, Block Gallery. North Western University Press, pp. 9-11.

Benjamin, W. (1977/ Orig. 1963) "Kleine Geschichte der Photographie", in: Benjamin, W., *Das Kunstwerk im Zeitalter seiner technischen Reproduzierbarkeit*, Suhrkamp Verlag, pp. 45-65.

Böhme, G. (1998) "Die Atmosphäre der Stadt", in: Böhme, G. *Anmutungen über das Atmosphärische*. Edition Tertium, pp. 49-70.

Bourdieu, P. (1991) „Physischer, sozialer und angeeigneter physischer Raum", in: Wentz M. (ed.) *Stadt-Räume. Die Zukunft des Städtischen. Frankfurter Beiträge, Bd. 2*, pp. 25-34.

Bruce, V., Green, P. R. and Georgeson, M. A. (eds.) (1996) *Visual Perception. Physiology, Psychology, and Ecology.* 3rd Edition. Psychology Press Taylor & Francis.

Burgin, V. (ed.) (1982) *Thinking Photography.* Macmillan.

Burgin, V. (1996) *In/Different Spaces. Place and Memory in Visual Culture.* University of California Press.

Chaplin, E. (ed.) (1994) *Sociology and Visual Representation*. Routledge.

Clarke, D. B. (ed.) (1997) *The Cinematic City.* Routledge.

Downs, R. M. and Stea, D. (1982) *Kognitive Karten: Die Welt in unseren Köpfen.* Harper & Row, Publishers

Flick, U., Von Kardorff, E. and Steinke, I. (eds.) (2000) *Qualitative Forschung. Ein Handbuch*. Rowohlt Taschenbuchverlag.

Foucault, M. (1991) „Andere Räume", in: Wentz, M. (ed.) *Stadt-Räume. Die Zukunft des Städtischen. Frankfurter Beiträge, Bd.2*, pp. 65-72.

Giddens, A. (1984) „Zeit, Raum und Regionalismus", in: Giddens, A., *Die Konstruktion der Gesellschaft*, Campus Verlag, pp. 161-185.

Goffman, E. (1997) *Das Individuum im öffentlichen Austausch. Mikrostudien zur öffentlichen Ordnung*. Suhrkamp Verlag.
Gombrich, E. H. (1994) "Zur Psychologie des Bilderlesens", in: Gombrich, E. H.: *Das forschende Auge. Kunstbetrachtung und Naturwahrnehmung*. Campus Verlag, pp. 11-19.
Groh, R. and Groh, D. (1992) „Naturerfahrung", in: Groh, R. and Groh D. (eds.) *Weltbild und Naturaneignung*. Suhrkamp Verlag, pp. 92-108.
Harper, D. (1998) "An Argument for Visual Sociology", in: Prosser, J. (ed.) *Image-based Research. A Sourcebook for Qualitative Researchers*. Falmer Press, pp. 24-41.
Harvey, D. (1989) "The Experience of Space and Time", in: Harvey, D. *The Condition of Postmodernity*. Cambridge University Press, pp. 201-225.
Häußermann, H. and Siebel, W. (1987) *Neue Urbanität*. Suhrkamp Verlag.
Hawking, S. (2001/ Orig. 1998) *Eine Kurze Geschichte der Zeit*. Deutscher Taschenbuch Verlag
Ipsen, D. (1998) „Die Landschaft der Stadt", in: Ipsen, D. and Wehrle, A. (eds.) *Stadt und Natur, Kunst und Ökologie*. Suhrkamp Verlag, pp. 11-25.
Kofka, K. (1990) „Psychologie (Teil II)", *Gestalt Theorie* Vol. 12, Nr. 4, pp. 241-283
Kostof, S. (1991) *The City Shaped. Urban Paterns and Meanings through History*. Little, Brown and Company.
Lefebvre, H. (2001, orig.:1974) *The Production of Space*. Blackwell Publishers
Löw, M. (2001) *Raumsoziologie*. Suhrkamp Verlag.
Lynch, K. (1989/ Orig. 1960) *Das Bild der Stadt* (The Image of the City), in the series: Bauwelt Fundamente, Heft 16, Vieweg Verlag.
Merlot–Ponty, M. (1966) „Jeder Sinn hat seine Welt. Die Kommunikation der Sinne. Die Vorgängigkeit des Empfindens vor den Sinnen. Die Synästhesien", in: Merlot–Ponty, M. (ed.) *Phänomenologie der Wahrnehmung*. Walter De Gruyter & Co, pp. 260-269.
Neisser, U. (1978) "Perceiving, Anticipating, and Imagining", in: Wade Savage, C. (ed.) *Perception and Cognition. Issues in the Foundation of Psychology*. University of Minnesota Press, pp. 89–105.
Pred, A. (1990) "Making Histories and Constructing Human Geographies", in: Pred, A. (ed.) *Making Histories and Constructing Human Geographies. The Local Transformation of Practice, Power Relations, and Consciousness*. Westview Press, pp. 3-18.
Prosser, J. (1998) "The Status of Image-based Research", in: Prosser, J. (ed.) *Image-based Research. A Sourcebook for Qualitative Researchers*. Falmer Press, pp. 97-112.
Psenner, A. (1998) *4/5 New York. Eine Situationsstudie*. Thesis at the TU-Vienna
Psenner, A. (2001) *Wahrnehmung im urbanen öffentlichen Raum. Ein Feldforschungsprojekt in der Praterstraße in Wien/ Leopoldstadt*. Doctoral thesis at the TU-Vienna
Psenner, Angelika (2002a) "Stadt – Raum – Wahrnehmung", *dérive* nr. 7, pp. 28-31
Psenner, Angelika (2002b) "'Also unten ist's schön und oben ist's Bibione' (Visuelles) Wahrnehmen im urbanen öffentlichen Raum", SWS Rundschau, Heft 1/2002, pp. 29-52
Reichert, D. (1996) „Räumliches Denken als Ordnen der Dinge", in: Reichert, D. (ed.) *Räumliches Denken*. vdf Hochschulverlag AG an der ETH Zürich, pp. 15-55

Riis, J. A. (1971/ Orig. 1890) *How the Other Half Lives. Studies Among the Tenements of New York*, Dover Publications, Inc.

Rudofsky, B. (1995/ Orig. 1964) *Strassen für Menschen*, Residenzverlag.

Rykwert, J. (1990) „Für die Stadt – Argumente für ihre Zukunft", in: Rykwert, J. (ed.) *Die Welt der Stadt*. München.

Simmel, G. (1999/ 1957) „Die Philosophie der Landschaft", in: Riedel, J. (ed.) *Schriftenreihe des Forschungsschwerpunkts Kulturlandschaftsforschung*. Christian Brandstätter Verlag, pp. 26-31.

Smith, N. (1993) "Gentrification in New York City", in: Häußermann, H. and Siebel, W. (ed.) *New York, Strukturen einer Metropole*. Suhrkamp Verlag, pp. 182-204.

Waldenfels, B. (1986) „Gänge durch die Landschaft", in: Smuda, M. (ed.) *Landschaft*. Suhrkamp Verlag, pp. 29-43.

Wentz, M. (ed.) (1991) *Stadt-Räume. Die Zukunft des Städtischen*. Frankfurter Beiträge, Bd. 2. Campus Verlag.

Winston, B. (1998) "The Camera Never Lies. The Partiality of Photographic Evidence", in: Prosser, J. (ed.) *Image-based Research. A Sourcebook for Qualitative Researchers*. Falmer Press, pp. 60-68.

The Rise of Urban Symbols through Cultural Policies
Three Flagship Cultural Projects between Internationalisation Strategies and Local Resistance

Brigitte Schwab

Introduction: Cultural policy and urban development

In this contribution to the book on city images and urban regeneration, we shall analyse three major cultural policy projects in Switzerland, which can be considered city marketing strategies.

A sterling example of a major cultural initiative in Switzerland is the construction of the Lucerne Cultural and Convention Centre by the Lake (*Kultur und Kongresszentrum Luzern* known by the German acronym KKL), which was completed in 2000. Designed by the French architect Jean Nouvel, the multipurpose complex with a roof jutting extensively out over the lake, is home to the famous classical music festival *Lucerne Festival* [1]. The centrepiece of the building is the concert hall, with world-class acoustics and a seated capacity of 1800. In addition to the concert hall, there are also two smaller conference halls, equipped with the latest audiovisual installations, as well as an art museum and a restaurant. The building cost SF 250 million (€ 170 million) making it the most expensive building that the city, which has only 61,000 inhabitants, ever commissioned.

There had been talk of a "theatre revival" in Zurich at the end of the 1990s, as the city's cultural policy in general was experiencing a new awakening. The city managed to appoint the internationally famous and successful director Christoph Marthaler as artistic director in the year 2000. With the new cultural centre planned already by his predecessor in the former Escher-Wyss industrial estate, which Marthaler would turn into a new playhouse with three stages shortly after his arrival, it now

[1] *Previously Luzerner Internationale Musikfestwochen*

has four theatres with 1600 seats[2]. Subsidies were increased several times for the Marthaler era up to 40%, and ultimately to SF 30 million (€ 19,3 million). Marthaler received the prize for best German-speaking theatre twice in a row.

But yet, the local theatre-going audiences stayed away of his very critical theatre, the number of subscription tickets dropped by 40%, while the costs could not be kept in check, in spite of the cash injections.
Things came to a head on 1 September 2002. The five-year contract with Christoph Marthaler was terminated early by the board of directors at the end of the 2002/2003 season. The news was received with lack of understanding and derision, and gave rise to rallies of solidarity and protests and resulted in serious damage for the image of Zurich and of Switzerland.
In the third case study, we analyse the establishment of French Ballet choreographer Maurice Béjart and his troupe in Lausanne in 1987. In the spring of that year, Béjart announced that he intended to move his contemporary *Ballet du XXème siècle* from Brussels.

The Lausanne authorities were able to seize the opportunity, initiating negotiations and concluding agreements in record time to get *Ballet Béjart Lausanne.* The first performance of the Ballet took place in

---

[2] *In addition to the traditional Pfauen Theatre (800 seats), the Schiffbau with three theatres (Schiffbau hall: 500 seats; Box: 200 seats; Atrium: 100 seats).*

Lausanne already at the beginning of the following year. Béjart also founded his *"Ecole Rudra"* ballet school in Lausanne and, together with Phillipe Brunschwieg the "Prix de Lausanne" talent competition.

In the context of increasing city competition at the national and international level, the question arises as to what extent such cultural initiatives can be considered city marketing strategies, and what the related challenges are. Compared on an international scale, the Swiss urban network is characterised by relatively small, but closely situated cities, and sound stability (Kuster and Meier 2000). Even so, the formation of metropolitan areas has in the last twenty years been a sign of an increasing polarisation of the polycentric city network. Increasingly smaller conurbations are emerging in the immediate vicinity of a larger metropolitan area, thereby becoming a sort of satellite conurbation. A vertical integration takes place (Kuster and Meier 2000) to the benefit of Zurich in particular[3].

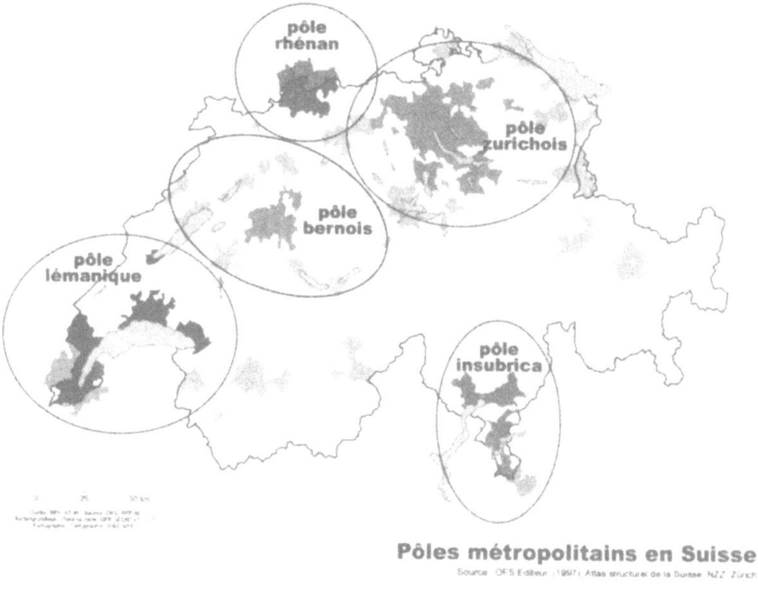

Pôles métropolitains en Suisse

Source: OFS Editeur (1997): Atlas structurel de la Suisse, NZZ Zürich

---

[3] *The causes of this phenomenon are deindustrialisation and the structural change of the economy in favour of the service sector (tertiarisation) as well as the improvement of inter-regional transport connection. The increasing commuter flows from increasingly more remote cities to the central city is typical for this development.*

Zurich, Geneva and Basel are the three Swiss cities with an outstanding international dimension (Brugger 1992), the only ones that can be said to have a role to play on the European horizon. The predominance of the Zurich, Geneva and Basel conurbations is not related only to their population density and territorial expansion, but also to their economic potential, as their inhabitants generate 43% of the net income of households, although only 38% of the population lives in these conurbations (Kuster and Meier 2000: 64)[4].

As to our three case studies of major cultural project in the cities of Zurich, Lausanne and Lucern, the given urban context is the following. Zurich is the only city of considerable European importance in our sample, and can be compared with cities such as Lyon or Turin (Conseil Fédéral 1999: 12). It is by far the largest Swiss city in terms of population (340,000 inhabitants) and also the financial centre of the Swiss economy. It is also the undisputed centre of the greater Zurich metropolitan area. Lausanne can be compared at European level with Liverpool, Thessalonica or Nancy. From the economic point of view, the service sector is very pronounced here too, although less geared to financial services than Zurich or Geneva. From a national perspective, Lausanne is in the "*aire métropolitaine lémanique*"[5] in which it vies with Geneva for dominance as the centre – a contest it appears to have lost. Finally, Lucerne must be designated as an "isolated" city (Schuler, Huissoud et al. 1997). It is located outside the metropolitan areas and is also a small city in terms of population (60,000 inhabitants).

***Kultur und Kongresszentrum Luzern* KKL; from calls for a new concert hall to a Jean Nouvel prestige building**

At the beginning the line of argument ran that if the *Lucerne Festival* was to maintain its international reputation, it had to have a bigger and more festive concert hall. The city marketing pitch was also present from the outset, but gained continuously in importance during the planning process. The call for a new concert hall, supported by a motion in the

---

[4] The number of positions in the service sector with higher increase in value is also typical; in 1991, 51% of such positions were concentrated in urban areas in these three conurbations. The structural and economic strengths of Zurich, Base and Geneva is moreover reflected in their appeal to international companies: 17% of the headquarters of multinational companies, and even 40% of all mainly foreign firms, are located in these three central cities (Brugger 1992).

[5] *Lake Geneva metropolitan area*

city's Parliament for a spatial design for cultural events, led to the creation of a work group on this issue and several interventions in the municipal parliament, amounting to a downright "cultural offensive" (as mayor Franz Kurzmeyer called it) in the City of Lucerne (Bühlmann 1998: 47).

The Lucerne cultural area planning initially favoured the idea of renovating the "Meili Building" (named after the architect), where the *Lucerne Festival* had been held hitherto. But personalities like the former mayor and the head of the Landis & Gyr cultural foundation, threw their weight behind the construction of a new "large-scale building." On August 1986, the Lucerne cultural area planning work group presented a report relating the various claims from different cultural groups that have raised since de beginning of the cultural debate in Lucerne and reached the conclusion that a professional planning firm had to be consulted for the coordination, elaboration and planning of the different cultural projects. In a motion on 15 October 1986 the firm *Hayek Engineering AG*[6] was entrusted to conduct a "Draft study on how to optimise the allocation of cultural areas in Lucerne"[7].

The publication of this study on 24 May 1988 gave rise to rosy dreams on the one side, and boundless outrage on the other, giving the culture debate in Lucerne a completely new impetus. The study evaluated the various ideas and projects and quantified the costs. The town council had counted on cultural investments of about SF 50 million (€ 35 million). The Hayek Report however stated that the renovation of the Meili Building alone would cost SF 96 million (€ 62.7 million). The study put a multi-purpose concert, municipal and convention hall, to be situated next to the railway station on the lake, at the top of the list of recommendation. At the same time, the report recommended that alternative culture projects were to be supported with subsidies of SF 1.5 million (€ 1.2 million) as well. This proposition of a garnered support immediately among wealthy personalities. For instance, Alice Bucher[8] offered the architectural competition to the City of Lucerne, who decided to organise a popular vote on this donation, in order to guaranty the democratic legitimacy of the process, which gave a 62% approbation on 5 of April 1989. As well a newly established *Lucerne Concert Hall Foundation* already allocated sizeable sums of private funds for the project to construct a new building rather than renovating the old concert hall.

---

6 *Consulting firm founded by Nicolas Hayek (the inventor of Swatch) in 1963.*

7 *"Konzeptstudie zur Optimierung der Bereitstellung von Kulturräumen in Luzern" Draft study to optimise the allocation of cultural areas in Lucerne"*

8 *former publisher of the « Lucerneer Neuesten Nachrichten » and owner of the Druckerei C.J. Bucher [printing works]*

Impressive projects were submitted to the architectural competition, especially the winning project "Opus" by French architect Jean Nouvel. Preference, however, tilted towards the third-place project by Lausanne architect Rodolphe Luscher, because the first two projects had not met the conditions concerning costs and the utilisation of the lake. This preference for the Lausanne architect angered the jury, however, and Jean Nouvel filed a complaint against the city for contempt of the competition. Faced with this mess, the city decided to have further professional planning carried out, and appointed Thomas Held[9] as general coordinator. In the summer of 1991, he submitted a "general design for a cultural and convention centre on the lake," which provided for a multi-purpose new building, with optimal use of space, built in two stages for SF 180 million (€ 116 million) with a concert hall, a medium-sized and a small hall for various purposes, as well as conference rooms, a restaurant and the art museum.
To sum up, we can note that under the influence of millions already collected by the concert hall foundation, the gift of Alice Bucher, and the vision of the consultant Thomas Held, the project went from renovating the existing concert hall, to the prestige building for the Lucerne cultural and convention centre designed by Jean Nouvel. The private funds from the *Lucerne Concert Hall Foundation* and Alice Bucher played an important role in exerting pressure for a new concert hall building. This was also in line with the reasoning of the town council concerning the postponing of the Pro Arte project[5]: there were no other important co-financiers. All three Pro Arte exponents withdrew in protest and disappointment. They were also sharply critical of the "international lobby, which not least owing to altogether direct financial and economic entanglements, exerted such great pressure, that it succeeded in having its way"[10].

***Schauspielhaus Zürich;* The theatre revival, the unplanned *Schiffbau* hall and the damage to Zurich's image**

The initial project for the Zurich Theatre was to build a new cultural centre. Local relations at the *Pfauen*-theatre were so bad, that studios had to be rented at all ends and corners of the city. Concentrating in one

[9] *Thomas Held is known in Switzerland as a leader of the 1968 movement in Zurich, but then changed completely his political orientation. He worked as consultant at Hayek Engineering and then founded his own consulting firm. Actually he is the director of the first Swiss Think-Tank "Avenir Suisse" financed by the Swiss employer organisation "EconomieSuisse".*

[10] *Vaterland, 4 December 1990*

location was expected to result in savings of some SF 700'000 (€ 450'000) per year. A suitable plot of land was soon found on the former Sulzer industrial estate at the Escher-Wyss Platz. Architectural firms worked out studies for the planned new centre. The competition description mentioned already that a "Centre Pompidou" was to go up in West Zurich[11]! In fact, the design now already foresaw, in addition to an off-theatre a restaurant, the Moods Jazz club, as well as private offices for architecture, graphics, stage construction and computer technology. An in place for insiders, a cultural centre as a pulse-taker of Zurich, the epicentre of the national, if not the international theatre world (NZZ 28 May 2001).
Concurrently with the construction of the cultural centre, the board of directors initiated a procedure to find and select a new artistic director for the Zurich Theatre. On 4 October 1997, the chairman of the board announced to the international press the appointment of Christoph Marthaler. Marthaler had signed a five-year contract the evening before. On 4 October 1997, the NZZ waxed with euphoria, calling the appointment the "event of the century;" for Marthaler was at the time touted as the "cult director of the 1990s" in Germany. As manager and artistic director of the Zurich Theatre, Marthaler was to stage two of his own productions a year. This would enable holders of subscription tickets to get to know him, while attracting greater international attention on the theatre.
A downright "theatre revival" was under way: To provide "start-up help for Marthaler," on 15 April 1999, the general meeting of the theatre voted to tripe the share capital from one half to 1.5 million Swiss francs (€ 966'000). Positive commitment signals were also sent by the canton, which had hitherto held no theatre shares; the city and the canton wanted to hold half of the shares in the future. Furthermore, the theatre was to get a total of two million francs (€ 1,2 millions) more from the city and canton coffers for the 2000/2001 season.
The application for an increase in subsidies submitted to the local council of the City of Zurich in the beginning of 2000 (before Marthaler took over as manager and artistic director in the summer) stated that, under the new director, the theatre would acquire a Europe-wide renown and attraction. That is why it was necessary to reach deep into the pockets, because in order to be able to build the theatre that Marthaler had in mind, the then annual budget had to be increased from around 39 million francs (€ 25 millions, whereby the number of seats would go up by 56%, and the number of performances by 25% (NZZ, 19 January

[11] *Neue Zurcher Zeitung (a local daily, known by the Germany acronym NZZ), 28 May 2001*

2000) explain mayor Josef Estermann, who thought it was right for the City of Zurich to compete with and be comparable to other European cities not only on the economic front but also in the cultural sector.
Yet it was not merely a matter of a theatre revival; the entire cultural policy was awakening after a "long sleep." After the lean 1990s, where emphasis was on maintaining current standards, the cultural budget for 2001 was increased by SF 7 million (€ 4'5 million). Culture had in the meantime emerged as an important location factor for tourism and economic appeal.
These were the conditions under which Marthaler began his tenure as manager and artistic director in the summer of 2000; and the presentation of the first programme gave rise to the highest expectations, when the Marthaler era was ushered in officially on 21 September 2001 with the leading business and political personalities in attendance, with the gentle satire on Switzerland "Hotel Angst"[12]. In spite of a few financial problems that still had to be dealt with, the prevailing opinion was that Zurich had entered the golden age of a European theatre Eldorado. "Everyone was in raptures that Zurich was now playing in the Champions League of German-speaking theatre"[13]

International reviews initially raved too, praising the excellent working conditions that Marthaler found in Zurich, comparing the city with Berlin and its legendary Schiffbauerdamm Theatre. The international hymn of praise was equally laudatory when it singled out Marthaler's theatre in the summer of 2001 and 2002 as the "best theatre in the German-speaking world," a distinction supported by invitations to the Berlin theatre festival. When owing to persistent financial problems (in spite of the increases in subsidies) and a precipitous drop in the audience figures, the board of directors decided to dismiss Marthaler at the end of the 2002/2003 season, Zurich's image was seriously tarnished. Actually, Marthaler's early dismissal was announced on 1 September 2002, only one week after Marthaler had been singled out for the second time in a row for the best German-speaking theatre. The newly elected mayor, Elmar Ledergerber, adopted the following stance: „I am grateful to Christoph Marthaler, for bringing to Zurich a theatre of European calibre. And I would like to congratulate the team for earning the distinction of best theatre in the German-speaking world. But the finest theatre is of no use to us, when even the New York Times is reporting that in spite of the increased subsidies, it is going bankrupt. That would create a gap in the cultural life of the city, one we simply cannot accept. The damage the

[12] *Anxiety Hotel*
[13] *Zurich daily „Tages Anzeiger", 2 September 2002.*

city's image from the loss of Marthaler is great, but that damage would be even greater if the theatre were to go bankrupt."
The reaction in the local press was one of sheer disappointment: "Zurich is being ridiculed in the international press. Once again, it comes across as small-minded and provincial"[14]. The Austrian dramatist and Büchner Prize winner Elfriede Jelinek interpreted Marthaler's dismissal as an "expression of Swiss self-hatred," which "throws its best artists and thinkers in the dustbin," and "if a mirror is held up to them, they prefer to discard it." In the German weekly "Die Zeit," Thomas Hürlimann wrote that the "ruling class of this city could not bear this great, exciting, shimmering and disturbing theatre." The case was mentioned in line with many such other Swiss disasters[15] (-- the long awaited cure for which would require a Marthaler!

***Ballet Béjart Lausanne;* The coup under cover of darkness the relocation of Maurice Béjart's ballet troupe in Lausanne**

At the origin of Béjart's move to Lausanne was his desire to leave Brussels. He justified the choice of Lausanne as follows: "[Lausanne is a] lively, nice, welcoming city, well situated for transport and communications, and at the same time sufficiently quiet and out of the way for creative and productive work. That is more important to me than big capitals where you risk tackling too many things at once. They are more suitable for dissemination rather than creation"[16].
This was an unexpected, yet welcome opportunity, one which the Lausanne authorities did not let go by. The driving forces were led by mayor Paul-René Martin, the Minister for Finance Yvette Jaggi and the official responsible for culture, Marie-Claude Jéquier. They conducted the negotiations with Béjart in record time. The Lausanne authorities found out about Béjart's intention to come to Lausanne, the negotiations were conducted in a small circle among the aforementioned individuals, yet an indiscretion leaked the news early. On June 12th, the headlines in the local press read: "Béjart préfère Lausanne" *24 heures*, "Béjart à Lausanne" *Le Matin*, "La valse de Béjart" *La Suisse* (Pastori 1998: 7). In Belgium, on the other hand, the news broke like a bombshell. The daily *Le Soir* wrote immediately that no effort must be spared to prevent Béjart from treating himself to a golden retirement in Lausanne (Pastori 1998:

---

[14] *Opinion in the Sunday NZZ, 1 September 2002.*
[15] *the grounding of Swissair, Switzerland's involvement with the Nazi regime in World War II, bank secrecy, money laundering , the Crossair crash, unconventionally reprimanded Ambassador from Berlin, the crazed rampage in the Swiss parliament, etc.)*
[16] *L'Illustré, 24 June 1987.*

7). In fact, Mr M. Philippe Monfils, Minister President of the *French-speaking Community of Belgium* travelled to Lithuania in an effort to exhaust every possibility to persuade Béjart to change his mind. At a press conference, he underscored: "Béjart is not in serious difficulty in Belgium. There are no financial problems. I am ready to add millions if need be. I hope that Béjart will not lose out by going to Lausanne or elsewhere. In Belgium he has the means and resources, autonomy, independence and an audience"[17].
It is interesting to point out that during the media briefings and also at the local council debate, which was held only on September 8th, after the troupe had already occupied the provisional premises, the city marketing line of marketing was kept in the background. The impact of the ballet troupe's arrival on the Lausanne cultural scene was stressed instead, with reassurances that the corresponding subsidies would not be provided at the expense of the other culture creators. However, at the creation of the foundation on 28 September 1987, the city's name featured in the in the new name of the troupe: *Ballet Béjart Lausanne.* Furthermore, an article of the foundation stipulated that the troupe could not perform in other Swiss cities without the foundation's consent. The city marketing through guest performances by the ballet was first stressed in the 1990s. For instance, in the *Journal de Genève et Gazette de Lausanne* of 29 May 1996, in which Maurice Béjart said: "I carry the name of Lausanne far and wide. When I work with the Ballet at the Paris Opera, Béjart Ballet Lausanne is in Copenhagen. Another day, it is in Tokyo or in Italy. The city is promoted everywhere. Lausanne has – and will have a name insofar as it boasts exportable cultural institutions." This effect appears to be recognised by other cities, in which Béjart gives guest performances, who are courting him to relocate to their city. In 1996, for instance, there were rumours that Béjart wanted to become the company in residence of the *Berliner Staatsoper,* but he dismissed them at a press conference, saying that he felt very attached to Lausanne, but did stage productions in major venues such as Paris and Berlin. As a result, the *Berliner Staatsoper* broke off all cooperation with Béjart, as they were disappointed and felt betrayed. The incident is an indication of how fierce the clashes round the 69-year choreographer were. Yvette Jaggi was relieved therefore that Béjart would be staying[18]. In the same year (on 4 December 1996), Béjart was made an honorary citizen of Lausanne, though this distinction stood only in little stead: "The citizens of Lausanne are proud to have their name placed next to yours,"

---

[17] *Gazette de Lausanne, 20 June 1987*
[18] *NZZ, 29 May 1996*

said Yvette Jaggi, now the mayor of Lausanne, "This homage is a way to show our gratitude to the ambassador you have become."

Conclusion: Cultural projects as city marketing strategy

Strategies can be grasped at the cognitive level through rhetoric. Among our three cases, the city marketing rhetoric was most pronounced for the Zurich theatre.

In the mid 1990s, it was the hiring of Christoph Marthaler as artistic director to the *Schauspielhaus Zürich* that bolstered the image-rhetoric for the City of Zurich: he enjoys worldwide attention, and with two new productions a year, the Zurich theatre landscape was to regain international acclaim. Investments flowed in and the Schiffbau-building originally considered as a work centre turned out to be a genuine cultural centre with two theatres, a restaurant and a Jazz club. There was talk of a "Centre Pompidou" and an "Epicentre of World Culture." The argument, put forward in particular by mayor Josef Estermann, was that Zurich should try compete with and be comparable to other European cities not only on the economic front but also in the cultural sector[19]. At the beginning of Marthaler's tenure, everyone in Zurich enthused that the city was now playing in the Champions League of German-speaking theatre[20].

In the case of the KKL in Lucerne, the city marketing pitch was there from the outset, though it picked up momentum during the planning phase. Plans for the Lucerne cultural centre were initially focused on the simple renovation of the antique concert hall. It was select personalities and the professional turn of the debate around the cultural centre that gave preference to the idea of a new, multipurpose building. The result was the prestige building by Jean Nouvel, in which the economic multiplier effect, as well as the international renown gained importance compared to the original idea.

Finally, in Lausanne, the relocation of Maurice Béjart and his troupe was concluded in record time away from the prying public eye. In the local council debate, people argued that the Ballet Béjart Lausanne would enliven the local cultural scene. It was only in the course of the year that the city marketing pitch veered more to the centre, culminating in making Béjart an honorary citizen of Lausanne. The city's mayor called him an "ambassador" for the great contribution he had made to Lausanne's international renown.

---

[19] *NZZ 19 January 2000*

[20] *Tages Anzeiger 2 September 2002*

It can be noted that the rhetoric justifying major cultural policy projects has changed, ant that in the light of our case-studies Bianchini's thesis is correct that during the 1990s, cultural policy was discovered more as a localisation factor in a context of growing globalisation, whereas formerly the integration function of culture (after the 1960s) and economic utility (in the 1980s) were more prominent. The change observed in the justificatory discourse to this city marketing rhetoric, as well as the importance it acquired in the expansion of the Zurich theatre, encourage such visibility.

In view of the current constellation in the Swiss city competition, these city-marketing projects certainly make sense. Thus, Lausanne, which has already all but lost the competition with Geneva for supremacy in the leman metropolitan area, it has ventured in the dance niche; for it cannot catch up with Geneva when it comes to the opera or conventions. Lucerne, which is in a poor initial position geographically, since it is outside the metropolitan areas, staked the highest wager, but pulled off a courageous but also successful coup with the convention and cultural centre. Competition with other Swiss convention cities (Geneva, Basel, Zurich) is very keen, however, and it remains to be seen whether the small city has not ventured out of its league. Finally Zurich, which started from the best initial position in the Swiss city hierarchy, appears not to want to specialise, but has invested in different fields (bringing the opera house under the purview of the canton, increasing the subsidies of the concert hall, and expanding the theatre).

In conclusion, it can be said that in the case of Béjart, as with the KKL the plans were successful, whereas the "theatre revival" in Zurich wound up as a disaster for the city's image! The poor communication form of the board of directors of the theatre was partly to blame, however it must be said that music and dance are far more suited to city marketing strategies than theatres (in particular of the Marthaler critical variety!) City marketing must project beautiful and positive images to the world in order to attract international attention. This must not be limited to bringing big artistic names to the city (like Christoph Marthaler), but must include a certain content. The board of directors of the theatre was in fact reproached because Marthaler's dismissal was not about money, but about the censorship of a certain type of critical theatre.

An important factor for the success of such city marketing cultural projects is the local embodiment of the projects. These cultural policy initiatives are geared to an international, mobile public and are very expensive. However, they are paid for by the city itself where, in the case of Marthaler, the public was left totally out of the picture, and stayed away from Marthalers productions. In the case of Béjart too, criticism were raise about the argument that the local dance scene is being stimulated by Béjart, and doubts appeared on what the thirteen productions performed by Béjart in Lausanne per year really bring to the city. In the case of the KKL the Lucerne Society was promised before the vote on the construction of the KKL, that the premises could be used under favourable (non-commercial) conditions. Regulations concerning the right of use were enacted, stipulating that the halls must be made available for 198 days under non-commercial conditions; however, an event in the concert hall under these conditions still costs SF 2'900 (€ 1'860), and entails only the basic equipment[21]. Under these conditions, the KKL is prohibitively expensive for most associations in Lucerne, what the local daily commented as follows: "The city had actually 'bought" their vote"[22].

The discrepancy between the international orientation and low local embedment fosters the line of argument, that cultural institutions with cross-regional renown must be financed by larger regional authorities than by the city alone. Thus, the opera house has already been overtaken by the canton of Zurich, and the idea propped to do the same with other important cultural institutions. In Lausanne and in Lucerne as well, the Béjart and KKL projects have encouraged inter-municipal agreements on the regional financing of urban culture (the *Fonds intercommunal de soutien aux institutions culturelles lausannoises*[23] and the *Regionalen Kutlurkonferenez Luzern*[24]). The new federal project of equalisation of revenue and costs between the cantons which is actually discussed, also provides for an inter-cantonal financing of cultural institutions of supra-national importance.

References

Brugger, E.-A. (1992) *Weltstädte - Schweizer Städte. Die Funktion schweizerischer Grossstädte im weltwirtschaftlichen Kontext.* NFP 25, Schweizerischer Nationalfonds zur Förderung der Wissenschaftlichen Forschung.

Bühlmann, K. (1998) *KKL - Kultur und Kongresszentrum Luzern. Die Geschichte seines Werdens, die Zukunft seiner Idee.* Rotkreuz, Zürcher Druck und Verlag AG.

Conseil Fédéral (1999) *Rapport sur les centres urbains.* Bern.

Kuster, J. and H. R. Meier (2000). *La Suisse urbaine, évolution spatiale et structure actuelle*. Berne, Office fédéral du développement territorial.

Mayntz, R. and F. Scharpf, Eds. (1995) *Gesellschaftliche Selbstregelung und politische Steuerung.* Frankfurt/New York, Campus.

---

[21] *standard lighting, as well as the obligation to use and to pay trained KKL hall staff*

[22] *Beilage der Lucerneer Zeitung, 21 March 2000*

[23] *Inter-municipal support fund for Lausanne cultural institutions*

[24] *Lucerne Regional Cultural Conference*

Pastori, J.-P. (1998) *Béjart Ballet Lausanne, 10 ans de création*. Lausanne, Fondation Béjart Ballet.
Schuler, M., T. Huissoud, et al. (1997) *Atlas structurel de la Suisse*. Zurich, Verlag NZZ.

Newspapers:

Neue Zürcher Zeitung
Tages Anzeiger
Luzerner Neueste Nachrichten
newspaper articles from the City Archive of Lausanne

Creating "Spatial Identity": A Way to improve the Periphery?

Lars Bölling

Zwischenstadt

After decades of 'inward-focus' the centre of attention of town planning has shifted since the 1990s to the expansion of the cities into their surroundings. The many and varied assessments of this phenomena are mirrored in the variety of terms used to describe it: Whilst labels like "periphery" and "suburbanisation" are still defined with reference to the traditional city centre, newer terms have been gaining ground which examine the increasing independence of (sub)urban structures emerging between the cities. The expression "Zwischenstadt" coined by Thomas Sieverts[1] represents this point of view. According to Sieverts, new structures of settlement can no longer be classified under the conventional concepts of 'town' and 'country'. The "Zwischenstadt" is no longer hierarchically dependent upon the city centre as the first generation of suburban settlements once was.

The first indications of a more independent identity are beginning to emerge, fragments of urbanity that have little in common with the traditional 'image of the city'. A new vocabulary needs to be developed to describe this new type of city.

Experts are agreed that it is necessary to improve this (in urban-terms) unplanned emerging structure. The continuing 'periphery debate' is proof of an increasing awareness of the functional, economic and ecological as well as social and aesthetic challenges presented by the "Zwischenstadt".

Ladenburger Kolleg

The "Zwischenstadt" is the focus of the research project 'Ladenburger Kolleg', financed by the Gottfried Daimler and Karl Benz foundation. As part of the research project ten universities and research institutes throughout Germany and Switzerland are undertaking interdisciplinary investigations into strategies for improving the former suburban structures that have rapidly grown in the second half of the 20th century.[2]

---

[1] *Sieverts, Thomas: Zwischenstadt: Cities without Cities: Between Place and World, Space and Time, Town and Country. Routledge 2003*

[2] *this contribution summarises the first results of the 'urban-design' part of the project by Prof. Wolfgang Christ (teamleader) and Lars Bölling at the Bauhaus-Univesity in*

Rhine-Main-Area

The Rhine-Main area serves as a reference area of study. Symbolically represented by the Frankfurt skyline and economically highly interconnected, this region is perceived from outside as a unit. However, from within there is only a fragmentary awareness of regional identity. The Rhine-Main area extends across three German states. Unlike other urban regions it is not mono-centric but encompasses six further large towns in addition to Frankfurt, two of which are local state capitals. Political and planning initiatives to promote regional integration have failed or succeeded only partially. The fragmentation of this space corresponds to the major inter-municipal conflicts, for instance between the city of Frankfurt and its neighbouring municipalities.

As a result of decades of suburbanisation of housing, but also of workplaces, shopping and leisure the hierarchical relationship between the core of the city and the former outskirts has changed fundamentally. The core has not become unimportant but is no longer necessarily the only centre of functional density and economic activity.

Figure 1: Centre of Rhine-Main area

Weimar which aims at identifiing strategies to improve the spatial quality of the Zwischenstadt

Figure 2: Centre of Rhine-Main area with area of study

Despite the shift away from the centre to the regions, the perception of the city as a whole is still related to the city centre. This perception is further influenced by the way city maps are drawn. As soon as we realise that the typical, concentric map is just one way of representing the urban structure of a polycentric, interdependent region, we become aware that the city can also be seen from different points of view. This idea has motivated us to 'read' the city in a new way – starting from its edges.
As a result, those areas of the city or region in which the highest levels of activity and transformation can be observed become the centre of attention, areas which seen traditionally lie on the edge of the city.

For the purposes of the research project a typical section was taken across the centre of the Rhine-Main region that is defined by a planned railway connection, the "Regionaltangente West" (RTW). The new railway represents a semi-circular connection between important centres of employment and housing in the area surrounding Frankfurt and fulfils increasing tangential (i.e. not concentric) transport demands in the region. Across much of its length it follows the western border between Frankfurt and its independent and prosperous neighbouring areas. It defines a space which has experienced nearly a century of suburbanisation and as such ideal for the study of prototypical structures of the "Zwischenstadt".

The 'urban-design' part of the project undertaken at the Bauhaus-Universität Weimar [3] examines strategies for developing spatial qualities for the area of study. The first step aims to decode the "spatial identity" of this particular Zwischenstadt by the means of "Drawn Hypotheses". The result is a new kind of atlas of the "Zwischenstadt" whose centre is not the traditional core but motorway interchanges and their accompanying suburban residential, commercial and retail centres.
Based upon this atlas as well as an investigation of international reference examples, the project attempts to investigate the transformation processes of the Zwischenstadt as a result of structural changes in society.
The second step aims at identifiing and developing design characteristics for the improvement of the Zwischenstadt. In a final step these models are used to develop and assess exemplary transformation scenarios for the area of study.

Area of Study
The area of study comprises municipalities and districts typical of the Zwischenstadt. Bad Homburg and Oberursel, both much-in-demand residential areas bordering the Taunus hills, are some of the most prosperous municipalities in Germany and are becoming increasingly important as commercial centres. The suburbs of Frankfurt with Ernst May's neighbourhoods and the "NordWestStadt" in the northern part of the area of study represent different phases of suburban housing development. By contrast Eschborn, due largely to its position, has become synonymous with growing service industry and commerce in suburbia. It provides 30.000 workplaces but has only 20.000 inhabitants. Together with the suburban commercial centres at Frankfurt-Rödelheim and Sossenheim, a considerable concentration of trade and commerce has become established around the Northwest junction of Frankfurt in the middle of the area of study. Sulzbach is well known as the location of the first suburban shopping centre in Germany, with its own direct motorway access built in the 1960s at the edge of the Frankfurt suburb Hoechst which, with its now defunct paint-works, was once one of the

[3] *by Wolfgang Christ and Lars Bölling*

most important suburban industrial areas in Frankfurt. Kelsterbach with an employment growth of 130% since 1980 is one of the most dynamic neighbourhoods in the area, due to its proximity to the airport. The airport itself, the single largest local employer in the area, has become a key point in the region due to its nodal transport function as well as an increasing reputation as a congress and leisure area. The final stop of the planned RTW and the edge of our area of study is Neu-Isenburg, with over 20.000 tax-paying employees a further service-oriented commercial centre at the edge of Frankfurt.

Figure 3: Spatial characteristics of the area of study

Topology
Developing a common spatial identity for this highly functionally-interconnected space is hampered by its political fragmentation. The perception of space is characterised by driving on the motorway, i.e. primarily through large-scale symbols in space. The Taunus-hills on the north-west horizon, the skyline of Frankfurt's financial skyscrapers and the take-off and landing of aircraft at the airport are key points of orientation from almost anywhere in the area of study.

The area of study was divided into a southern area dominated by the airport and a northern area between Bad Homburg and Frankfurt Hoechst for the purposes of detailed study. This area is characterised by a shift in the relationship between figure and ground in the urban grain, a typical characteristic of Zwischenstadt with amorphous clusters of building and infrastructure enclosing pockets of remaining open space.

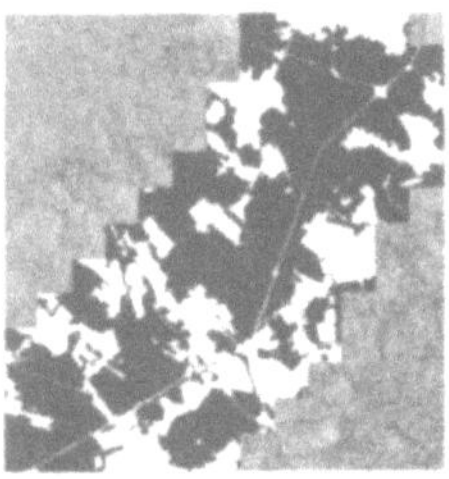

Figure 4: Northern area – figure and ground

Structures
Only 100 years ago this area was solely agricultural land. The oldest settlements are therefore villages whose locations were determined by topography and the pattern of rivers. The building of the motorway in the 1930s was the basis for all further growth and suburbanisation that followed after the war. The village centres are no longer points of reference, in fact they are typically not even directly connected to the transport infrastructure. Residential areas have sprung up around these, particularly single family housing from the 50s to the 80s but also multi-storey dwellings. Alt-Niederursel next to the Nordweststadt is a good example of the lack of structural interconnection that characterises the Zwischenstadt.

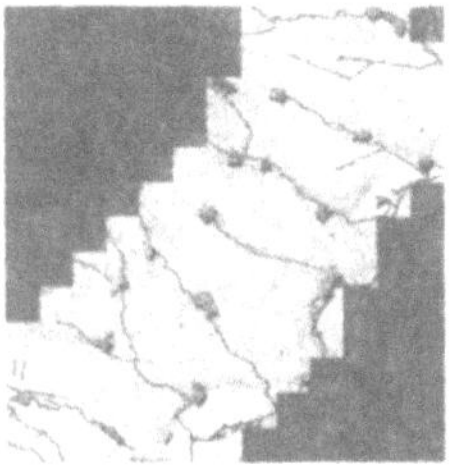

Figure 5: Northern area – former centres and rivers

Figure 6: Niederursel and the "NordWestStadt"

'functional' residential areas
From the 50s to the early 80s large numbers of individual family houses were built which characterise whole areas yet, despite an attempt to make each house individual, could be almost anywhere. These areas provide safe private realms with gardens, the paradigm of a fordist society with a clear spatial separation between work place and private dwelling. Public space is reduced to rational access ways for serial rows of individual houses.

Figure 7: "Cloned living"

Addresses
But in the last 15 years newer patterns of living have emerged which in spatial terms appear quite different to their 'functional' neighbours. We have introduced the term "address" to help describe this tendency. It stands for a comprehensive change in the originating conditions and the demands and expectations placed on suburban residential housing.

Here it is less the individual house and more the place – the address – of the residential area that is visually differentiated from its neighbours, a means of generating identity in the surrounding mediocrity of monofunctional centres. Addresses are 'created' through a variety of staged constructs using spatial, image-oriented or associative means. The area of study includes a variety of 'thematic settlements', perhaps most obviously the "ParkStadt 2000" in Frankfurt-Riedberg which uses pictorial elements to awaken associations with favourite holiday destinations.

Figure 8: "Address" in Sulzbach

Figure 9: "Parkstadt 2000"

Commercial areas

Similar tendencies can be observed in commercial developments. Most commercial areas in the area of study are monostructural, typically located at excellent transport locations. Examples, such as the particularly successful office area "Eschborn-Süd", demonstrate the reduction of local consideration to a minimum. It is the fordist pendant to the single family housing areas, monocultural office space reduced to the factors accessibility and maximum floor area.

Figure 10: Office Park Eschborn-Süd

However, companies are increasingly looking for locations which serve also as a representative address and a number of 'thematic work environments' have sprung up to meet this demand. As in the residential housing sector, this too reflects a change in the conditions and demands placed upon suburban commercial centres as a result of comprehensive structural change in the employment and business sectors. Towns such as Bad Homburg or municipalities on the edge of the Taunus hills have a 'home-advantage' combining good location with a 'good name' as well as a pleasant landscape. In respect of the ubiquity of "hard factors", the qualities of such addresses can become decisive location factors for businesses most notably those with highly-qualified staff.

Figure 11: Offices in Bad Homburg

Clusters

With its suburban concentrations and its new transport, commerce and business "centres" the area of study demonstrates clearly the growing 'emancipation' of the Zwischenstadt. Public space is no longer concentrated in the centre as in the traditional city, rather it has become established in new locations with all kinds of functions, for example the university in its own campus in green space.

Taken together the spatial-functional areas which are examined in the research project are indicative of a regional area with a comprehensive mixture of functions.

Figure 12: Northern area: clusters

In terms of quantity, the monofunctional areas dominate, products as it were of a 'spatial-functional division of labour'. These areas also dominate the public discussion of the Zwischenstadt – primarily negatively. However these areas have been joined by a whole range of new structures that go much further than purely functional aspects for which we have introduced the term "addresses".

A "Mature Periphery"

These developments provide clear indications for the maturing of former suburban structures. The older suburbanised zones of the expanded city often reach a phase of consolidation after a period of over 50 years rapid growth. The heterogeneous structure of these spaces have become independent of a direct dependency upon the city centre: This Zwischenstadt is no longer a temporally-defined place of dwelling but a formative and experiential environment, a natural habitat as it were of several generations. Growth is here too a similarly complex process as in the traditional city. The spatially determining structures of this Zwischenstadt have expanded and the different suburban areas have grown or are growing together.

Restructuring forces

This presents us with the a variety of challenges:

The pattern of structural change in society is the motor of structural transformation of these "mature peripheries": New media, an inter-permeation of living and working, increased leisure time, non-linear career development etc. provide impetus for restructuring forces in the monostructural residential, business and commercial areas in the periphery. Single family house estates, built under the paradigm of a fordist society, no longer automatically fulfil the demands and expectations of a service and leisure society. Similarly the monofunctional industrial estates built during the sixties to the eighties now have to compete with new "Business Parks" with an identity and address, and the typical suburban shopping centre must compete with new all-inclusive malls and revamped inner cities.

Parallel to this, the generation that 'built' the Zwischenstadt is retiring and the first wave of inheritancies, sales and change of ownership is beginning in the single family housing areas of the sixties and seventies. Industrial and commercial property from this time have now been written-off and are increasingly left to waste. In addition, increasing tangential traffic in the region also places new demands on regional infrastructure.

To summarise, large-scale transformation processes are at work that provide a central potential for an improvement of the Zwischenstadt.

Four models for an improvement of the Zwischenstadt

An analysis of international examples and of the area of study shows prototypical spatial transformations from which four models for an improvement of the Zwischenstadt have been identified.

1. "Addresses": The 'thematic staging' of spatial identities by means of image-associative, thematic or functional enrichment of suburban location.

The creation of "adresses" is the most obvious qualifying strategy that can be observed in the Zwischenstadt. Many international as well as

individual cases within the area of study indicate clearly this development [4]. It represents the comprehensive change in requirements a suburban neighbourhood is expected to fulfil as a result of progressive structural change in society: not only purely residential but also monofunctional industrial neighbourhoods must fulfil the requirements of a service, leisure and increasingly aging society and provide complex environments that are not only private 'cell' or workplace but also provide a sense of identity – an address.
The examples show that this development changes the appearance of suburban patterns of settlement. The demographic shift as described above also means that the older residential and industrial areas are primary areas of potential transformation.
In order to investigate the resulting potential of this development, the area between Bad Homburg and Frankfurt Hoechst was further divided into three 'districts'. Each district is characterised by building structure around an 'empty' centre, frequently bisected by infrastructure.

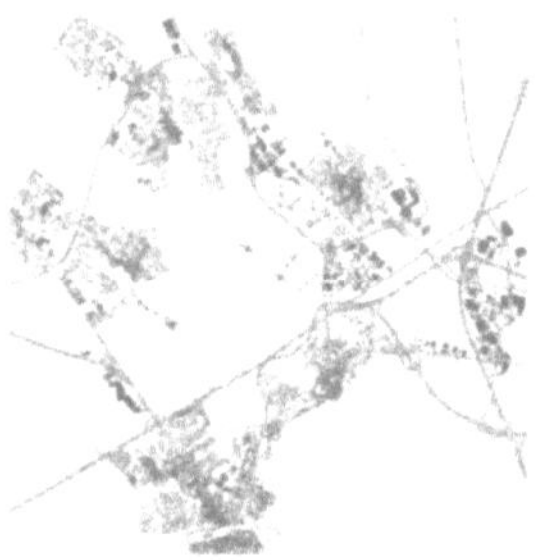

Figure 13: District – South ring

The picture shows clearly the quantity alone of the single family housing estates in the southern area between Eschborn and Frankfurt Hoechst which are potentially affected by forces of transformation. International examples demonstrate how such often 'faceless' areas can be transformed into places with an adress, whether through the revamping of public space, increased density and/or introduction of further functions.

"joints and gaps": Improving the 'already built' periphery
In view of the slow process of growing together of structures in the 'mature periphery' it is the edges of existing developments and the joins between areas which offer most potential for the insertion of

[4] *compare with the discussion of New Urbanism*

development strategies. The edge, once simply the end of an area followed by a gap in readiness for future expansion, can be used for a conscious intervention, a transition area between two areas and a potential carrier of "address" qualities.

Figure 14: Edge

In the area of study it is usually the edges between built areas and open landscape which are most suited for such qualifying strategies. These edge-situations today demonstrate clearly the lack of relationship between the different systems: residential culture and agriculture meet abruptly. The design potential inherent in such spaces is just as evident.

Practical research at the Bauhaus-University

A central aspect of the practical research at the Bauhaus-University Weimar is to transfer the qualitative models to the area of study. Together with architectural students, interpretations, impulses and designs for typical situations within the Zwischenstadt were developed.
Two older single family housing areas in Schwalbach and Bad Soden were chosen as objects for studying the model "addresses". In Hattersheim the possibilities of converting a suburban industrial area to a new quarter in the Zwischenstadt was investigated. The creation of an "address" was achieved by drawing associations with the industrial heritage, through a differentiated design of public space and the articulation of a transitional area to the neighbouring open land and the planned Regional Rhine-Main Park.

Figure 15: Design project Hattersheim

Joins
It is not just edges that offer potential for a qualitative improvement of the "mature periphery" but also the joins between areas which have grown or are growing together. A noteworthy example of such a join in the area of study is the area around the Nordwest junction in Frankfurt. Between Eschborn and the Frankfurt districts Sossenheim and Rödelheim different areas have grown together to form an intensified commercial concentration in the periphery providing over 40000 workplaces. The excellent access conditions together with the planned RTW, which will cut through the middle, offer ideal potential for the creation of a new centre, a centre which corresponds to a second model:

Figure 16: area around Nordwest Junction Frankfurt

2. "Nodes": Multifunctional centres in the Zwischenstadt
This model describes the transformation of monofunctional office, commercial, infrastructural or conurbations to multifunctional nodes with the character of a centre in the regional environment. The USA has witnessed this kind of development in which sprawl has developed into so-called "Edge-Cities" [5], where monofunctional suburban office areas have been transformed into places with commerce, leisure as well as residential character. The research project investigated the theme of 'nodes' using the join in the vicinity of the Nordwest Junction in Frankfurt under the title "Downtown Eschborn-Sossenheim". Key aspects included identifying necessary functions and how such a multifunctional centre will be perceived in the Zwischenstadt.
The pictures of the student's work show exemplary approaches to these tasks. The first example[6] attempts to combine the heterogeneous structures around the motorway interchange into a monumental ring surrounding an open park through which the motorway crosses and which characterises the "address" of the node. The authors of the

[5] *Garreau, Joel: Edge Cities - Life on a new frontier. New York 1991*
[6] *by C. Hong, T. Kleinsteuber, T. Papp, S. Trovato*

second project[7] wanted to make the character of the individual structures more evident by strengthening their edges. The join between areas serves as a potential building block whose prominent centre together with the infrastructural elements also serves as a gateway into the landscape.

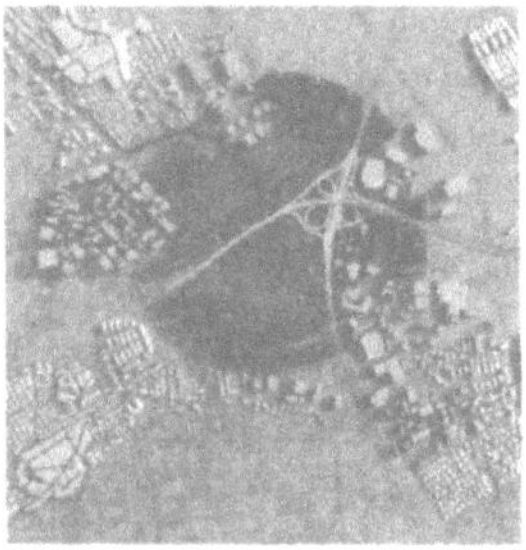

Figure 17: Project Downtown Eschborn Sossenheim

Figure 18: Project Downtown Eschborn Sossenheim

In the near neighborhood the Main-Taunus Centre (MTZ) represents a similar 'nodal' situation. The MTZ was built as the first german suburban shopping mall with its own motorway access in the sixties just outside the boundaries of the city of Frankfurt. Many similar shopping malls of this period in the USA are being renovated in order to be able to compete with newer "all-inclusive experience malls" or the rediscovered old town centres. A whole series of different approaches have resulted in recent years ranging from the insertion of leisure, work and residential uses to complete renewal.
Using the MTZ and referring to international examples, the research project investigates ways of transforming monofunctional shopping malls. The Frankfurt district Hoechst lies directly adjacent to the centre and offers the possibility to look at the direct relationship between the

[7] *by J. Mieskes, J. Müller, A. Nielson, F. Schiavello*

suburban and the old centre. In addition the question of how to articulate the edge situation of the MTZ with regard to the changing landscape is investigated.

Figure 19: Main-Taunus-Centre

In Europe the development of such nodes can best be observed at transport interchanges such as large airports. The once monofunctional infrastructure has become enriched with various new uses, most notably shopping and leisure facilities as well as business and short-stay residential facilities. It was therefore logical to examine the Rhine-Main Airport in the area of study. Under the working title “Airport-City-Rhine-Main” the students examined which functions are necessary to transform an airport into a ‘nodal point’ in the Zwischenstadt and how such a node can be articulated. The investigations of the design project also showed that again the edge of the airport, particularly to the motorway, offered the most potential as a ‘visiting card’ for the airport. The example[8] shows how this edge situation is developed as leisure facilities that connect the Airport with the Rhine-Main urban landscape via a series of experiential stations. A second project[9] signalled the address of the Airport with a large-scale form on a former military area adjacent to the motorway junction Frankfurter Kreuz.

Figure 20: Project Airport-City-Rhine-Main

---

[8] *by P. Brummermann, N. Köplin, N. von Brandis*
[9] *Student's name*

Figure 21: Project Airport-City-Rhine-Main

3. "Myths": Identify and thematise the aura of place in the Zwischenstadt
The strategies of the address and the node imbue an area with hierarchy and therefore an importance that was previously not evident. The increasing 'manufacture of place' in the Zwischenstadt offers new possibilities for designing structures of local and regional relationships. Identifying and engineering the 'aura of place' becomes a decisive strategy. Landmarks, markers, historical, social, economic or cultural 'solitaires' can be interconnected in a network to constitute a new form of regional identity.
Which situations offer the most potential for engineering such mythical auras in the Zwischenstadt? Much as with the traditional city it seems obvious to explore the specific history of place. Old village centres become anchors of identity in the muchness of the suburban surroundings and are in reality already often the subject of affectionate self-presentation.
Historical analyses also uncovered the 'mythical potential' of former connections and paths. For example the historic "Elisabethenstrasse", once an important trade route in roman times and now covered over by motorway and parking spaces, connects important elements within the area of study.

Figure 22: Elisabethenstrasse today

In other regions[10] it is the relicts of the industrial age which become subject to 'mythical' transformation, and the Rhine-Main region now too has its own "Industrial Heritage Route". However a more pertinent question is whether it is not more appropriate to explore other 'myth

---

[10] *see also the strategies employed in the IBA Emscher Park*

potential' in areas of the Zwischenstadt not quite so endowed with historical monuments. Perhaps suburbanisation itself is a suitable topic for thematisation. Numerous situations offer potential within the area of study, ranging from workers' neighbourhoods in Frankfurt-Hoechst from the turn of the 20th century to Ernst May's urban expansion programme or satellite towns such as the Nordweststadt and the Limesstadt.

Figure 23: Frankfurt Roemerstadt by Ernst May

However, today it is the economic relationships that accord the study area its functional meaning and importance, and it is these which are less easy to perceive in space. The picture highlights which firms operate within the otherwise relatively faceless industrial estates between Eschborn and Frankfurt-Sossenheim. The act of "making visible" the enormous economic potential could also animate the companies to take part in the qualitative renewal of space in the Zwischenstadt.

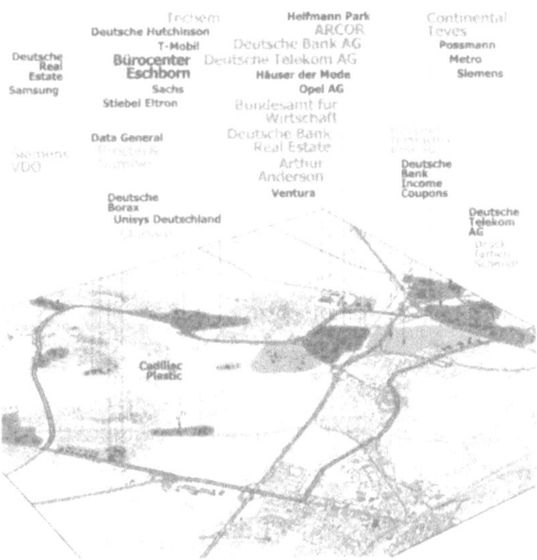

Figure 24: Companies around Eschborn

The 'myth' model leads us to a central fourth model for the qualitative improvement of the Zwischenstadt.

4. "Network": Combining heterogeneous regional structures with an "image of the region".

The model "network" attempts to integrate heterogeneous regional structures associatively with a "regional image". Design efforts aim to uncover and recognise open and hidden 'structures of meaning' in the Zwischenstadt, whether these are addresses, nodes or myths, and to connect them with one another in an identifiable network. The aim is to create a "spatial identity" of the Zwischenstadt which can be experienced.

Landscape

In view of the heterogeneous nature of the 'clusters' of the Zwischenstadt, it seems natural that the landscape can act as a connecting element and basis for an 'integrative culture'. The notion of a Regional Park as a 'backbone' for heterogeneous urban landscapes is one often used in network-strategies employing landscape. [11]

Existing regional infrastructure

Experience has shown that due to conflicts of interest landscape is not always capable of forming an 'integrative culture' on its own. The perception of the Zwischenstadt is primarily experienced through using the infrastructural connections. Question can be raised, for instance, for instance, how can motorways become 'boulevards' through the region rather than the closed-off monofunctional corridors they often are.

New regional infrastructure

A central means of integration in the Zwischenstadt is the development of new regional infrastructure. The shift of hierarchical interdependencies between the centre and edge areas means that the concentric structure of the city becomes increasingly overlaid with tangential relationships. From a certain point onwards the development of 'regional' traffic and transport infrastructure becomes necessary and can be used as an important strategy for the qualitative improvement of the Zwischenstadt, most notably around the new stations and nodal points. The planned Regionaltangente West aims to do just that for the Rhine-Main region. The practical research at the Bauhaus-University

---

[11] *see also IBA Emscher Park, Filderpark Stuttgart, Regionalpark Rhein-Main etc.*

aims to investigate ideas for spatially experiencing the new regional transport route RTW and correspondingly development patterns for the Zwischenstadt. In addition to the motorway the RTW has the potential in future to act as the backbone of the region by networking individual building blocks along a new 'regional experiential line'.

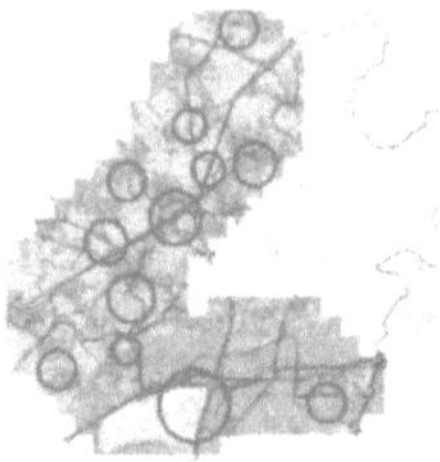

Figure 25: Networking

The research projects demonstrate clearly, in different situations throughout the area of study, how the models can be applied, whether they are 'thematic addresses', possible regional 'nodes' or 'myths' that can be connected in a 'network'. These can contribute both to a qualitative improvement in space as well as to a regional identity for the Zwischenstadt.

All Figures by the author

Viewing Gentrification
A Photographic Study of Prenzlauer Berg in Berlin

Julia Müller

In the progress of urban renewal inner-city quarters become revalorised and experience a change of social, cultural and built environment. The image of the quarters change, often from a neglected place to a trendy quarter or to a popular living area for the new urban professionals. Rising rents and the transformed living space often lead to the displacement of the original inhabitants. This phenomenon is called *gentrification*. The following article deals with this change of inner-city urban space. There are many ways to notice it: renewal of facades; modernisation of apartments; rising rents; new inhabitants with higher income and "new" lifestyles; "new" stores with exclusive selections; an increasing number of visitors from other parts of the city; or the redesign of public spaces. This process affects the complex urban space. Though photographs have the ability to compare, to document and to describe complexity, the photographic analysis is currently missing in the discussion on gentrification.

Through a photographic study of three redevelopment areas in Prenzlauer Berg in Berlin I wish to contribute an additional view[1]. The study is based on theories and methods from the field of visual sociology and follows the results of existing studies on gentrification. It deals with the relevance of the visual transformation of the urban space within the gentrification process. Therefore the change of lifestyles of the inhabitants plays an important role.
The visual sociology refers to the method of photography as a scientific tool and improves the methodology for the sociological field. For the following analysis a corresponding procedure and structure has been developed. The aim of the study is the connection of theory and photography. In this way the critical aspect of photography, the subjectivity, can be marginalized and the results of the visual research can be put in context of the discussion on gentrification. The visual perspective on the highly discussed topic of gentrification shall encourage a closer look at the city and the rethinking of the existing city images.

---

[1] *This article is based on "Quartiersansichten im Prenzlauer Berg – Photographische Betrachtung eines gentrifizierten Quartiers", Julia Müller, master theses 2003, European Urban Studies, Bauhaus Universitiy Weimar.*

Gentrification
"Gentrification is the invasion of a higher class population in a living area of a lower class population and the linked revalorisation of the built environment and public facilities." (Dangschat/Friedrichs 1988, p9 - translation by the author) The term "gentrification" was coined by Ruth Glass (1963). The process of gentrification is linked to the revalorisation of the built environment and the (re-)investment in housing and public facilities (Blasius 1993: 14).
As a result of numerous definitions and theories (Hamnett 1984, Marcuse 1992, Smith 1993, Friedrichs 1996 etc.) models were developed to describe the course of the gentrification process: the model of the transformation of neighbourhoods (Berry 1985) and the model of the double invasion-succession-cycle (Dangschat 1988). The double invasion-succession-cycle, which is modulated according to the old ecolological paradigm of the Chicago school, is presented here as an example. The process of gentrification is divided into five phases, within which the population is exchanged twice.
(1) First a group of young, highly educated people with low income, called "pioneers", move to a run down area and make it attractive through cultural activities. (2) Through this development, further pioneers and public facilities, fitting their lifestyle, are attracted. This leads partly to the displacement of original inhabitants. The area becomes increasingly interesting for people from external areas. (3/4) Then the group of so-called "initial gentrifiers", people in a financially and professionally established position with an individual lifestyle, are moving in. This leads to a more distinct physical and infrastructural change and finally to the displacement of original inhabitants and even pioneers. (5) Further gentrifiers settle. Transformation and displacement are accelerating. Increasingly more rental apartments are becoming freehold flats.
This model gives an opportunity to describe the theoretical progress. In reality the phases are, however, difficult to identify; they overlap and are developing separate from each other.

Gentrification in East Germany
In the beginning of the nineties, shortly after The Wall broke down, the historical parts of the East German cities were in a bad physical state and had an underdeveloped network of infrastructural support. Urban renewal and gentrification in East Germany had, and still has, special conditions and dimensions:
(1) The redevelopment areas includes all historical city parts, not only some. The reason for this strong decline of the physical substance was not only the financial situation, but also the result of rejecting all signs of

the capitalistic class society. Only in the eighties did the redevelopment, instead of replacement by prefabricated concrete buildings, of single historical buildings begin. (2) In contrary to the social homogeneous structure of inhabitants in West German redevelopment areas – workers, older people, foreigners and poor people – the inhabitants of these areas in East German cities were quite heterogeneous. There the old city parts had been developed to niches for all population classes within the GDR-system: workers, intellectuals, artists, students, dissidents. (3) The structure of properties changed through the restitution of nationalised buildings. (4) For the current urban renewal the public funding was, and is, quite low; with special write-offs the government tried to interest private investors. (5) Moreover the bad image of the historical city from the time of the GDR, the change from the planned to market economy, the new mobility etc. influence the behaviour of the inhabitants. The indicators for gentrification become distorted. (Häußermann / Kapphan 2000, Harth 1996)
These aspects have to be considered when studying the gentrification process in Prenzlauer Berg in Berlin.

Visual Sociology
The city image shall be redrawn in this case study through the means of photographs. However, in order to put a photographic study into a theoretical context, structures for the interpretation are necessary. The visual sociology deals with the interpretation, qualities and problems of photographs in sociological studies.

Sociology and photography both originate from around 1830 and among other things both deal with the society as an object.
Photographic work often can be called a sociological analysis because of a detailed documentation of current social problems. However, due to selective publication, lack of interpretation and the fact that most photographs show only a moment instead of a long-term view, they are not studies in a sociological sense.
In sociology the focus lays on the achievement of theoretical knowledge and the interpretation of study results. Sociologists trust too much in the truth of the photographs and overlook the influence of the photographers experience and equipment on the quality of photographs. They underestimate the subjectivity of photography (Becker 1986: 223-271).

The visual sociology requires a combination of photographic studies with a technical and aesthetic quality and sociological studies on a high theoretical level (Becker 1986: 245). According to the visual sociology a scientifically applicable photographic study (1) has to choose a sociologically relevant topic. (2) The most controversial aspect of the scientific photography is the subjectivity. On one hand it is conditioned by the selection of motive, time, place, perspective, light etc. On the other hand the act of seeing and interpreting is subjective, because it is influenced by the photographers theoretical background, experience and equipment. The theory serves in this context for the establishment, selection and interpretation of motives and therefore for the framing of the subjective view of the researcher. (4) The photographs should be taken with a sociological and photographical consciousness, that means that weakness and strength of photography must be taken into consideration. (5) Photographs enable new perspectives and are contributing to the rectification of prejudgements. (6) The photographs should be seen as supplementary source of information. (7) The truthfulness and acknowledgement of the photographs should have priority to the aesthetic. (Harper 2000, Gordesch/Salzwedel 1993, Becker 1986)

The Structure of the Study

The photographic analysis[2] is based on an approach of integrating visual sociology and the discussion on gentrification. The study is subdivided into a theoretical and an interpreting part. The photographs are categorised in built environment, uses, atmosphere and people. These categories can be derived from the definition of gentrification.

Three study areas in Prenzlauer Berg were chosen. To make the study of each area comparable and to be able to describe complexity and contexts of the urban space the following structure was developed: Panorama views show the spatial context of the studied area. Together with photographic details they form the basic structure. To show the transformation and to put the study into a chronological context, photographs of the same situation from the beginning of the nineties and today are compared. The interpretation of the photographic analysis, which draws on current gentrification studies, characterises the research areas.

[2] *time of study: July and August 2003*
accomplished by foot, with a digital camera, coloured photographs

Study quarter: Prenzlauer Berg, Berlin

The quarter of Prenzlauer Berg was chosen because of the amount of current studies and discussions already available; so the photographic research can make use of them and provide a new insight regarding the visual development of this area.

Figure 1: Prenzlauer Berg in the context of Berlin

Prenzlauer Berg was developed within 50 years according to the scheme of the engineer James Hobrecht (1862). In the beginning of the 20th century it was the densest residential area worldwide with 300,000 inhabitants.[3] Today Prenzlauer Berg is the biggest "Gründerzeit"-area[4] with a still intact structure, escaping much of the destruction during Second World War. Characteristic for this area are eaves the height of 22 meters according to the Hobrecht Plan. Large chessboard-like blocks of flats with one or more small and narrow backyards and a dense building structure with spars green and open spaces are characteristic for the city image. Still one can find a mixture of renovated and not renovated facades in a single block. Prominent for this district is the differentiation of apartment qualities and sizes. It is the result of the building structure with front houses, backyard houses and side wings. The apartments in the front houses are larger, lighter and often better equipped. Those in the back yard houses, by contrast, are smaller and darker. Encircling the single neighbourhoods in Prenzlauer Berg, radial routes, tram tracks and subways permit each one to develop its own character,

---

[3] *1925 as working class area: 326.311 inhabitants; 1987: 157.791 inhabitants; 2000: 134.934 inhabitants (Statistisches Landesamt 2000,as quoted by STERN) in the last years first increase of population (Asum 2002: 69).*

[4] *A period of economic boom during the industrialisation in the 19th century, influencing society, city development and architecture.*

Since the fall of The Wall 1989 Prenzlauer Berg has changed a lot: from a run-down area to the "hottest address in middle Europe" in 1990 (Kil 1992: 511) and today a popular and parent-friendly residential area for students, dinks and young families (Berliner Zeitung 12/06/03: 3).
In the beginning of the eighties Prenzlauer Berg became, similar to other historical areas in the GDR, a place of refuge for those who did not want, or were not allowed, to live in the new, better equipped prefabricated accommodations. Intellectuals, students, dissidents and artists mixed with workers and poor people and created niches within the socialistic system. With the end of the GDR, the hotbed for these niches vanished. In a "short winter of anarchy" (Kil 1992: 511), when Prenzlauer Berg was a scene for the cultural liberation and the public political action, numerous provisory pubs, shops, galleries and cultural institutions set up and more and more students, artist, alternative people etc moved in. Despite the bad physical state[5] Prenzlauer Berg became ever more popular to live in, first for the "pioneers", with the rising amount of redeveloped buildings also for the "gentrifiers". Within the process of redevelopment, the population in Prenzlauer Berg changed from a heterogeneous mixture to a more homogeneous population, especially consisting of new, financially well-situated inhabitants. The rents often reach above-average levels (Asum 2002: 45). Describing the inhabitants of today, these are mostly younger (between 27 and 44 years), high-educated people, living tendentiously in single households without kids. Astonishing, is the above-average high number of children under 6 years.

Prenzlauer Berg is the quarter with the clearest tendency of revalorisation in Berlin (Borst/Krätke 2000: 256) and can be classified in the pioneer-phase of the gentrification process. With 90% of the building structure emanating from before 1920 this area shows what the "new" households appreciate: flats with the typical layout of old buildings in an attractive residential environment of the Gründerzeit.

---

[5] *In the beginning of the 90's around 80% of the flats were coal heated, 18% had neither bath nor toilet (Bernt 1998: 22)*

The three study areas

Figure 2: The redevelopment area Prenzlauer Berg and the three study areas

Selection of the study areas

In Prenzlauer Berg there are five redevelopment areas showing different levels of renewal and phases of gentrification[6]. To meet the variety of Prenzlauer Berg, three quarters with different characters were chosen: Kollwitzplatz, Helmholzplatz and a part of the Winsstrasse.[7] As study areas the centres of these three quarters were selected: the ensemble around Kollwitzplatz, around Helmholzplatz and along Winstrasse. Being the central places of the single redevelopment areas, they are the condensate of the characters of each quarter and therefore very suitable for a visual analysis.

Figure 3: The three study areas out marked in dark grey shade

---

[6] *comp. Argus 2000, Asum 2002*

[7] *Because of the existing data and the better comparability only quarters within the redevelopment areas were considered as study areas.*

Kollwitzplatz

Kollwitzplatz, the second largest redevelopment area[8], is the supraregionally most known part of Prenzlauer Berg and is described and analysed strikingly often. Actually, the area around Kollwitzplatz is what outsiders used to know as Prenzlauer Berg and became mythical. "This myth became the actual reason for investments into pubs, galleries, travel guides, city walks..." (Bernt 1998: 31).

Kollwitzplatz was laid out as a city square between 1870 and 1900. Some streets had been redeveloped already in the time of the GDR for the 750th anniversary of Berlin. The old Jewish residential area is dominated by elegant facades, wide streets with trees and big, but not necessarily better equipped, flats. Here, building structures with only one backyard are predominating and therefore the area is less dense and much better lit (Häußermann 2002: 39; Asum 2002: 15).

Considering Kollwitzplatz as urban space, it is characterised by the green atmosphere of the square and the adjoining streets. Prominent is the partly costly redevelopment of nearly the whole building ensemble. Three new, discussable buildings are an alien contribution to the square. In contrary to the other areas there are big stores on the ground floors and some studios under the roofs. Already in the beginning of the 90's Kollwitzplatz experienced a big transformation because of the establishment of trendy bars and stores during the ecstasy of awakening. Rising rents for business space and flats made Kollwitzplatz an area for posh people and city jet set ("Hauptstadtschickeria" Spiegel 1998: 49): elegant stores and restaurants displaced "conservative" stores (Franzmann 1996: 233) as well as trendy bars, e.g. the post office was replaced by a Caribbean restaurant.

Once a place for students and alternative people to move to, Kollwitzplatz gained, with the increasing number of redeveloped buildings and the resulting rising rents, attraction also for people with high income[9]. The obvious increase of children under 6 years of age, the rising income and the lowest number of single households (48%) show the trend to settled inhabitants: the gentrifiers (Asum 2000: 17f).

Helmholzplatz

In the time of the GDR tendentiously socially weaker people lived in the area around the Helmholzplatz. Some studies prophesised devaluation. In the last years, it experienced great changes and developed to a hip

---

[8] *with 6.8300 flats and 9.531 inhabitants (Kollwitzplatz – Senat 2001)*

[9] *state of redevelopment 2000: 52,7% (Asum 2002)*

area. Helmholzplatz is with 13.200 flats and 16.582 inhabitants the most dense and largest redevelopment area. Besides the costly front houses one finds, as embodiment of the *Mietskaserne*, more than average many backyards, backyard houses and side wings with lots of small flats. Relatively small trees characterise the streets. The redevelopment quote in 2000 reached 51,7% (Asum 2002: 14/15).

Only in the mid nineties the trendy bars at Kollwitzplatz, where the customers vanished and the rents became too expensive, slopped north to Helmholzplatz. Today you can find also chic stores, restaurants and bars, which "do not distinguish at all to the pendants at Kollwitzplatz" (Bernt/Holm 2002: 21). The vivid short sides of Helmholzplatz contrast to the calmer long sides. Characteristic is the heterogeneity: intimate or uncomfortable, chic or homeless, exciting or boring, deserted or crowed.

Salient in the Helmholzplatz quarter is the coexistence of all classes and ages: children on the playground next to homeless people with dogs and beer bottles. It is the only redevelopment area with a continuing decline of population[10] and a stagnation number of children under 6 years. With 25% the number of children drop above average. Moreover, the incomes with 54% of the inhabitants earning less than €1,250, are significantly below the average and the quantity of students and single households is unusually high (Asum 2002: 39).

Winsstrasse

In the GDR time, the quarter around Winsstrasse was a bourgeois district. The flats were better equipped and the area was not as run down as the other parts of Prenzlauer Berg. However it did not have the niche character of the Kollwitzplatz and the Helmholzplatz (Bernt 1998: 22). After 1989 the need for redevelopment was lesser than there.
The atmosphere can be described as heterogeneous, quiet, ordinary and not very green. Especially in the north, the lack of trees is striking. The state of facades and building structure varies between badly maintained and costly redeveloped.

With 4,850 flats and 7,781 inhabitants Wisstrasse is a middle-sized quarter. There you find the largest apartments of the redevelopment areas (Asum 2002: 27,34). Winsstrasse is inferior to the other redevelopment areas in its renewal state with only 24.6% (Asum 2002: 15). Significantly, many building sites suggest an ongoing renewal. In

[10] *1993 18.923 inhabitants, 1999 16.582 inhabitants (Helmholzplatz-Senat 2001)*

comparison to the rest of the quarters in Prenzlauer Berg the district Winsstrasse has no central square. In 1999 the 5,000 m² square "Marie" was laid out in the Marienburgerstrasse as a green and open space for the district with a sports ground, playgrounds and lawns. It is surrounded by firewalls and a school.
In contrary to the calmer northern part the ground floors of the southern area accommodate more stores, restaurants and bars, offices etc. Nevertheless, the vacancy rate is comparatively high. The share of "conservative" stores and traditional restaurants is much higher compared to Kollwitzplatz and Helmholzplatz. Though you can find wine stores, an ecological shop, espresso bars etc.

The social structure is quite young with the lowest share of pensioners and an over average number of children under 6 years (Asum 2002: 17, 25). Only 6.7% of those moving away are students: significantly less than in other areas[11]. The coexistence of different users and residents creates an environment for a broad palette of inhabitants.
An architectural revalorisation and a transformation of the public affairs can be stated.

Photographic documentation and evaluation of the study areas

The Photographic study (panoramas, details, transformation) is an attempt to make "a 'pictureistic' ('bildwirksam') diagnosis of the reality", as Klaus Honnef describes the virtues of the photographic media (Honnef 1977: 33).
The photographs in the following section are a selection from this study.

Corner Panoramas

The panoramic views of the street corners of the three study areas provide an overview of the examined urban spaces. In one single picture they make special contexts visible that one might perceive in real life, but not in this simultaneous complexity. The "parallel view" of all corners allows a first characterization of built environment, utility, atmosphere and people in the study area.

[11] *in comparison: Kollwitzplatz 11,4%, Helmholzplatz 11,9% (Argus 2000)*

Figure 4: Kollwitzplatz: Husemann-/Wörtherstrasse (top). Wörther-/Kollwitzstrasse (bottom)

Despite the rather homogeneous atmosphere - describable as chic, cultivated, intimate but also welcoming and alive - it is apparent that the corners of the excessively green square are of different character. The corner of Husemann-/Wörtherstrasse (fig 4, top) is the aesthetic centrepiece with numerous cafés and the costly *gründerzeit* houses. The western corner differs through exclusive shops and a calmer atmosphere. The eastern corner (fig 4, bottom) breaks the structure with its two unspectacular new buildings and a renewed fallow site, offering space and air.

The high level of redevelopment, the specialized stores and the cultivated atmosphere suggest high rents and therefore economically strong households. The extraordinarily well-visited playground indicates many families (fig 4, bottom left hand). The large menu boards and closely placed tables in front of cafés and restaurants imply a clientele enhanced by tourists. Consequently, no alternative cafés, electronic stores or homeless persons are to be seen here. The Kollwitzplatz isn't thoroughly chic though with its graffiti, badly maintained buildings and the new mundane yellow house accommodating a supermarket (fig 4, bottom right hand).
The square and its architectural structure, uses and atmosphere appear to be a diverted reflection rather than a mirror of the social structure.

Figure 5: Helmholzplatz: eastern Raumer-/Dunkertstrasse (top). western Lychener-/ Lettestrasse (bottom)

The architectural structure surrounding the oblong square doesn't form an ensemble with the trees on it, but a fragmented and very heterogeneous formation around the "untamed vegetation".
Whereas one can characterize the western half of the square as a lively stroll and café area (fig 5, bottom), the rest of it has a heterogeneous and more quiet ambience with a supermarket, hobby store, pharmacy etc. but also exclusive shops like a chocolate store. The tendency towards the innovative and individualistic is observable in multi-coloured houses, graffiti etc.
This polarisation is also reflected in the built environment, which appears much more renovated and elaborate in the west (fig 5, bottom) than in the east (fig 5, top).

The heterogeneity of the study area is an indication of an equally heterogenic population. While the one café lies next to the other on the Lychenerstrasse the homeless and their dogs meet at the corner.
It is possible to reach a conclusion about the social situation of Helmholzplatz by the architectural and atmospheric structure.

Squares

Additionally the squares themselves are documented.

Kollwitzplatz

Figure 6: Kollwitzplatz: meadow, square with memorial, playground, market

The eastern and northern parts of Kollwitzplatz are, in contrary to its otherwise introvert character, relatively open, bringing the life from the playground to the street. (fig 6, middle) Particularly in the late afternoon the playground gives the impression to be as much an important meeting place for the ever-young parents as a place for the children. One meets at the playground just like in a café or at the chic Italian. As a contrast to the playground, the rest of the square is calmer with a meadow, benches and a memorial. (fig 6, top)

The ecological and weekly markets accentuate the lively ambience in the north-eastern corner on Thursdays and Saturdays. Here conspicuously many young "dads" and "mums" purchase products of high price and quality. (fig 6, bottom)

Figure 7: Helmholzplatz: homeless people, pavilion, playground, the center,

The discussion about the design of the in 1902 first outlaid Helmholzplatz - and the related question of how to handle the problem of the coexistence of green areas, a playground and a meeting place for homeless people (dogs and alcohol) – goes back to 1993. Renewal measures were begun in 1999, and in July 2001 the "square for everyone" was completed.

From the outside the square seems mostly introverted, rejecting or solitary (fig 7, top). A reason is surely the fence protecting against dogs, the different levels of the street and the square and the dividing stripes of unrestrained greenery. Only at the eastern half does it invite passers-by to linger on the meadow. The centre is the corridor from the north to the south (fig 7, bottom): a playground, table tennis, benches and a pavilion for special events make it a place for hanging around for children and parents as well as homless people (fig 7, middle). The playground hasn't the self-evident and lively character of the one at Kollwitzplatz. Next to the meadow is the newly rebuild transformer building with a modern, open appearance, currently serving as setting for a chic-alternative store selling "Recycled Fashion for Kids".

Details

For the registration and the analysis of the urban space, photographic details as the “footprints” of the social, architectural and infrastructural composition are necessary, besides the portrait of the coherent space. The framework – the panoramic views – is completed by the detailed “mosaic stones” to a picture: the portrait of the study area. Details show, in contrast to the panoramas, selected information, but nevertheless make a rather complex statement. Therefore they require a comment e.g. through subtitles or categorisation. They give qualitative information, but can merely imply quantitative tendencies.

Spatial succession

Arranging the photographs successively, corresponding to the studied area, the details integrate themselves into the context and provide information about relations and the character of the whole area. The succession of uses, the heterogeneity, the monotony of parts of the area etc. remain readable despite the detailed perspective. These details clarify the heterogeneity of the Helmholzplatz through the great variety of facades, graffiti, advertising, balconies, café tables, shop-indows, the mixture of stores and services etc..

Rows of Details

Furthermore, series of photographs of restaurants, uses, balconies, windows, doors, exterior advertising are put together for each single area. The spectrum of quality of the particular aspects – in context of lifestyles - becomes readable. The rows of details show the photographs beginning with the “traditional” examples, then the “alternative” and finally the “gentrified” ones.

Figure 8: Restaurants and bars – Kollwitzplatz
The Kollwitzplatz is the most homogeneous area. The “gentrified” restaurants predominate.

Figure 9: Balconies – Helmholzplatz
The Helmholzplatz is characterised by the wide range from “traditional” over “alternative” to “gentrified”, here the balconies as an example..

Figure 10: Stores – Winsstrasse
In the Winsstrasse there are above average many “traditional” facilities, here the row “stores”.

The photographs convey the character of the study area and clarify the strong influence only of the share of cafés, restaurants and snack bars on the atmosphere and the urban space. Advertising, colours, café tables, sunshades, menus, streetlights, store names, balconies etc; these are signs that, on one side, create atmosphere and urban space; on the other side they reflect the lifestyles and offer identification and communication. If an area is predominated by a certain lifestyle, and one does not belong to this group, one might feel excluded because of not knowing the corresponding signs.

Comparison: 10 years ago and today

Next to the documentation of the recent status the transformation of the area plays an important role for the understanding of the development. The gentrification of an inner city quarter is a process, which cannot be described only by snapshots. Long-term studies would have exceeded the time frame of this analysis. Therefore exemplary photographs of the study areas, from the archive of S.T.E.R.N. (company for urban renewal Berlin), of the time from 1991-1996 were used. The transformation becomes readable through photographs of the same situations from the summer of 2003. Aerial photos of each area from the beginning of the nineties and from 2000 offer an overview.

Winsstrasse

Figure 11: Four situations from around 1994 (left) and in 2003 (right) at Winsstrasse

Even if the old and the new photographs seem to be rather similar, architectural renewals like roof additions, balconies and buildings sites (photo 2, 3) can be discovered when looking closer.

As far as the uses are concerned, not much difference can be noticed. In 1996 there were already a "new" Irish pub and an alternative furniture store there. The pub at the corner Immanuelkirch-/Winsstrasse has become a club (photo 1). Besides the revalorisation of single buildings more green influences the atmosphere of the area now (photo 1,4).

Kollwitzplatz

Figure 12: Four situations from around 1994 (left) and in 2003 (right) at Kollwitzplatz

Initially with a building structure in a quite different state, nearly the whole building structure is redeveloped today, somewhat very costly. Besides roof additions and new balconies, the new buildings (photo 1) catch the eye.

Instead of daily life stores and cultural institutions (e.g. a hair dresser, the children's library or the citizen office), above-average many restaurants have moved into the ground floors (photo 1-4). The vacancies on the ground floors, especially in the Knaackstrasse (photo 4), have vanished and the building gaps are filled with new buildings (photo 1) and a new designed open space.

Earlier provisory, coloured facades and the mixture of badly and well-kept buildings were characteristic for the visible urban space. Heterogeneity and vividness characterised the atmosphere. Today in contrast, the light and friendly redeveloped building structure and the crowded terraces of the cafés form a quite homogeneous image.

Résumé of the photographic analyse

Kollwitzplatz

Kollwitzplatz is the most gentrified of the study areas. Evidence is provided by the elevated uses mainly in the field of restaurants and bars, the visible high level of redevelopment and the resulting cultivated atmosphere. Other characteristics for the quarter are children in the streets and plentiful green.

Helmholzplatz

Concerning Helmholzplatz it can be spoken of a revalorisation and the pioneer phase of gentrification. This can be read out of the heterogeneous - with a tendency to alternative and innovative - character of the building structure, uses, people and atmosphere. Even if the redevelopment level is comparable to that of Kollwitzplatz, the photographs clearly show the different manners of renewal. Redevelopment does not equal redevelopment.

Winsstrasse

Winsstrasse is in an early state of the pioneer phase. The lower status of the redevelopment and the higher number of building sites imply a continuing renewal process. The clearly smaller share of restaurants and cafes and the ordinary atmosphere confirm this conclusion.

Because of the relatively high income and the rising number of children it could also be spoken of a pioneer phase skipping the gentrifier phase.

What are the additional benefits of photography?

The photographic study regards the urban space with a new perspective. The analysis focuses on the urban space. Important are the visible and readable aspects, not the theoretical reflection or the view behind the facades. The photographic study demands an accurate view on, and a direct discussion about, the urban space.

But what are the additional benefits?

The urban space becomes perceptible. Lifestyles, uses, building structures, people and atmosphere become simultaneously visible.

Relations within and between the single areas become noticeable: e.g. spatial polarisations, boundaries, and continuities.

The textually described atmosphere is made more understandable by photographs providing an additional dimension.

Photographs also capture temporary and flexible aspects e.g. “traces” of visitors.

The choice of format, the angle of view and framing make new perspectives possible. Wide-angle panoramas, e.g., make hardly ever seen relations visible.
Moreover photographs can serve as a visual basis for discussions that is objective despite the subjective interpretation. Descriptions, e.g. "a traditional bar", can be assigned a face.

Conclusion

Photography as a method in urban sociology requires an appropriate structure and interpretation to achieve, besides numerous photographs, a certain conclusion. The confrontation of the photographic analysis with existing studies establishes a relation between photography and theory. The visual view of the urban space often confirms, but also supplements, the results of these non-visual and more conventional studies. In the visible urban space the transformation conditioned by the process of gentrification manifests itself. The photographs presented in the study of Prenzlauer Berg are showing the qualities and nuances of the ongoing social and spatial transformation of the quarter. The visible urban space is a "reservoir" of gentrification, in which many indicators of gentrification are recognizable. The process of photographing provides a new perspective on the city. The photographic act makes the photographer see the whole context. One becomes aware of boundaries between public and private space, how urban life is depending on the time of day, season, and weather. First impressions are confirmed through reviewing or refuted after a more precise analysis.
This paper aimed at presenting a starting point to describe and value a gentrifying area in transformation by a photographic method. In the process of transformation, besides the hard factors like rents and flat layouts, also the soft factors like atmosphere and image are important to observe and analyse. It is difficult to get a grip on the urban space, but it is a significant factor in the process of gentrification.

References

argus GmbH (2000): Wohnmobilität in Sanierungsgebieten, Wegzugsmotive von Haushalten aus den Sanierungsgeben in Berlin-Prenzlauer Berg 1994-1999, Berlin

ASUM (2002), Mieterberatung Prenzlauer Berg: Fortschreiben sozialer Sanierungsziele und Mietobergrenzen, Berlin

Beauregard R.A. (1986): The chaos and complexity of gentrification. In: Smith, N.; Williams, P. (eds.) (1986): Gentrification of the City, Boston: Allan&Unwin

Becker H.S.(1986): Doing things together, Photography and sociology, Illinois, pp223

Bernt M. (1998): Stadterneuerung unter Aufwertungsdruck, Sinzheim: Pro Universitate Verlag

Bernt M. / Holm A. (2002, im Erscheinen): Gentrification in Ostdeutschland: der Fall Prenzlauer Berg,

Blasius J.(1993): Gentrification und Lebensstile. Eine empirische Untersuchung, Wiesbaden: Deutscher Universitäts-Verlag
Borst R./ Krätke S (2000): Berlin – Metropole zwischen Boom und Kriese, Opladen: Leske + Budrich, p211-285
Dangschat J. / Friedrichs, J. (1988): Gentrification in der inneren Stadt von Hamburg. Eine emipirische Untersuchung des Wandels von drei Wohnvierteln, in Hamburg: Gesellschaft für sozialwissenschaftliche Stadtforschung
Dangschat J.(1994): Lebensstil in der Stadt. In: Dangschat J./ Blasius J.(1994) Lebensstile in den Städten, Konzepte und Methoden, Opladen: Leske + Budrich, p336-354
Franzmann G. (1996): Gentrification und Einzelhandel. Gibt es die „neuen" Geschäfte? in: Friedrichs / Kecskes (1996), p229-258
Friedrichs. J./ Kecskes R (1996): Gentrification: Theorie und Forschungsergebnisse, p 13-40, in: Friedrichs / Kecskes (eds) (1996) Gentrification, Opladen: Leske + Budrich
Gordesch J. / Salzwedel H. (1993): Fotografie und Symbol, in: Europäische Hochschulschriften 22, Bd. 237, Frankfurt / Main, p2-46, pp99
Harper D. (2000): Fotografieren als sozialwissenschaftliche Daten, in: Flick U., von Kardorff E., Steinke I. (eds): Qualitative Forschung. Ein Handbuch, Reinbeck bei Hamburg: Rowohlt, p402-416
Häußermann H. (2002) Stadterneuerung in der Berliner Republik, Opladen: Leske + Budrich
Häußermann H./ Kapphan A.(2000): Berlin – von der geteilten zur gespaltenen Stadt? Sozialräumlicher Wandel seit 1990, Opladen: Leske + Budrich,
Honnef K. (1977) Katalog der Dokumenta 6, zitiert nach: Carolin Ferster: Architektur in der Zeitgenössischen Fotografie, in: Bauwelt 47/2002 p33
Harth A., Herly U., Scheller G. (1996): Ostdeutsche Städte auf Gentrificationskurs? in: Friedrichs J./ Kecskes R. (1996) S 167-192
Helms H.G. (1992): Die Stadt als Gabentisch. Beobachtungen der aktuellen Stadtentwicklung, Leipzig: Reclam-Verlag
Kil W. (1992): Prenzlauer Berg. Aufstieg und Fall einer Nische. In: Helms H.G. (1992) S 508-519
Rada U. (1997) Hauptstadt der Verdrängung. Berliner Zukunft zwischen Kiez und Metropole, Berlin: Verlag Libertäre Assoziation
Senatsverwaltung für Stadterneuerung 2/2001: Stadterneuerung – Sanierungsgebiet Prenzlauer Berg – Helmholzplatz / Kollwitzplatz Berlin, Bezirk Pankow
Smith N. (1979) Toward a Theory of Gentrification: a Back to the City Movement by Capital, not by People. In: Journal of the American Planning Association 45
Spiegel (1998) Der Charme des Maroden, Hamburg, 19 / p48-50

Figures

Figure 1: Map Berlin, Falkplan 60. edition, 1996/97, worked by the author
Figure 2: Redevelopment areas, Berlin Prenzlauer Berg, quoted as Asum 2002, source: S.T.E.R.N. 2002, adapted by the author
Figure 3 Figures adapted by the author

All photographs taken by the author in summer 2003
Figure 12 / 13: Exceptions are the photographs from the years 1991-1996, which had been placed by S.T.E.R.N. to the authors' disposal

The European City in Transition

Edited by Dieter Hassenpflug und Frank Eckardt

Vol. 1 Frank Eckardt / Dieter Hassenpflug (eds.): Consumption and the Post-Industrial City. 2003.

Vol. 2 Frank Eckard / Dieter Hassenpflug (eds.): Urbanism and Globalization. 2004.

Vol. 3 Frank Eckardt / Peter Kreisl (eds.): City Images and Urban Regeneration. 2004.

www.peterlang.de